AN INTRODUCTION TO
HUMAN GEOGRAPHY

D0258155

Geography

———

Editor

PROFESSOR W. G. EAST

*Professor of Geography
in the University of London*

AN INTRODUCTION TO HUMAN GEOGRAPHY

J. H. G. Lebon

Reader in Geography, School of Oriental and
African Studies, University of London

HUTCHINSON UNIVERSITY LIBRARY
LONDON

HUTCHINSON & CO (*Publishers*) LTD
178–202 Great Portland Street, London W1

London Melbourne Sydney
Auckland Bombay Toronto
Johannesburg New York

First published 1952
Second (revised) edition 1959
Reprinted 1961, 1962
Third (revised) edition 1963
Fourth (revised) edition 1964
Fifth (revised) edition 1966
Reprinted 1968
Sixth (revised) edition 1969

This book has been set in Times, printed in Great Britain
on Smooth Wove paper by Anchor Press, and
bound by Wm. Brendon, both of Tiptree, Essex

09 031610 x (cased)

09 031612 6 (paper)

To the memory of
Arthur Oliver Cattell-Jones
1 8 8 9 - 1 9 3 7

CONTENTS

FIGURES

PREFATORY APOLOGY TO THE SIXTH EDITION

This little book, originally written some eighteen years ago, now needs substantial revision for like any other branch of knowledge, human geography has been undergoing growth and change. Reappraisal of its aims and scope is timely.

In 1950 the dominant position of the French school seemed confirmed by the publication of Sorre's magistral volumes; and when I wrote *An Introduction to Human Geography* I necessarily based it upon that notable work and its predecessors. That French conceptions have not lost their validity and appeal is amply evident in recent works by my university colleague Emrys Jones and by Perpillou, cited in my bibliography. But in the course of reading, observation, reflection and teaching through the years, I have come to adopt an alternative standpoint, from which human geography is viewed as the comparative study of major societies in the areas of their characterisation. This view was first expounded (so far as I am aware) by Schmitthenner in 1936, and developed in an historical analysis by Toynbee and in an anthropological analysis by Kroeber. Accordingly, in my first chapter I attempt to justify this newer definition and to examine its connections both with the ideas of earlier authorities and with modern doctrine on the nature of geography. Inevitably, these considerations lead to a broad, ecological and holistic treatment, which, in outline, must become somewhat impressionistic. I must leave it to my reviewers and critics to judge whether so paradoxical a proceeding has any merits or must be condemned. If some sections seem merely skeletal, may I refer the reader to my bibliographies, which include books and articles relevant to most topics adumbrated in the text.

My thought might perhaps not have evolved thus but for my years of residence and travel in Asia and Africa when I was working in new universities in Ceylon, Iraq and Sudan. Living within the Hindu, Islamic and African civilisations, and, at Khartoum, made aware of the tensions inherent in the palpable cultural frontier dividing Islam from Negroid Africa, I could hardly avoid realising that earlier, when my studies and travel were confined to Europe and North America, many realities of non-Western societies had eluded me. Moreover, I have returned to a School in my university in which the autonomy of Oriental and African civilisations is accepted and is indeed the basis of departmental organisation.

I have also been a beneficiary of American liberalism at Southern Illinois, Columbia and Michigan universities, where I was invited to teach courses in cultural geography. Thereby, I was committed to the salutary task of making my ideas comprehensible to students. I hope this little book will be regarded as a tribute to my friends and colleagues of those brief yet rewarding visits, and to their great, welcoming academic communities.

I am grateful to Professor Charles A. Fisher for permission to quote two extracts from *South-East Asia*; to Professor W. M. Macmillan for the quotation on page 192 from his *Bantu, Boer and Briton* and to Professor A. Boyd and Messrs A. Tiranti for permission to base Fig. 11 on a diagram in *Chinese Architecture and Town Planning*.

I am much indebted to Professor W. Gordon East for removing some obscurities by suggesting improved wording for a number of phrases, to my colleague Mr J. M. D. Freeberne for his criticisms of my first draft on the Sinic civilisation, and to Mr A. F. de Souza, whose patient craftsmanship transformed some crude drafts into elegant maps.

July, 1969   J.H.G.L.

I

THE NATURE OF HUMAN GEOGRAPHY

The trend towards chorology

In 1950 the editors of this series wrote an introductory volume called *The Spirit and Purpose of Geography*. Admirable both in its defence of the integrity and intellectual standing of geography, and as a quickening and illuminating guide to the entire post-war generation of British undergraduate students, this work never-theless left some aspects unexplored. Despite its series of chapters on the principal systematic branches—physical, cartographical, historical, economic and political—it gave little attention to human geography. In the chapter on regional geography, the authors went so far as to 'reaffirm our former conclusion that there is, as yet, no such subject as a generalised human geography'. The 'former conclusion' had been reached in their second chapter after a brief allusion to a French work (*La Géographie humaine* by Brunhes) which, as will be shown later, deceived by its title; a longer discussion of an American work concerned more with physical than with human geography; and the dismissal of cultural anthropology as an ally of geography because primitive peoples are so rapidly disappearing from the earth. Professor Wooldridge, however, generously conceded in argument that he and Professor East were not altogether impartial in their treatment of human geography, and readily consented to the inclusion of a volume about it in this series.

Perhaps unconsciously, they depended more upon their German than their French predecessors and contemporaries. This is par-donable, if we reflect that modern geography originated in the

life-work of Ritter and Humboldt during the first half of the nineteenth century; and the French school, under Reclus and later
Vidal de la Blache, blossomed during the second half of the same
century. Further, the German mind takes readily to the theoretical.
Germans, therefore, were not only the first in the field of modern
geography but have cultivated its theory. Between about 1905 and
1930, Hettner came to occupy an almost papal eminence in German geographical thought. He was, however, elaborating the
doctrines expounded by leading German geographers after 1870,
including von Richthofen (as early as 1863), Supan and Albrecht
Penck, and supported by most of his contemporaries, such as
Passarge, Krebs and Philippson.

There was another reason for the bias towards German rather
than French thought in England immediately after the Second
World War. Geography had come of age in America. The steady
German immigration into the United States after the failure of the
'48 and the suppression of liberalism by Bismarck influenced the
trends of American intellectual life, and was not counterbalanced
by any corresponding influx of Frenchmen or French ideas.
France contributed less than any other European country to the
peopling of the Middle and the Far West. The 1913 International
Geographical Congress brought a group of eminent German
geographers to the United States; and a few years later, Isaiah
Bowman became Director of the American Geographical Society
in New York, which he organised as a geographical institute of the
continental type. Leading universities began to broaden their
curricula in geography, which till then had been restricted largely
to courses in physical and economic geography. An article by Carl
Sauer, published in *California Papers in Geography* (1925), summarised German orthodoxy for the American student; and P. E.
James, followed by others, produced textbooks suitable for the
American undergraduate, but inspired by German concepts.
Coinciding with the outbreak of war in 1939, the Association of
American Geographers devoted two numbers of its *Annals* to a
treatise on the 'Nature of Geography', by Richard Hartshorne,
who had spent some time studying in Germany. This was
America's first full-scale work on the scope and method of geography, and it is based essentially upon the German sources that
greatly predominate in its bibliography. Grounding in Hartshorne's work became a *sine qua non* of the aspirant American
geographer. And in the absence of any other comparable work in

the English language, it was widely read and influential also in Britain.

Hence, it is not surprising that in both Britain and America, the German conception of geography prevails. Geography is the systematic, mainly scientific, study of areal differentiation. It observes, describes, explains and interprets the complicated range of features observable on the earth's surface. It is the study of lands, and the distributional relationships of peoples to lands. Its primary facts are part of the landscape. The geographer is mainly interested in certain results of mankind's work. The German proclivity for inventing new compound nouns produced new terms—*Länderkunde*, literally 'lands-knowledge', and *Erdkunde*, 'earth-knowledge'—which many writers used in preference to the older Greek word geography, or the also earlier Greek, but by then archaic, word chorology. One of the leading German journals of the subject is significantly entitled *Erdkunde, Archiv für wissenschaftliche Geographie* (records of scientific geography). It is implied that an older, mainly descriptive subject has been replaced, in the modern age, by a better-organised, more methodical, more scientific branch of knowledge.

Among the influences tending to transform geography into chorology or *Länderkunde* were first, the progress of the natural sciences, especially geology, meteorology and botany, and, secondly, advances in surveying and map-making. Geology, between Hutton and Suess, progressed to the stage at which it could explain the origin of landforms on the earth, and assess climatic action upon the weathering, transport and erosion of rocks. Modern surveying, from its beginnings in the eighteenth century, provided an increasingly accurate and detailed delineation of the earth's surface and man's multifarious works thereon. And the range of maps was widened by the expansion of official statistics, which could be used as the raw material of many thematic maps, of which those depicting the distribution of population, industries, crops, etc., appear in almost every geography book. Courses in natural sciences and surveying became part of the training for the explorer from the time of Humboldt and Livingstone. Some leaders among German geographers, notably von Richthofen and Albrecht Penck, were geologists before they became geographers. Von Richthofen was also the outstanding nineteenth-century explorer of China.

Physical geography and map study in field and laboratory

largely displaced travellers' narratives and descriptions as the primary sources of geography. The map, rather than the written source,
increasingly dominated geographers' research. Much modern geographical writing is commentary upon and interpretation of maps,
including both large-scale topographical maps and thematic maps
based either upon analysis of topographical maps, or statistical
sources. Modern geographers have written many books characterised by the integration of text with maps and photographs. The
most recent writers exploit the aerial photograph as an aid to
analysis and illustration.

Orthodox method proceeds from the static and permanent to
the mobile and changing. The 'physical basis', including geology,
landforms, climate and hydrological phenomena, is treated first.
Then attention is turned to vegetation, usually combined with an
account of soils, the properties of which depend upon climate,
vegetation and parent rock. At this point, man's works are introduced. The constraints and opportunities offered by his habitat
are examined in relation to his technical attainments and culture.
Description and interpretation of the results of human activity
upon the landscape may follow. This relates to the nature of agriculture, pastoral activity and forestry, mining and industry, the
distribution and forms of rural settlements, the nature, location
and function of towns and cities and the communications network.
These all fall into a rational and ordered analysis of the human
modification of the earth, demonstrating the intimacy, variety and
reciprocity of the relationship between societies and the lands they
occupy. This is the *Zusammenhang* (literally, coherence, interdependence) of the German geographers.

As a subject, geography is not easily accommodated in schemes
of knowledge, or library classifications. It is largely scientific and
indeed the competent geographer needs more than mere acquain-
tance with geology, pedology, meteorology, ethnology and anthropology. Since the past is so often the key to the present—for the
human impress upon the landscape is generally lasting—historical
sources, especially social and economic, are often indispensable.
Some of the earlier British geographers, notably Mackinder, regarded geography as a bridge between the humanities and the
sciences. But the place of geography in knowledge was more clearly
discerned by Hettner, who, following German epistemologists,
pointed out that the external world can be studied, first, by categories of objects, as in natural and social sciences; secondly and

historically, as a sequence of events; or thirdly and geographically, implying that the pattern of the earth's surface is an aspect of reality not comprehended either systematically or historically. The three categories of study are not mutually exclusive; rather, they are modes of apprehending the external world. There are similar implications in defining geography as the study of interaction of the atmosphere, the lithosphere, the hydrosphere and the biosphere at the surface of the earth.

The intellectual appeal of geography is not confined to the library or study. It is also an outdoor pursuit. The field days and expeditions arranged by school and university teachers train pupils and students in observation and reasoning. They also prompt questions for research. The mature geographer, whether professional or amateur, has acquired the power rationally to perceive the nature of a landscape or a region that illimitably enhances the enjoyment of travel. His reflections and judgments upon international affairs and regional problems will be informed by his understanding of the meaning of location, of areal relationships, and of the environmental factor in human efforts and achievements.

This chorological view of geography has also proved to be extremely apposite to the present age, in which the growth of population and the greatly intensified use of natural resources in Western countries have created new problems in the sphere of government, arising from competition for land and the choice of the best use for it. Town and country planning has become a new profession to which many young university-trained geographers have been attracted. Realising the advantages of importing a vocational content to their teaching, many academic geographers have emphasised the chorological content of their subject.

In *Länderkunde*, the effects of human activities upon the earth's surface form a separate class of facts, which are also the avowed subject-matter of Brunhes' treatise. For he stated that he was writing about three categories of essential facts: (1) the unproductive occupation of the soil—houses and highways; (2) the conquest of the vegetable and animal kingdoms; and (3) the destructive occupation of the soil, including the exploitation of minerals. Clearly, he was classifying the elements of landscape arising from man's work upon the earth. In German terminology, this is *Kulturgeographie*, which is a distinct subdivision of *Länderkunde*. In French, however, Brunhes could find no better equivalent than *géographie humaine.* Doubtless he rejected the term *géographie culturelle* because he believed that the French conception of culture is more intellectual and aesthetic—is more the product of *l'ésprit humain*—than the German *Kultur*, which at that time in France as well as in England was deemed to be fundamentally materialistic and aggressive. In French, the scope of Brunhes' work demanded a phrase in the absence of a suitable term. For he was really investigating *'l'œuvre de l'homme sur la terre'*—the effects on the earth's surface of man's work; and evidently he could not think of a phrase conveying this meaning brief enough to be used as the title of a book.

His inappropriate title was literally translated into English in 1920. It would have been far better if the translators (E. C. Le Compte, I. Bowman and R. E. Dodge) had used the term cultural geography, as a fair English equivalent of *Kulturgeographie*, which (as has been already shown) is really what the book is about. In America, little harm has been done, because the term cultural geography is commonly used, and Brunhes' book is often included in recommended reading. In England, however, human geography is often indistinguishable from cultural geography; but sometimes may be or may include human geography in alternative senses. The present work seeks to elucidate an alternative conception.

Human geography defined

To understand this distinction between cultural and human geography, we must turn to the work of Vidal de la Blache. By common consent his greatest work was the *Tableau de la géographie de la France*, published in 1911 as the first volume of a series on the history of France under the editorship of E. Lavisse. Now, in the *Tableau* he adopts the orthodox German view of the nature of geography. He is interpreting the land of France as a 'medal stamped in the effigy' of a people (to repeat an oft-quoted phrase from the introductory section). He surveys France, region by region, shows how the landscape has evolved through the centuries as a result of human efforts, and considers the rôle of each in French and European history. It was the product of a lifetime of close study and intimate knowledge based upon prolonged field work. Profound erudition and literary brilliance gave it the rank of a masterpiece among French geographical writings.

He must have been thinking of his aims in the *Tableau* when he wrote in an article in 1913 that 'geography is the science of places not of men'. This is quoted approvingly in the *Spirit and Purpose of Geography*; but it does not epitomise all Vidal's work. In the *Tableau* he was writing *Länderkunde*; later, in his last book, published posthumously, he saw a geography that is not primarily a study of the land. He regarded human geography as a comparative study of human societies. It originally arose from man's curiosity about other peoples: about their ways of living, their customs and institutions, which indeed is most apparent in the greatest of the ancient treatises, Strabo's *Geographia*. Vidal seeks to interpret differences between societies in terms of their relationships with environment. In the successive sections of the *Principles*, he considers (as the leading aspects of societies) the density and distribution of population, tools and raw materials, the means of sustenance, building materials, forms of settlement and communications. These are to be interpreted in terms of the resources, the limitations, or the advantages of environments. In one of the 'Fragments', unfinished at his death, and appended to the work by his editors, he considers also racial differences.

He points out that such a study could be undertaken in the modern age for two reasons: first, the expansion of human knowledge about the peoples of the world, as a result of explorations from the Age of Discovery until the end of the nineteenth century; secondly, the insight into the infinitely complex connections between man and his habitat, revealed by the progress of biology, emphasised in the work of Darwin and termed ecology since Haeckel's day. Some aims of human geography are coincident with human ecology. 'The phenomena of human geography . . . are everywhere related to the environment, itself the creature of a combination of physical conditions.'

Vidal regarded Ratzel as the founder of human geography: Ratzel invented the term for the first volume of his work *Anthropogeographie* in 1882. Ratzel's environment was mainly the physical. He inquired into the rôle of rivers, mountains, islands, coasts, deserts, etc., in human affairs. Vidal saw him also as a successor of earlier, pre-Darwinian writers (including Ritter), who had speculated upon the influence of lands upon history. He mentions among these Buckle, and, as well he might (being a Frenchman), Montesquieu. But Ratzel took the world as a whole. Vidal, as early as 1890, and on several occasions afterwards, emphasised 'terrestrial unity' as a cardinal principle of geography. 'Friedrich

Ratzel very wisely insists on such a conception, making it the cornerstone of his *Anthropogeographie*.' The phenomena of human geography are related to terrestrial unity, 'by means of which alone can they be explained'. Earlier writers restricted their comparisons to ancient and modern Europe together with the Near East. Not only does Vidal interpret important aspects of society in terms of the non-human features of environment, but he compares civilisations. He draws attention to the zone stretching across the old world north of the tropic, in which early forms of civilisation developed on a larger scale than elsewhere: 'domains ready-made for great empires, as well as for the great religions which there succeeded one another. A long period of synthesis has resulted in the formation of social groups summed up in such words as Islam, Christian Europe, Hinduism, China—centres of influence which are composed of many lesser centres, but which appear to be homogeneous.'

This evolution in thought about human geography can be summarised in a simple table.

THE EVOLUTION OF HUMAN GEOGRAPHY

Early writers Classical, e.g. Thucydides; Modern, e.g. Montesquieu, Buckle, Ritter	The influence of lands upon history.
Later writers Ratzel	Wider conception of environment; but still viewed mainly physically. Principle of terrestrial unity.
Vidal de la Blache	Society, viewed ecologically, and terrestrial unity as the twin principles of human geography.

One of Vidal's most distinguished pupils was Maximilien Sorre, who towards the end of a long life productive of much scholarly work, wrote the most comprehensive treatise on human geography yet to appear, in three volumes, of which the first was published in 1943 and the last in 1952, called *Les Fondements de la Géographie Humaine*. Whilst it is not a masterpiece, because its approach is partly conventional, its breadth and the original treatment of biological foundations in the first volume place the work among the outstanding achievements of French geography, which must be recognised by any author writing about the evolution of geographical thought. It was the omission of any reference to it by Professors Wooldridge and East which first prompted the present author to think that there might be room in this series for a book on human geography, distinguishing it from geography (chorologically conceived) and to introduce French work, more particularly Sorre's, to the English-speaking world.

Sorre's first volume is devoted to 'the study of man as a living organism subject to determinate conditions of existence and reacting to stimuli received from the natural environment'. In it he considers, first, the effects of terrestrial climates upon the anatomy and physiology of man, and hence, ultimately, upon the origin and function of racial differences. Then he turns to the relationship between man and disease-producing micro-organisms, themselves subject to environmental influence, and called by Sorre 'pathogenic complexes'. (Here, and generally in this book, 'race' and 'racial' are to be understood in their anthropological sense, as referring to the physiques of human groups, not to their arts, customs or institutions.)

The second volume (in two parts) is devoted to the techniques of social life. He asserts at the outset, that 'we put man in the centre of the picture, with all his power of invention, with all his initiative in the pursuit of the conquest of the globe, to transform it into the *oikumene*. The composition is certainly of an ecological order, but on a larger scale. It comprises not only the most elementary and primitive forms of activity but all the most evolved. Its pursuit leads to the geographical explanation of the world.' In elaborating this theme, he first adumbrates 'essential facts' (surely in order to emphasise the gulf separating him from Brunhes). For Sorre's facts relate not to the landscape; but to the forms of society, language, religion, economy, population density and political organisation.

For both Vidal de la Blache and Sorre terrestrial unity implies a perspective of mankind that is not only ecological but is also evolutionary. Human society has attained its extraordinary complexity because human intelligence can devise means of adaptation to almost the entire environmental range offered by the earth. Hence, change has been incessant, though its nature and effects in the present age differ from those in the past. When mankind was young, small social groups extended the bounds of the *oikumene* or inhabited world, devising new means of living as they encoun-

tered new resources, losing touch with those behind. It was a
world of self-sufficient groups living in isolation, such as were
discovered in remoter continental areas during the explorations
of the period between 1500 and 1900, and very locally in the
twentieth century: for instance, in New Guinea. More recently, as
the means of transport have improved, terrestrial unity has been
increasingly realised in growing economic interdependence and
diffusion of knowledge. Yet there is little diminution of regional
disparity, because locally the web of relationships with environment becomes more complex. Some nineteenth-century writers
believed that the progress of mankind would reduce differences
between groups and lead to a world society. But today, many believe that disparities are still increasing, more particularly between industrialised regions and 'developing' societies. Can the
contemporary challenge to geographers be the interpretation of a
paradox: a world increasingly unified yet becoming more diversified?

The problems of human geography

Human geography, then, at its emergence under Ratzel, viewed
human society as a whole, in all its diversity and ecologically. And
the culmination of exploration not only provided this new opportunity for geographical scholarship, but also initiated the classical
period of ethnology and anthropology. Hence, human geography
can also be regarded as a new branch of geography called into
existence by the rise of these new cognate social sciences. (Earlier,
physical geography had arisen from the impact of geology and
meteorology upon the older, more descriptive geography.)

By the beginning of the present century, a very large number of
primitive societies, in all continents, had been described; and some
anthropologists became engaged by problems of classification. It
was realised that the most fundamental division arose between
societies that collected and hunted, and those that produced their
food supplies by means of cultivation, pastoralism, or a combination of both. Mankind could be divided between a small minority
of hunters and food collectors and the greatly preponderant
majority of the food producers.

Further subdivision of these two main categories was devised
by several authors; and an attempt was made by Hobhouse,
Wheeler and Ginsberg to establish correlations or connections
between institutions and the several types both of producers and

non-producers. Somewhat later, C. D. Forde in a work entitled *Habitat, Economy and Society* provided an introduction to modern ethnology in the shape of studies of selected societies, chosen to exemplify the range existing within both the producing and non-producing societies. As its title implies, its approach was ecological; and the book was widely used for introductory reading in connection with courses both on ethnology and of human or cultural geography. The work of Hobhouse and Forde influenced the classification of societies developed in the earlier editions of the present book, in which the geographical concept of terrestrial unity was given effect by bringing the major civilisations, Western and Oriental, into a scheme that included also categories of more primitive societies. The concept was also illustrated in fields quite untouched by Hobhouse and Forde, by considering the results of human migrations and the diffusion of cultivated plants and domesticated animals. Other aspects of the economy and ecology of societies were also considered briefly. These included the forms of settlements and communications. Seen in retrospect, this work represented fairly enough on a small scale the conception of human geography developed so much more fully by Sorre; but to some extent it still remained entangled with ethnology and anthropology (when dealing with simpler societies) and with Brunhes' chorological type of human (cultural) geography on the other: an entanglement which, incidentally, Sorre did not entirely avoid, particularly in his treatment of production and transport (which is essentially descriptive economic geography) and of settlements, rural and urban, in his third volume. Here, and substantially, he slipped away from his avowed objectives (see p. 21) into cultural geography.

Now the continuing task of geography is to describe and understand the contemporary world. Its subject-matter evolves with mankind. In an age of revolutionary change, such as the present, its content can alter radically within a life-time, if not within a decade. It is therefore important to recognise and define the current tendencies within, and the characteristics of human society, viewed ecologically.

The most important recent change has already been mentioned. The internal combustion engine, used as the source of power in aeroplanes and motor vehicles, has completed the revolution in transport begun by the railway and steamship more than a century ago. World trade has greatly increased, and so has the interdependence between regions and countries. The movement of persons and goods locally and internationally is continually expanding. New world trade currents have appeared.

Modern forms of transport were Western inventions. Their diffusion throughout the rest of the world has catalysed non-Western societies. Most primitive societies have now passed from self-sufficiency into trade. They now produce surpluses of agricultural or pastoral products, which they sell for money and use to purchase exotic goods. Others have been even more profoundly altered by the introduction of large-scale Western enterprise, in the shape of plantations to produce tropical crops like tea, coffee, sisal, sugar or rubber; or of mining concerns, winning copper, petroleum or iron ore. In non-Western societies that had already become commercial, the character of trade has changed, and craftsmanship has been partly supplanted by modern manufacturing in factories. In short, the world today is in the throes of the industrial and agrarian revolutions, which, after transforming western Europe and North America, are now permeating all other countries, regions and continents.

In all the continents we find primitive societies drawn inexorably into this main stream of human progress. The Eskimos of the American Arctic are representative of hundreds of tribal peoples who until recently lived apart from the rest of the world. Their traditional and specialised mode of living has often been described by geographers and ethnologists. To the former, who often classify economies in terms of the major climatic zones, the Eskimos exemplified adaptation to extremely cold climates. Their main sustenance was obtained from marine Arctic mammals, which they hunted with the greatest skill and with ingenious weapons fabricated largely from driftwood. They could paddle across open water in skin-covered small boats. They habituated themselves to a meat diet. They used animal oil for cooking, heating and lighting. They built their winter homes of ice blocks. They used furs for clothing and bedding. In summer, they moved away from the coast to hunt caribou and to gather wild fruits, sheltering themselves in skin-covered tents. They lived and migrated in small groups or single families.

It is clear from recent studies, such as the series on *Eskimo Administration* published by the Arctic Institute of North America, that the traditional Eskimo way of life has been quite superseded. The first stage was passed when they were drawn into the fur trade.

They ceased to practise a subsistence economy. They were encouraged to produce a surplus, beyond their own requirements, of
the skins of fur-bearing animals. These they sold, and bought not
only imported utensils, foods and drink, but new types of trap.
However, this did not bring an improved standard of living; and
the Eskimo came increasingly to depend upon allowances paid by
the American or Canadian governments to ensure that he could
obtain at least the bare necessities of life. The Eskimos were im-
pelled a stage further from their original subsistence economy
during the Second World War and immediately afterwards, when
military bases were built in the Arctic, and minerals began to be
exploited. Eskimos began to live in prefabricated houses in the
settlements adjoining airfields, radar stations and mines.

But they remain on the fringe of Canadian and American life.
It is unlikely that they can all find modern forms of employment
in the far North providing a standard of living comparable with
North America as a whole. The Arctic Institute's reports recom-
mend improved education, to ensure that children learn English
well, and improved vocational training. An Eskimo would then
be able to rise above the unskilled worker's position in Canada.
And both the more able and ambitious, as well as others for whom
no livelihood can be found in the North, could migrate south and
become assimilated into the larger societies of Canada or the
United States. The future for the young Eskimo is epigrammatised
as 'get educated and go south'. Eskimos have now advanced so far
in the transition from isolation to absorption within modern
north American society that knowledge of their original life will
be soon confined to the antiquarian. Those still following hunting,
fishing and trapping are probably to be numbered only in hundreds, and will doubtless continue to diminish.

The universal growth of towns and cities is another dominant
social trend of the present age. Urban communities seem first to
have appeared at a few places in the Near East during the Neolithic period, e.g. at Jericho. By the middle of the fourth millennium B.C. small towns had been founded in Mesopotamia and
Egypt. Later, they spread to the Indus valley and China. The first
towns of the New World were established by the inhabitants of
what is now Mexico about two thousand years ago. Until the end
of the Middle Ages, urban communities were confined to Europe,
northern Africa, the Orient and Central America. The European
expansion across the oceans and into Siberia after the age of

Columbus caused many new cities to be founded in colonial regions. But everywhere, in the regions of ancient and more recent urbanisation alike, the proportion of population living in towns and cities remained small. The majority of men lived in the countryside.

But again, as a concomitant of the industrial and agrarian revolutions, town gradually gained over the countryside. The process began first in England towards the end of the eighteenth century; and by 1900, the proportion of the population living in towns in Great Britain had reached four-fifths of the whole. Since then, it has remained almost stationary. Other similarly industrialised countries in western Europe and North America have also attained much the same degree of urbanisation. The United States, where in 1800 less than 10 per cent of the population was urban, had in 1960 70 per cent of its population living in towns.

More recently, the same trend has been revealed in the extra-European world. It has been most marked in Japan, where in 1875 about 15 per cent of its population lived in towns, and it now has an only slightly smaller (65 per cent) proportion than the United States. Brazil, relatively advanced by 1940, when 30 per cent of its population was town-dwelling, had reached 45 per cent by 1960. Egypt, with 25 per cent in 1935, had increased its urban population to 38 per cent by 1960.

Evidently, the urbanising tendency is universal. Where society has been completely transformed by the industrial and agrarian revolutions, three-quarters to four-fifths of the population lives in towns. At the present time, some 25 to 30 per cent of the world's population is urban. But a century ago the proportion was only about 3 per cent. In the last century, therefore, the proportion of the world's population living in towns and cities has increased tenfold. Hypertrophy of cities is a now well-established and irreversible characteristic within human society.

The growth of urban populations is taking place at a time of accelerated expansion within the entire human family. From the emergence of *Homo sapiens* at a still undetermined date in the Pleistocene period, the number of human beings increased relatively slowly until about A.D. 1820, when, it is estimated, the total reached 1,000 millions. This resulted from the extension of the inhabited world by migration from the original home of mankind in the Old World, and the adoption by most societies of food production instead of hunting and collecting. Agriculture, as it came to be practised in the Monsoon Lands, Egypt and some parts of Europe gradually attained the capacity to support quite dense populations. But by 1820, accelerated population growth had already begun, under the twofold influence of the industrial and agrarian revolutions and improvements in medicine. The former influence increased the production of and trade in foodstuffs. The latter conquered disease. Not only have modern drugs overcome epidemic diseases that formerly decimated whole populations, but public health measures arising from knowledge of the true causation of diseases have reduced the incidence of illness. These advances in medicine have been particularly effective in combating the infectious diseases of childhood, which until the last century so greatly reduced the numbers of infants reaching adulthood as to prevent populations from increasing fast. They have also been an effective passive agent permitting the urban growth so actively promoted by industrialisation. Large cities and conurbations could not function unless the population is guaranteed immunity from epidemics by public health measures.

Beginning in western countries last century, and extending to the remainder of the world in the present century, the world population has increased astonishingly. The total reached 2,000 millions in 1930, 3,000 millions in 1960 and it is estimated that it will attain 4,000 millions by 1975.

Since the Second World War, it has been realised that this multiplication of human beings imperils the future. Many countries are now desperately struggling to avert imminent decline in living standards and widespread malnutrition. The population problem looms in sociology, government, international relations and economics. But it has only recently become universal; and in the past was correspondingly subordinate in the social sciences. To Vidal de la Blache it was the local concentrations of population in Europe and the Monsoon Lands that invited inquiry and explanation. Otherwise, in geography the distribution and numbers of the population were simply essential aspects of man's relationship with his environment. Population increase or, occasionally, decrease or stability, was touched upon for the sake of completeness; but rarely needed to be considered as a major problem of a country or region, except perhaps for China, India and Egypt. Sorre had less to write about population even than Vidal, despite the greater scale of his treatise. Seen in this light, Sorre's work is the culmination of a past phase of geographical thought rather than a pioneer work of the present. It is not surprising that population geography has become a new specialism.

Major societies in the post-imperialist age

The present is an epoch in world history for reasons additional to the spread of Western technology and the accelerated growth of population and towns. Among these the end of European expansion is the most important. Four-and-three-quarter centuries ago, Columbus reached the New World, thus heralding the Great Age of Discovery. Thereby two great currents of human migrations began: the European and the Negroid. These profoundly altered the distribution of races, particularly in the New World, but also in Africa and Australia. He also initiated the age of European overseas empires, by claiming Haiti for the King of Spain. The Spanish and Portuguese world empires were accompanied by Dutch, British and French. Russia simultaneously began an overland expansion into Siberia and North America. Almost the entire extra-European world came under European rule. The only exceptions were all—except one, Liberia—in Asia: Arabia, Turkey, Iran, Thailand, China, Tibet, and Japan. Two centuries ago, with the Declaration of American Independence, the break-up began. During the nineteenth century, disintegration (especially in Latin America) was counterbalanced by the further expansion of the imperialist era in Africa and Asia. But in the twentieth century, the British empire evolved into the Commonwealth of independent nations; and this movement was paralleled in the surviving overseas colonial empires: Belgium, France, and the Netherlands. Only Portugal retains sizable colonies; for Britain and France now rule but a few fragments. The only European empire (though not so called) to survive intact is the Russian.

Overseas dependencies of European powers fell into two categories. In the first, their rule was established over numerous and often advanced peoples, mainly in subtropical and tropical regions. Into these dependencies, the volume of European immigration was never large. Into the second category, in temperate lands, usually thinly-peopled, was directed—as a distinguishing characteristic—a much greater volume of emigrants. Here, daughter-states of the European mother countries were founded, which in the course of time became independent.

The downfall of the colonial empires resulted from the reaction of indigenous peoples to alien rule, prompted by the example of the United States of America, Latin America and the 'old' dominions of the British Empire. It was begun by the Congress movement in India; and spread to the Arab world and South-east Asia in the present century. China also, which underwent penetration by competing European imperialisms, and also a Japanese conquest, has recovered her autonomy, and is now assimilating the industrial and agrarian revolutions in her own way. Indonesia has shaken off Dutch authority. And in the mid-twentieth century, the anti-colonial movement has spread throughout Africa. Within a decade, French, British and Belgian colonies have become independent. The withdrawal of imperial rule has left the world's major societies more clearly revealed. In Asia, the Far East and the Indian subcontinent each contain a substantial portion of the human family, conscious of its distinctive institutions, traditions, history, arts and economy. Each is not without internal diversity. The Far East (or Sinic) region is composed of the larger China and the smaller Japan, Korea and Vietnam, having many characteristics in common, but also important regional differences. Farther west, in the Middle East and North Africa, is a less numerous and more scattered population consciously sharing the common inheritance of Islam; but Islamic unity does not bring social conformity. Arabic is the dominant language; but others flourish, notably Turkish and Persian. In the South Asian subcontinent, Pakistan and India now stand apart. Ceylon is an adjacent island, socially akin to India.

In the peninsular and island world of South-east Asia, a group of peoples including the Burmese, the Thai, the Malays, the Javanese and the Filipinos are now experiencing independence in the modern world. Most of them were strongly influenced by Hinduism and Buddhism in the Middle Ages, and by Islam since the sixteenth century. They are not, however, a part either of the Islamic or the Hindu society today. There is too much that is indigenous in their way of life and outlook.

Recovery of political autonomy by these great Oriental civilisations has also brought partial political reintegration. The most outstanding instance is China, where the authority of the central government has been restored, not only within China proper but also in some of the historic dependencies in central Asia. The unity of Chinese civilisation has always been greater than that of either India and or the Islamic world. And, undoubtedly, the Peking government is fostering nationalism to underpin the foundations of strengthened central government.

The unifying influence of the Arab League in the Middle East and North Africa must not be underrated, despite evident dissension about many issues. In Arab lands, the 'unity of the Arab nation' was an aim of the pioneers of self-determination and the revolt against colonial rule. Pan-Arabism, not negligible as a political force, has fostered much sympathy and co-operation between the scattered Arab peoples.

If one is inclined to stigmatise the political rupture of the Indian subcontinent as declension from the unity achieved in the Indian Empire, it should be remembered that the present Indian federal constitution provides a more coherent framework for modern government than the fragmentation left by the demise of the Moghul Empire, so sedulously preserved by British rule. And the struggle for self-determination waged for so long by the Congress movement has imparted awareness of the nature and range of Hindu civilisation, which only educated Brahmins previously understood, and then in traditional religious terms. Local language, caste and village community are still strong bonds in an individual's loyalty in India; but in addition he is now a member of an Indian nation.

Alongside these Oriental civilisations stands the Western. European in origin, it has now become well-rooted in other continents, especially in the New World, as a result of overseas emigration and colonisation by European peoples from the sixteenth century onwards. Moulded by Graeco-Roman civilisation and by Christendom, it entered upon a particularly rapid social and economic evolution when the agrarian and industrial revolutions arose within. Like the Oriental civilisations, it is not without diversity and deeper cleavages, such as that subsisting between the Eastern Bloc and the rest. The characteristics of Western civilisation will be examined more fully later. Here, only the introductory problem of terminology will be faced. The adjective 'Western' has several meanings. It is often equated with the countries of the 'Atlantic alliance', as the rival power-group led by the United States to the countries headed by the USSR, sometimes referred to as 'Eastern Europe' or 'Socialist Europe'. Sometimes the 'West' is identified with western Europe and lands overseas now inhabited by the descendants of European emigrants, or in which Europeans are dominant. Thus, much or all of South America and Central

America would be included. But the meaning to be attached to the term 'Western' in this book is wider still, because it includes Eastern Europe, which with western Europe has its historical roots in Greece, Rome and Christianity; and is also far advanced on the path of industrialisation. A writer is confronted by a dilemma. The only two suitable available terms are 'European' and 'Western'. The former seems to ignore the nations of the New World and elsewhere that are offshoots from the European stock. 'Western' suitably emphasises the separate identity of the civilisation, in contrast especially with Oriental; but it suffers the handicap that it is also used in a more strictly political context to signify the non-Communist portion. The use of either term is to some extent an arbitrary decision. Perhaps the disadvantages of 'Western' are fewer than those of 'European'; and so the former will be used henceforward in this book.

In addition to these four major civilisations of the Old World, the observer of the contemporary human scene must recognise a nascent civilisation in tropical Africa. Here is another new element in the post-Imperialist world. Negroid peoples in Africa have realised their affinity. Alike, they have sought independence of foreign rule. And they face similar social and economic problems, arising from common characteristics of their societies before the colonial period, and their economies. Their newly-discovered mutual sympathy has been expressed politically in the Organisation of African States. An Economic Commission for Africa has been founded as an organ of UNO. Tropical Africa was previously a major ethnic province; but its peoples had little if any awareness of one another. They were illiterate, and had horizons limited by their tribal membership. They may have had some inkling of the nature and effects of colonial government; but colonial subdivision inhibited any pan-African tendencies. Only at the end of colonial rule, and with the introduction of modern education and politics, have Africans become aware of their continental unity.

The developed and the developing worlds

The recovery of autonomy by the Oriental civilisations and the rise of an African civilisation are not the only principal consequences of the altered political relationship between the Western peoples and the rest of mankind. For the present age is witnessing a changed attitude towards the diffusion of Western technology and institutions. In the past, the non-Western world was subjected

to the effects of the agrarian and industrial revolutions as an in-
escapable consequence of European emigration, imperialism and
commercial expansion. Generally, the results were localised.
Japan was the single non-Western country to be transformed by
the adoption of Western technology and institutions before the
present era: a portent of the future during the climax of the
colonial period. In Ceylon, the plantation economy, though extensive, was confined to the hills and the Wet Zone of the
south-west. In India, too, plantations were localised along the
Himalayan foothills, in Assam, and in the hill regions of the
southern peninsula. Industries were most active in and near
the great ports of Calcutta, Madras and Bombay. In Africa, the
Copperbelt and the Highlands of Kenya were separated by an
expanse of bush, either uninhabited or occupied by tribes obtaining
their livelihoods in traditional ways. In the East Indies, Java was
thoroughly transformed by Dutch colonial enterprise; but the
remaining islands of the archipelago were hardly touched.
Neighbouring Malaya was an admixture of rubber plantations, tin
mines, Malayan cultivators or fisher-folk, adjoining Singapore, a
colonial maritime metropolis and entrepôt; but here the intrusion
of Western enterprise was greater than generally in, what was then
called, Indo-China. In the Middle East, the oilfields of Iran and
Iraq were the more isolated from the indigenous population because they are for the most part in thinly-peopled or uninhabited
arid regions. Characteristically, colonial rule, and the application
of Western techniques to undeveloped resources, was the work of
small, transient European minorities, composed of individuals
who, after spending part of their working lives abroad, returned
to their European country of origin to retire, or to continue their
careers. Whilst many alien administrators, educators, and other
residents were sympathetic students of the peoples among whom
they were living, and often cultivated friendships with the 'natives',
the relationship always remained artificial. They could not fully
accept or be accepted by the non-European majority.

In addition to non-Western regions, parts of the Western world
also reveal uneven and retarded development. South and Central
America have generally been backward, but in varying degrees.
Recently some countries, e.g. Argentina, Brazil, Venezuela, Chile
and Mexico, have recorded substantial increases in national income. Eastern Europe, also, lagged behind Western Europe and
North America; but during the past two decades has made con-

spicuous progress industrially. These developmental peculiarities within the Western world will be examined more fully later.

Social changes accompanying the march towards independence not only illuminate recent political history but also explain the universal demand in the non-Western world to develop or to be developed economically. Colonial governments and Western enterprises needed educated indigenous persons in subordinate positions. Therefore, they founded schools providing at first elementary technical training and the rudiments of literacy; but later, secondary and higher education. Political movements aiming at liberation from foreign rule were then founded—almost everywhere within the small minority that had received the more advanced forms of Western education. At this stage, when literacy had become thinly yet widely diffused, the printing press and improvements in communications enabled political leaders to arouse indigenous peoples and to claim both independence and better standards of living. Films, imported from the West, as well as the style of living of the alien ruling minorities, created awareness of the gulf between Western and indigenous consumption. After independence had been obtained, the new leaders could use broadcasting, and in many countries television, as well as the press, to foster not only local nationalism but also to advocate development as the supreme goal of internal policy. Hence, the populations of former colonies are impatient to develop latent resources. They demand more education as a prerequisite of the march towards better living standards; and claim the right of access to Western scientific knowledge and capital. They assert that capital investment, instead of being determined by the politico-economic calculus of former colonial powers (which they stigmatise as neo-colonialism), should include criteria based upon the welfare of previously-dependent peoples. These claims are repeated in international assemblies, and have led to lengthy debates, such as those at Delhi during the UNCTAD conference of 1968.

Recent growth of the international community has been shaped by development problems. Several organs of UNO, especially FAO, the Economic and Social Council, UNESCO and WHO, exist mainly to foster progress in former colonial regions. New financial organs, of which the most important is the World Bank, have been created to manage investment. Enlargement of function is of the essence of the international organisation during the present era. Only a generation ago, the League of Nations fulfilled only

B

a limited, and mainly political, rôle. Moreover, this adaptation and expansion of international organisations have been supplemented by new government departments within the former colonial powers. The Ministry of Overseas Development in London is typical.

Most, if not all, developing countries have national plans drawn up by, or with the advice of, experts from the developed world. Many issues arise during investigations, and final decisions on the scope and aims of plans demand judgment in the light of all circumstances, including the political. Newly-independent countries in the 1950s were prone to insist that industrialisation was the open sesame to improved living standards. Since India was compelled, in its third five-year plan, to emphasise agricultural advance, there has been more widespread realisation that the countryside must become more productive before industrialisation can be a success. President Nyerere's Arusha Declaration is proving a turning-point in the history of African development policies.

Characteristically, national plans are composed of a list of schemes, local or regional. A new cash crop may be introduced somewhere. Dams, power stations, new industries and new irrigated tracts may be included in a plan for a river basin. New roads railways and ports may be constructed to facilitate both the export of agricultural surpluses and minerals. Plans for the remodelling and growth of towns are prepared.

Many plans are based upon integrated surveys of natural resources, or, for towns, upon urban surveys, produced by teams of experts, local and expatriate. Reports of these surveys are valuable additions to the range of existing sources on the countries or parts of countries concerned. Some lay the foundations of scientific knowledge where previously there was little or none. As such, they are extremely useful to the geographer.

New perspectives for geography are also created. Formerly, the goal was the rational study of the present. In countries with history, the past was often invoked to explain the existing. Nowadays the present must be viewed as the doorway into the future. Trends are as significant as facts. Moreover, the geographer's holistic, ecological principles give him a valid basis for independent appraisal of development. He can often undertake the salutary task of assessing and explaining shortfall in the results of past planning. He can contribute to public discussion with detachment, if he has not been involved in the planning process. He can contribute to education in developing countries by his understanding of the aims of current effort, the gains it is hoped to secure, and the interrelationships between human efforts and available natural resources.

Prolegomenon to a theory of human geography

Most of humanity is divided between five major societies: Islamic, Western, Hindu, Sinic and Negroid. All these societies originated in the Old World, and all except one are still located there. They have all grown from small beginnings. They can be traced to modest, very localised origins in the prehistoric era. They have all revealed remarkable capacity for internal evolution and also for geographical expansion, arising both from the absorption of adjoining societies and by acceptance of innovations from outside after long-distance intercourse had been achieved by land and sea.

Expansion has extended the influence of these major societies beyond the tracts they can properly call their own. Islam, for instance, is expanding in West and East Africa, in regions outside those hitherto regarded as Islamic. Chinese communities are active in many Pacific islands, the East Indies and in Central Asia—all well outside the Sinic region proper.

The combination of these tendencies to evolve, assimilate and expand suggests a fourfold zonation of the regions which they occupy. The place of origin of each civilisation is its *hearth*. This was the original, prehistoric seat of the embryonic society. Here the fundamental techniques in using resources were invented or first applied. Here enduring social, including religious, institutions were founded which contributed to cohesion and continuity through the historic period. For example, Sinic civilisation originated in the valley of a small tributary of the Hwang-ho—the Wei —in north China. Here were the first Chinese urban communities. Hindu civilisation extends throughout the Indian subcontinent. But if we trace it to its prehistoric beginnings, we find that it was born and nurtured in the Upper Ganges basin, at a period when the rest of India was non-Aryan. Western civilisation originated in the Levant, Greece and Italy. It spread only slowly into the rest of Europe.

In the course of their evolution, the major societies have expanded outside their hearths into their present *cores* or *core-regions*. These may be defined as tracts absorbed early into its occupied area by the growing society, and in which, today, it exhibits its most fully-developed form. Today, for instance, Western Europe is the core of Western civilisation.

Proceeding outwards from the core, we may next identify the *domain*. Usually this was incorporated in the course of fairly recent expansion; and some more ancient features preserved in the core may be lacking. Thus, Manchuria can be included within the domain of Chinese civilisation. It has been settled by Chinese since about 1900. But it is a 'new' Chinese country. Some of the old China has been left behind. The same is true of the regions of the New World and Australia recently settled by European emigrants. They undoubtedly form part of Western society; but they also bear the marks of their recent establishment. Within some domains, features of earlier cultures, not fully assimilated, may be in evidence, although incorporation is not in doubt. Such is apparent in north-west Africa, where the Berber societies of the mountains, though part of Islam, are loth to relinquish their languages and traditional social institutions, which, however, have been accommodated within the frame of Islam.

Finally, we may think of peripheral regions, influenced by a civilisation or major society, but not fully incorporated within it, as its *sphere*. Here, indigenous societies still exist, usually in course of transformation. Thus, the Andean highlands in South America are within the sphere of Western civilisation, rather than its domain, for substantial groups still speak Kichua (Quechua) and Chibcha, and maintain many customs and practices of the pre-Columbian period. The same is true in Mexico, where the Aztec and Maya peoples have not wholly disappeared. Moreover, the spheres of the major societies may intersect. Hindu, Islamic, Chinese and Western civilisations evidently meet in South-east Asia.

In one important aspect, the sphere of Western civilisation differs from those of the other major societies: it is world-wide. Not only has Western civilisation expanded more widely and rapidly in recent centuries, but its influence has become universal. This is a simple statement, in alternative theoretical terms, of the effects of the industrial and agrarian revolutions, which have already been outlined.

From this theory, two other concepts arise. Major societies in the course of their expansion come into contact with one another along often well-defined frontiers. One of the most significant and fundamental dividing lines in Africa is the frontier between the Islamic north and the Negroid centre, which cuts both Sudan and

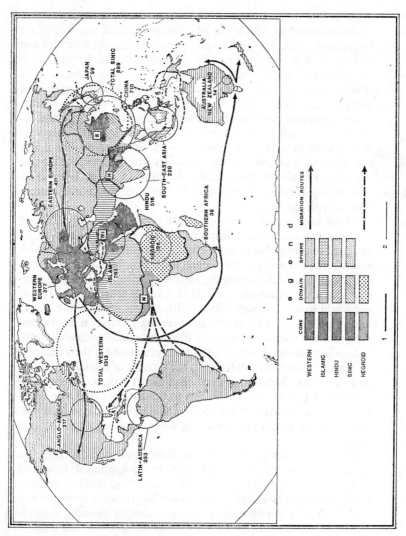

Fig. 1 The major human regions of the world

Areas of circles are proportional to the total population of each region. Hearths of the major civilisations are located by squares enclosing initial letters.

1 – boundaries between civilisations
2 – boundaries between the Soviet bloc and western Europe and between Latin America and Anglo-America

Nigeria into two. To the north, urban life, long-distance commerce, pilgrimage within the Muslim world, and nomadism are prominent in the way of living. To the south, until recently, hoe cultivation and tribal life in villages prevailed. The Levant is another zone of contact between civilisations. In its cities, such as Beirut, Istanbul and Cairo, the interaction of European and Islamic societies through the centuries can be studied. And Israel is an enclave of the Western world, conceived in Europe and intruded into the domain of Islam. In passing, it is worth observing that the Islamic frontier marches with those of all the major societies in the Old World. The frontiers with Negroid Africa and Europe have already been mentioned. But in India, Islam is involved with Hindu civilisation; in Central Asia and north-western China, with the Sinic.

Along such frontiers two or, more occasionally, three, major societies are in contact. But there are also regions not to be assigned to any major society, even as part of its sphere, in which several such societies are interacting. Southern Africa comes readily to the mind. European, Negroid African and Hindu communities are inextricably mingled in a social crucible. The rest of the world waits to observe the resulting alloy. Perhaps the largest and most varied of these cultural meeting grounds is South-east Asia and the Pacific. Here, some distinctive and relatively-advanced indigenous societies, like the Malay, still retain their identity, alongside more primitive tribes in the interior of the larger islands and the Indo-Chinese mainland. But Sinic, Hindu, Muslim and Western civilisations have all come to these shores, and a fascinating human kaleidoscope has resulted. Singapore, as one outcome, may perhaps claim to be the world's most cosmopolitan city (see chapter 5).

This conception of the essential division of mankind into five major societies was first developed in geographical terms by Schmitthenner in 1936. It is somewhat surprising that its introduction into human geography should have been so long deferred. For it is implicit in the awareness by Europeans of essential dissimilarities in the Orient. And among Oriental scholars, the need to recognise Islam, India and the Far East as civilisations *sui generis* has been accepted for at least a century. More recently, historical and anthropological thought has emphasised the significance of discrete societies and civilisations. Toynbee bases his *Study of History* upon the hypothesis that the unit of historical study is the civilisation. In his text he distinguishes a total of twenty-three; but of these at least sixteen are affiliated to earlier civilisations. His map of civilisations in A.D. 1952[1] shows: Western, Russian, Islamic, Hindu and Far Eastern. His theory that civilisations arise from response to challenge (often environmental) has naturally attracted much interest among geographers. A. L. Kroeber, a leading American anthropologist, in a posthumous work (*A Roster of Civilizations and Cultures*, 1962), attempted to identify the world's principal societies. He lists 6 European, 5 in Oceania, 7 African and 6 in the New World. For Asia, he lists 7; but this section of the book is incomplete; and he would almost certainly have amplified the number if he had lived longer. Again, he regards some societies as extinct.

Both Toynbee and Kroeber therefore regard discrete civilisations or societies as a primary feature of mankind on the earth. For Toynbee, also, there is a dynamic in all human civilisations. His work compares one with another to discover the laws of history. His attention is focused upon institutions and critical events. This puts him on a road parallel to, but distinct from, the human geographer, whose leading concepts are, as already stated, evolutionary and ecological. In the succeeding pages, the main objective will be to sketch the evolution of each major society and its interaction both with its habitat and with the rest of mankind.

One final question, of terminological import, arises. Does the prominence given to society in this theory justify the introduction of a new term? Bobek, for instance, in 1948 (see the bibliography) argued that social or socio-geography should be clearly distinguished from cultural geography. It is perhaps pertinent that many of his original investigations have been undertaken in the midst of a non-Western society, in Turkey and Iran. His argument has been supported in England. However, it should be remembered that whereas in Germany the nature of *Kulturgeographie* is understood and is circumscribed, in England and France human geography is a larger, more diffuse branch, which has been defined and expounded in a variety of ways. Some of the present work could form part of a more conservative and orthodox exposition. Hence, such a mode of treatment cannot be regarded as a distinct, new branch of geography in England.

[1] A Toynbee and E. D. Myers, *A Study of History, XI, Historical Atlas and Gazetteer*, 1959, map 4, p. 93. Tropical Africa, Papua and Melanesia are shown as "Primitive, uncommitted".

BIBLIOGRAPHY

THEORY OF GEOGRAPHY AND NATURE OF HUMAN GEOGRAPHY

BAGBY, P., *Culture and History,* 1958.

BEWS, J. W., *Human Ecology,* 1935.

BOBEK, H., 'Stellung und Bedeutung der Sozialgeographie', *Erdkunde,* **2**, 1948, 118–25.

BRUNHES, J., *La géographie humaine,* 1910 (translated Le Compte, E. C., Bowman, I. and Dodge, R. E., 1920; translated and abridged Row, E. F., 1952).

Eskimo administration: I, Alaska; II, Canada; III, Labrador; IV, Greenland. Arctic Institute of North America, *Technical Papers,* **10**, 1962; **14**, 1964; **16**, 1965; **19**, 1967.

FRY, E., 'Growing up in Canada's Frozen North', *Geographical Magazine,* **41**, 1968–9, 271–7.

HARTSHORNE, R., 'The Nature of Geography', *Annals Association American Geographers,* 1939 (reprinted 1958).

HETTNER, A., *Der Gang der Kultur über die Erde,* 2nd ed., 1929.

HOBHOUSE, L. T., WHEELER, G. L. and GINSBERG, M., *The Material Culture and Social Institutions of Primitive Peoples,* 1915 (reprinted 1965).

JONES, E., *Human Geography,* 1966.

PERPILLOU, A. V. (translated Laborde, E. D.), *Human Geography,* 1966.

SAUER, C. O., 'The Morphology of Landscape', *University of California Publications in Geography,* **2**, 1925, No. 2.

SCHNORE, L. F., 'Geography and Human Ecology', *Economic Geography,* **37**, 1961, 207–17.

SEMPLE, E. C., *Influences of Geographic Environment on the Basis of Ratzel's System of Anthropo-Geography,* 1911.

SORRE, M., *Les fondements de la géographie humaine,* 3 vols, 1943–52.
—*L'homme sur la terre,* 1961.

VIDAL DE LA BLACHE, P., *Principes de géographie humaine* (Ed. E. de Martonne), 1923 (translated Bingham, E. T., 1926).

WAGNER, P. L. and MIKESELL, M. W., *Readings in Cultural Geography,* 1962.

WAGNER, P. L., *The Human Use of the Earth,* 1961.

WOOLDRIDGE, S. W. and EAST, W. G., *The Spirit and Purpose of Geography,* 1951.

GROWTH OF POPULATION, URBAN GEOGRAPHY AND UNDER-DEVELOPMENT

BEAUJEU-GARNIER, J. and CHABOT, G. (translated Yglesias, G. M. and Beaver, S. H.), *Urban Geography*, 1967.

BECKINSALE, R. P. and HOUSTON, J. M. (Eds.), *Urbanization and its Problems*, 1968.

FRASER, D., *Village Planning in the Primitive World*, 1968.

HODDER, B. W., *Economic Development in the Tropics,* 1968.

MOUNTJOY, A. B., *Industrialization and Under-developed Countries,* 1966.

PHILLIPS, J. F. V., *The Development of Agriculture and Forestry in the Tropics,* 1961.

Political and Economic Planning (PEP), *World Population and Resources,* 1955.

RUSSELL, E. J., *World Population and World Food Supplies*, 3rd ed., 1961.

MAJOR HUMAN REGIONS

BROEK, J. O. M., and WEBB, J. W., *A Geography of Mankind*, 1968.

RUSSELL, R. J., and KNIFFEN, F. B., *Culture Worlds*, 1951.

SCHMITTHENNER, H., *Lebensräume in Kampf der Kulturen*, 2nd ed., 1951.

SOPHER, D. E., *Geography of Religions*, 1967.

The Times, 'In the wrong bundle', 22 February 1965.

2

CLIMATE AND MAN

The adaptation by which man is enabled to live in all climates of the world, except the very coldest, is of a dual nature, consisting of both physiological modifications and artificial devices which anthropologists associate with distinctive cultures. As an animal, man is capable of withstanding considerable variations of temperature and atmospheric pressure. His powers of invention have enabled him yet further to accommodate himself to the wide range of terrestrial climates. Houses and fires keep him warm during the Siberian winter: tents and loose garments protect him from dry air, dust and intense sunshine in the heart of Arabia. It may perhaps be thought that invention has accomplished more than physiological adjustment in aiding dispersion over the earth. For fire, clothing and shelter promote comfort and efficiency in regions which would otherwise be submarginal for physiological toleration, and even somewhat extend the range between the extremes which man can bear. Yet man's inherent powers of adaptation by physiological means are very great.

Climate and the human organism
Of the climatic elements, pressure, radiation, temperature, humidity and wind directly influence the human organism. Of these, change of air pressure is least important. Its effects can readily be isolated from the others and studied experimentally. It is insignificant to humanity at large, because changes of barometric pressure near sealevel are unaccompanied by any significant physiological effects. The top of the mercury column fluctuates between 950 and

1,050 millibars, or by about 10 per cent. Until the barometer was invented, men were unaware of it. On high mountains, however, air pressure is much more considerably diminished. At about 5,300m (17,500 ft) a barometer reads about 500 millibars, or about half the normal amount. At 9,100m (30,000 ft) the pressure is between one-third and one-quarter of that at sealevel. The extent of land above 3,000m (10,000 ft) is limited; but, nevertheless, small populations are permanently established, on the high Andes in Peru, and in Tibet, at altitudes of more than 4,500m (15,000 ft). In tending flocks or herds, and crossing passes, man may ascend to 5,500m (18,000 ft).

It is well known that an ascent from sealevel to about 10,000 ft produces mountain sickness, shortness of breath, headache, lassitude and faintness. At greater altitudes, prostration and death may follow. For long, ignorance of the cause encouraged the belief that high mountains were inhabited by malevolent demons; but in 1590 a Jesuit father, Acosta, suggested the true explanation. Since then, many experiments have shown that mountain sickness is due to lack of oxygen. It has also been realised that within certain limits the human body can adapt itself in a comparatively short time to a lower oxygen tension. The natives of Mexico and the high Andes are physically vigorous and perform the most arduous toil in mines or on the land, although not without the assistance of a drug (coca) and perhaps at the expense of longevity.

It was formerly thought that this adaptation to a rarefied atmosphere was partly the result of enlargement of the thorax by the processes of natural selection extending over many generations. Large chests are certainly a normal feature among the Bolivian Quechuas and other mountain populations; but they seem common also among nomads of central Asia living at low altitudes. And mountain sickness arises from rapid ascent. Climb a few thousand feet and remain at this height for some days; climb again, and go on repeating this procedure of ascent followed by a pause, to become accommodated to the lower oxygen tension, and you may remain vigorous at least up to 7,300m (25,000 ft). By this method, mountaineers have been able to ascend at least within striking distance of the summit of Everest without the use of extra oxygen. But this is very near the limit of adaptation. The body has compensated for the lack of oxygen in the air breathed by increasing the number of red corpuscles, which are the carriers of oxygen in the blood stream. There are no extensive tracts of land above

7,000m (20,000 ft), but only peaks largely composed of unproductive cliff, scree, ice and snow. Accordingly, we may regard the changes of atmospheric pressure which occur within the altitudes available for human habitation as no greater than the adaptive capacity of the human body.

Solar radiation and pigmentation

More complicated is the bodily reaction to solar radiation. The beneficial influence of light upon humanity has been firmly believed since very early times. To this day, pilgrims ascend Adam's Peak in Ceylon, to greet the rising sun with loud and fervent cries. To the Eskimos and the crews of Arctic expeditions, the polar night brings pallor, insomnia, indolence, dyspepsia and anaemia. The return of daylight renews vitality among the indigenous Arctic peoples almost to excess.

Yet the intensity of tropical sunlight can be harmful to human beings, apart from physiological changes having a defensive function. Prolonged, unaccustomed exposure to tropical sunshine causes blistering or even death to a white-skinned person. It is known that this effect is produced by radiation at the blue end of the spectrum, and beyond, in what is known as the ultraviolet range. (The wavelength of this radiation is about 3/10,000 parts of a millimetre.) But if acclimatisation is gradual, the skin becomes progressively darker and a person can spend whole days in strong sunlight without suffering harm. This was clearly proved during the war of 1939–45 when British troops, serving in India, became accustomed to intense radiation by progressively-lengthened daily exposure, thereby becoming dark brown like the indigenous peoples, and finally able to work or play out of doors clad only in shorts. Evidently, such pigmentation, albeit impermanent, protects the body from the effects of very strong sunlight.

Of a different character is the pigmentation of certain races, such as the dark brown of Dravidian peoples in southern India, the Malays and the Australian aborigines, or the black of Negroes and Melanesians. The colour of the skin is permanent; for the pure-bred Negroes have retained their pigmentation during several centuries in the temperate climates of North America. Among Negroes, the pigment, a substance called melanin, which is found in minute granules at the base of the epidermis, is especially abundant. It also occurs in the skin of the 'White' races, especially in brunettes; but is more widespread in the body and present in larger amounts in peoples of the tropics. Experiments with thermo-couples inserted into the skin have proved its efficacy in protecting deeper and more vulnerable tissues. Dark-skinned people also have much melanin in the irises of their eyes, where it serves a valuable function in defending the delicate structures of the retina from the harmful effects of exposure to excessively bright light. Melanin is found also in certain internal organs, to a greater extent in dark-skinned people than in 'Whites', for instance, in the *substantia nigra* of the mid-brain, but here its function is obscure. The unhappy lot of albinos, who are persons with a hereditary inability to synthesise melanin, are mercilessly burnt by the sun or unable to open their eyes fully in bright light, illustrates vividly the advantage of pigmentation to races living in areas where solar radiation is strong. Ancient beliefs that heat and sunshine produce black skins are thus largely confirmed by modern science.

Ambient temperatures and the human body

In order to survive, bodily temperature must be maintained near 37° C (98.4° F), in air temperatures which may fall as low as −68° C (−90° F) in northern Siberia, or rise as high as 130° F in the Sahara and Arabia. In the coldest climates, clothing is indispensable; though not in some cool climates, as is proved by the savages of southern Chile, who live naked in the rigours of the Antarctic westerlies in temperatures which vary between −4° C (25° F) and 9° C (48° F). Recent investigations have shown that the Alacaluf of southern Chile are physiologically adapted to low temperatures. Their basal metabolic rate is as much as twice the average for Europeans. They also have stout, short ankles and squat feet well insulated by a fatty layer beneath the skin. Peoples living in cold latitudes who employ furry animal skins as a protection against frost do not depend wholly upon their cultural devices in order to survive. The Eskimo, eating the whale, seal and bear, can digest quantities of fat that would be impossible to other races. They consume precisely those foods capable of producing the greatest amount of energy. Moreover, they accumulate a reserve of fat underneath their skins. For the conductance of the skin, i.e., its power to transmit heat from the deeper layers to the surface, has been experimentally proved to be lower in fat people. With the tendency to adiposity go massive jaws and teeth, the better to masticate tough food, which is often eaten uncooked. Thus, races of man living in very cold climates have become adapted to low temperatures partly by the same means—the development of fatty tissue—as the animals they hunt and by a body shape which gives the lowest surface area per unit mass, and hence minimal heat loss.

Some anthropologists, among them Buxton, have suggested that the long noses and narrower nasal passages which have appeared among some races living in colder and drier climates serve to warm and humidify respired air before it reaches the throat and lungs. This theory postulates also that this characteristic is of recent development; because the Eskimo nose is as short as the Negro's. Both of these races are thought to be more archaic than the European or the Mongolian.

At high temperatures, the body must dissipate heat, not conserve it. The heat generated in vital processes and muscular activity cannot readily be dispersed. In part, it may be evacuated by an increased rate of respiration. The everted and enlarged lips and nose of Negro races may thus be adaptive, and may be related to the greater importance of exhalation in transmitting bodily heat to the surrounding air.

But there is another cooling agency. The evaporation of liquid water from the skin lowers temperature, because considerable heat is required to make water change from its liquid to its gaseous phase, which is taken from the body. The Negro sweats more readily than a European. He has slightly more sweat pores in each unit area of skin, and these pores are larger. Moreover, his capillaries are more numerous and dilated, bringing blood very freely to the surface of the body. Experiments have shown that for the same amount of work, the Negro exudes sixteen per cent more sweat than a European. It is not surprising that he is a great drinker.

Basal metabolism, or the heat generated in vital processes, such as maintaining the circulation, the heat of the body and in breathing, is reduced in hot climates. Most peoples show a preference for a vegetarian diet and aversion from fats.

Recently Dr Carleton Coon has examined racial differences in the light of generalisations formulated by biologists from observations of animal species widely distributed over the earth. His comments on Gloger's rule, relating to pigmentation, confirm the remarks made earlier in this chapter (p. 44–5). He finds much evidence for Bergmann's rule, relating body weight inversely to temperature, though he also notes anomalies. And Allen's rule, that protruding body parts lengthen in hot climates, he finds justified by the long arms, legs and necks of many Negroid peoples and Australian aborigines, which aid perspiration by increasing the area of skin at places where sweat is normally exuded most freely.

The evolution of man

Biologically, man is related to the apes of the Old World. Scientists generally hold that both apes and man diverged from a common ancestral species which, not greatly specialised, lived both upon the ground and in trees during the Tertiary era. Apes have become, on the whole, arboreal and vegetarian. By being able to move rapidly through a forest without descending to the ground, they are secure from capture by more powerful carnivorous land animals, such as the leopard or tiger, and can pluck shoots or fruits anywhere between the ground and the lofty canopy of tropical forests. They are essentially quadrupeds, and most species have prehensile tails. Man has become a biped, by forsaking trees for the land, and has no use for a tail. His feet have become fully adapted for walking or running, and the toes cannot grip a branch, as can an ape's. The hand, not required either for walking or for grasping branches during leaps from tree to tree, has become a precisely controlled organ, which, having the thumb opposed to the fingers (instead of alongside), can use a variety of tools. Adoption of an erect posture has been accompanied by enlargement of the brain, especially of the front, which is the seat of the higher intellectual functions. The eye has become elaborated, and human vision is fully stereoscopic, unlike that of any other animal. A diminution of the jaw and its controlling muscles appears to have accompanied the increasing variety of food which greater intelligence could command and, in the later stages of evolution, prepare for convenient eating. Thereby freer and more delicately controlled movements of the jaw, face and tongue are possible, giving man the faculty of speech. Compared with apes, the gestatorial period of the human infant is 280 instead of 240 days, and the child is dependent especially upon the mother but also, indirectly, upon the father for many years whilst its mental and physical powers slowly develop. Males and females therefore tend to specialise. The former obtain food and protect the family; the latter tend the young and prepare food. Thus the family finds its origin in the mutual dependence of male, female and the young.

The change of habitat to the ground from trees brought about a change of diet. To fruits, nuts and edible shoots were added animals, when primitive man became a huntsman. At the same time, hair growth was arrested, for modern man, apart from the head and certain other localised parts of the body, grows only sparse, very fine hairs. The skin, too, is thinner and less resistant to abrasion than that of the monkey.

The final stages of evolution as a separate species (*Homo sapiens*) took place mainly during the half million or so years of the Pleistocene period, during which the world's climates underwent great oscillations. For geological research has shown that throughout the preceding Tertiary era the land areas of the world, particularly in the middle and higher latitudes of the northern hemisphere, were less extensive than today, and the climate generally milder. Forests of a tropical or subtropical character were more widespread, and it may be inferred that the precursors of both modern apes and men were widely dispersed. But in the Pliocene period, great uplifts of land, constituting the final phase of recent worldwide mountain building, increased both the extent of land and its mean altitude. Larger areas became remote from the sea and some were shielded from rain-bearing winds by the higher mountains. Forests became savannas or steppes; and herbivorous animals, as well as the greater carnivores, multiplied. It was in such a world that man's ape-like forbears became wholly terrestrial and more carnivorous. The immediate ancestors of modern apes, however, keeping to the denser equatorial and tropical forests, preserved for species of living apes the tree-dwelling habit of existence. Reduction of hair-growth in human beings would be improbable in a more severe climate, which would tend to encourage a shaggier growth; and until perhaps the most recent stage in human evolution, during the latest phases of Pleistocene, when cultural equipment had become fairly elaborate, prehominids, or man-like apes, were confined to warm climates. Thus we may infer that as savannas, grasslands and steppes became more extensive towards the close of the Pliocene period, ape-men ranged in the outer regions of the tropics and in subtropical latitudes in Asia, Africa and Europe, for fragments of very primitive skulls and other parts of skeletons have been found in China, central and western Europe, as well as in Africa. But their developing intelligence enabled them also to survive near the Equator, for some of the most significant remains have been discovered in Java. Thus, constitutionally, men became adapted to a fairly wide range of warmer climates, and towards the polar margins of his habitat must have become accustomed to seasonal changes of temperature.

Before they were able to make fire and skin animals—the latter, especially, requiring edged tools, including scrapers, such as appeared only during the Palaeolithic period—prehominids could hardly have survived a season with night temperatures much below 16° C (60° F), which, in a fairly equable climate, would be felt in a cool-season mean temperature of 21–24° C (70–75° F). To withstand lower temperatures (we have already inferred) at least a seasonal thickening of hair would be a likely adaptation, if ape-men had been free to drift slowly into higher latitudes and to remain in a cold climate. But the Great Ice Age prevented such a biological solution, and stimulated man to technical and social invention.

Four times the climate oscillated between mildness greater than today, when permanent snow and ice were uncommon even in Arctic regions, and severity which caused much of Europe, northern and central Asia to be covered by ice sheets. Arctic and sub-Arctic climates, such as today are largely confined to the regions within the Arctic and Antarctic Circles, prevailed as far south as latitude 40° in the northern hemisphere. The zone over which tropical and subtropical climates prevailed was correspondingly reduced. During milder interglacial periods, prehominids spread more widely, for fragments of primitive stone tools have been discovered in Europe and northern China, worn by the action of ice and running water. During the first three glacial periods, the ancestors of humanity were compelled to retreat towards the tropics. Thus each glaciation was a crisis not only for evolving prehominids, but for all forms of life, and many species of plants and animals which flourished at the end of the Tertiary era failed to survive into the Holocene (Recent). Ape-men, moving to and fro across the Old World, were confronted with new perils, and new economic crises, which their greater mental powers overcame. By the third interglacial period, between the Riss and Würm glaciations, they were sufficiently advanced to be able to fashion a variety of crude tools and weapons, although we can only guess at the range of their equipment, because only stone implements have survived, and we can but presume that they also used wood, bone and perhaps skins. Certainly during the fourth (Würm) glaciation, which began about 75,000 years ago and ended about 10,000 years ago, men differing but little from ourselves had spread widely in the Old World. They were able to survive in more rigorous climates, not by retreat into warmer regions, but to caves, where, by the use of fire and skin garments, they could continue to live close to the glaciers and ice-sheets. Among the best known of these early races was Neanderthal man, having larger bones and more powerful muscles than modern man, and possessing a more primitive skull, with protruding, massive jaw, a receding forehead and a very prominent bony ridge above the eyes. Neanderthaloids appear to have evolved as a separate race north of the Tertiary mountain belt of Europe and Asia. Their remains have been found in northern China as well as in Europe (Fig. 2).

Meanwhile other races had appeared, which are ancestral to most living races. Some crossed to Europe from northern Africa during a milder interlude in the last glaciation, by using land-bridges at Gibraltar and the Sicilian Straits. In what are now the deserts of northern Africa and south-western Asia, the art of fashioning flints with great deftness had been acquired. Some of these could be used for pointing arrows and spears. With these weapons, larger animals could be hunted, for the lands south and east of the Mediterranean were steppes rather than deserts. In France and Spain, which resembled the present tundra of northern Russia, remarkable cave drawings, amongst other evidence of the life of the times, have enabled us to learn much about this early race of modern man.

Mankind thus appears to have evolved, on the whole, south of the mountain zone in Eurasia, and to have lived in India, Java, western and southern Asia, and northern Africa before entering Europe, for, especially in south-eastern Asia and Africa, many skull fragments with rather primitive features have been unearthed. It seems that Neanderthaloid and more modern races lived together in Europe and south-western Asia during the latter part of the last glaciation, and although the more specialised Neanderthaloids have not survived as a race, some of their physical characteristics have been identified in living Europeans. Some authorities, including Weidenreich, believe that the Neanderthaloids of eastern Asia have contributed more to Mongoloid peoples.

The modern races of mankind

Europe was not the only goal for modern man. He spread throughout the Old World, wherever it was free of ice or snow, especially in Africa, which is very rich in Palaeolithic remains. But the distri-

bution of climates and vegetation types differed greatly from that
of today; and it is important to visualise the cradle-regions of
races as they were, because to their characteristics during the
Würm glaciation may be related the adaptations exhibited by
living races of man, which, we must infer, were beginning to appear
as the Würm ice-sheets were melting.

Great expanses of permanent ice and snow could not be occupied at all. These included north-western and central Europe,
most of European Russia and the plateaux of north-eastern
Siberia. The higher mountains of Europe, especially the Alps, were
also enveloped by extensive snow-fields or glaciers. The same was
true of the Himalayas and Karakorum ranges, the mountains to
the east of Tibet, and the high ranges of central Asia, such as the
Kuen Lun and the Altai. But in central Asia, distance from the sea
reduced precipitation, and the climate of plateaux at intermediate
altitudes was fairly dry, sustaining a natural vegetation resembling
a steppe. Westwards, in Asia Minor and in Europe close to the
margins of the ice, tundra prevailed. Rainy mountains in south-
western Asia and around the Mediterranean basin were forested
but lower ground was a kind of subtropical savanna, where both
trees and grasses flourished, including many plants to be found
nowadays on the littoral of the Mediterranean Sea. The Arabian
and Saharan Deserts were smaller and farther to the south than
today. Perhaps the only true deserts corresponded with the Libyan
Desert and the Rub al-Khali (the 'Empty Quarter') in Arabia. In
central Africa, savannas and forests largely covered the regions
they do today; but in southern Africa, the Kalahari Desert was
less extensive and less arid. Little is known of Australia but the
climate of its southern parts was probably cooler and more moist,
for small glaciers were nourished on the summits of the Australian
Alps. The 'Dead Heart' of Australia was correspondingly reduced.
South-eastern Asia was largely forested (Fig. 2).

The withdrawal of an immense volume of water from the oceans
to form the continental ice sheets and enlarged glaciers caused the
sealevel to fall about 180m (600 ft). Asia thus became connected
with North America by an isthmus where are now the Bering
Straits. The Mediterranean and Black Seas were reduced to a
series of lakes. Land bridges also connected Borneo, Java and
Sumatra to the mainland of Asia. (But sea still extended through
Indonesia along Wallace's Line, maintaining the separation of
Australia from Asia, which had begun at least very early in the

Tertiary era. For not only were mammals unable to reach Australia before the European settlement, but the precursors of modern man were also absent from this continent. No remains of apemen have been discovered.)

The dispersal of the primitive types of modern man over this vast land area and into the most diverse climates, when culture was still rudimentary and massive migrations impossible, allowed the modern types or races of mankind to be evolved, in relative segregation from each other. Keeping speculation within bounds, we may tentatively relate important physical characteristics of the main races to the environments in which they were appearing towards the close of the last glaciation.

In east-central Asia the climate was very cold, and, as the Würm ice sheets diminished, increasingly dry. Outblowing winter winds, laden with dust for thousands of years, have blanketed northern China with loess. Here, strains of Neanderthaloid man, less specialised than in Europe, with which were mingled newer types from the south and perhaps south-west, acquired the thickened, and hence yellowish, skin which is characteristic of Mongoloid peoples, and which may perhaps be deemed protective against cold and drought. The nose and mouth became small, which, as already suggested, may ensure that respired air is warmer and more humid when it reaches the lungs, and freer of dust. Perhaps the slit-like eyes and the epicanthic fold (or curl of the outer upper eyelid over the lower) may serve partly for protection from dust and very cold air. In addition, lank, straight hair and broad skull appeared, although these features are less readily related to the climate prevailing in the Mongoloid cradle-region.

In south-eastern Asia, India and the East Indies, the early types of modern man conserved primitive features in their skulls. The forehead recedes (among the groups isolated in remote forested hills from more recent immigrations of Mongoloid and White

---

Fig. 2 Conjectural vegetation zones of the world during the Würm glaciation

(after Charlesworth, Frenzel and Troll)

I–II Equatorial and subtropical rain forests; III Subtropical evergreen sclerophyllous forests and scrub; IV Temperate deciduous forests; V Northern coniferous forests; VI Tropical grasslands (savannas); VII–VIII Temperate grasslands and semi-deserts; IX Tundra, subalpine and alpine flora.

Fig. 2

races), the jaw is large and protruding, and the nose broad. The skin has remained dark brown, and the hair generally wavy or curly. Although dispersion within this area was aided, at the height of the Würm glaciation, by the lowered sealevel, it must have been necessary to make rafts to reach New Guinea, where very primitive groups have survived in the still almost inaccessible mountains. The overseas migration continued to Australia and Tasmania, where, practising a Palaeolithic culture, the peoples we now know as Australian aborigines remained in isolation from the rest of mankind until very recent times. Other strains, living close to the Equator in the East Indies, became almost black and grew hair in tight curls, which, so some physiologists have argued, both shades the scalp from strong sunlight and yet permits moisture to be evaporated from the sweat-glands.

In south-western Asia, northern Africa and Europe, important strains of modern man had already lost many primitive characteristics by the time they met the Neanderthaloids. A higher forehead, reduced brow ridge and jaws, smaller nose, lighter complexions and wavy hair have on the whole prevailed. Whilst the Würm glaciation was at its height groups could mingle across northern Africa, which was fairly thickly peopled for the times, if we may judge from the abundance of Stone Age implements. But as the Sahara was desiccated, a barrier was created between men living around the Mediterranean and those in central Africa. In effective isolation from the rest of mankind, the Negroes conserved and perhaps intensified their skin pigmentation, thick lips, broad noses, and tight-curled hair. It has been pointed out that two types of variation among the races of Africa appear to facilitate cooling of the body by the process of sweating, for which increase of skin area in proportion to body weight is clearly an advantage in hot climates. Among the Nilo-Hamites extreme slenderness of build is noteworthy; and among Pygmies all-round reduction of size (cf. Bergmann's and Allen's rules, p. 46–7).

But Africa, south of the Sahara, is large enough to permit more than one race to exist. To the great size of the second largest continent must be added the impenetrability of tropical forests. In the depths of the latter, in the Congo basin, the Pygmies became dwarfed. From the same or a similar stock (Negrillo), which must have been preserved from intermingling with the Negroes for a very long period by migrations to the extreme south of the continent, sprang the Bushmen, who are not only among the smallest of races but have peppercorn curls and other physical peculiarities. In the savannas of what was French West Africa, however, were bred the true Negroes, who have spread eastwards and south-wards along the open savanna lands of eastern Africa after contact with Hamites, although a great part of this movement was accom-plished within the past thousand years. The black or reddish-black skin of this race is accompanied by the other racial traits just mentioned, and some groups, especially in western Africa, are tall and finely muscular.

Further migrations and racial differentiation have ensued since the recession of the Würm ice sheets and glaciers. In Indonesia and the mainlands on either hand, the Andaman islanders, the Semang of Malaya, the Aëta peoples of the Philippines, the Kubu of Sumatra, the Toala of Celebes, increasingly isolated by the rise of sealevel, have come to exhibit a certain diversity within the range of characteristics known as Negrito; and, except where pre-served in remote islands or in jungle-clad mountains, have become mingled with later Mongoloid immigrants who have drifted into the East Indies from the north. But formerly Negrito and Austra-loid peoples must have been in sole occupation of a much greater area of southern India and South-east Asia.

The later dispersal of modern man

In eastern Asia, as the climate ameliorated, Mongolian men began to disperse. Moving southwards, they became darker and shorter, thus giving rise to the Malays, who have become established along the coasts, in the river basins of south-eastern Asia and upon some of the islands. Mastering the art of ocean navigation, a wide dis-persion to the islands of the Pacific (Polynesia) was also achieved by peoples akin to the Malays and Chinese, although before this movement took place, there must have been some intermingling with peoples like those of south-western Asia. Moving north-wards, Mongoloids dispersed through the forests to the Arctic coast and throughout the grasslands and semi-deserts in the heart of this continent. During historic migrations, some have settled in eastern and northern Europe. Others, crossing to North America, either on ice or before the Bering Straits had been formed, began to live in the New World. The earliest human remains yet discovered in North America are about 15,000 years old. The ancestors of the Amerindian peoples probably passed along a corridor formed when the north American ice sheets began to melt, along the present Mackenzie River valley. That Mongoloid man has occupied the Americas too recently to permit of effective adaptation to climates which are often in the greatest contrast with those of the cradle-lands was affirmed by the great naturalist Bates, who observed that the pale-skinned natives of Amazonia were even less able to bear the humid heat than Europeans.

In western Asia and Europe, several new types appeared. Around the Mediterranean Sea, the olive-skinned, dark, slight Mediterranean type became fully developed; and migrated thence to the coasts of western Europe, especially during the Bronze Age. Closely-related stocks also moved eastwards into India, where their descendants, much mingled with Negrito peoples as well as the Aryan immigrants of historic times, form the majority in that subcontinent. In Armenia and Anatolia, men became stockier and broad-headed. Migrating westwards to Europe, they are now known as the Alpine race, because, on the whole, they have kept to the mountain districts of central and western Europe, although they have also contributed a great deal to the ancestry of the Russian people. In southern Russia, as steppes appeared north of the Black Sea and the Caspian Sea, a tall, fairer, long-headed race appeared, which, later migrating to the cloudy shores of the Baltic Sea, acquired the extremely distinctive characteristics of the Nordic type—very fair hair, blue eyes, white skin—which are common today in Sweden, and northern Germany and eastern England.

Some migrations since 1500

The dispersion of modern man was succeeded by many later migrations, which have continued to the present day and have repeatedly modified the distribution of races. The peopling of North America and Australia by European settlers must be reckoned as a major movement of men. Moreover, in the last few centuries, racial groups have been transplanted into environments differing profoundly from their regions of origin, and have prompted scientists to ask whether groups long-conditioned by a particular climate are at a disadvantage when they go to live elsewhere. Communities derived from races long established in temperate regions have settled within the tropics. A more limited reverse movement—of tropically-conditioned races to temperate latitudes—has also been witnessed. If we postulate capacity to reproduce and increase as the best test of ability to withstand climatic change, then we must conclude that there have been both successes and failures.

The Negroes of western Africa have been bred in an equatorial climate, and the extent to which they are physically adapted to such an environment has already been discussed. The fine physique of several west African tribes suggests that here a strain of humanity has been evolved which is better fitted than any other to thrive in a hot, humid climate. During the period of slave trading, many thousands were shipped to the tropical regions of South America, the Caribbean and the southern United States. In the last-named country, they were henceforth to live in a region where the mean annual temperature is not less than 9° C (15° F) below that of their homeland, and where the winter is very changeable, with frequent severe cold spells. There they reproduce themselves, and are physically vigorous, in a way which is clearly demonstrated by the athletic prowess of their young men and women today.

Successful migrations from temperate to tropical regions have been accomplished by the Mediterranean peoples of southern Europe. In Cuba and Puerto Rico are white populations descended from the peasants of Spain and Portugal. In Cuba, the importation of Negro slaves ceased in 1841, and was succeeded by active and increasing immigration from Spain. The white population of Cuba has now become much more numerous than the Negro, and has a higher birth-rate. It may, perhaps, be argued that because immigration has been so active in the past two generations, the fact of acclimatisation has not been proved. But in Puerto Rico, where the white population is sixty per cent out of nearly two and a half millions, a greater proportion is descended from seventeenth- and eighteenth-century settlers, whose existence was precarious until modern hygiene reinforced them in their contest with tropical diseases. In recent decades, the rate of increase among whites has been greater than amongst Negroes, and some assert that the island is now over-populated. Both Cuba and Puerto Rico have mean annual temperatures 6° to 9° C (10–15° F) higher than Spain, and have no true cool season, although December and January are somewhat less hot than July. A smaller white community of similar Latin origin inhabits the tropical uplands of Costa Rica. Its existence is more precarious than those of Cuba and Puerto Rico, because Negroes are competing very strongly for the use of the land.

Northern Europeans in the tropics

When persons of Nordic or Alpine stock from England, France or the Netherlands live near the Equator, a rise in mean annual temperature of 17° C (30° F) or more must be endured, and a climate having marked seasonal and non-periodic changes exchanged for one which is uniform to the point of monotony. Many are the examples scattered around the world, from the West Indies and Africa to the Philippine Islands and Queensland, which may be examined in order to arrive at a verdict upon the vexed subject of the capacity of the northern White races to survive in the tropics. Among these are successes and failures; but it is not so easy to distinguish the respective rôles of climate, disease and historical vicissitude.

In the seventeenth century, England, France, Holland and Denmark seized islands in the Caribbean Sea and 'planted' colonies. Barbados and St Kitts, the two most important English settlements each had more than 30,000 White persons by about 1640. In the former, the White population has now been reduced to little more than 10,000; in the latter, to only 1,000. The chief causes of this decline appear to have been the introduction of Negro slaves into both islands, bringing low living standards, hookworm, bilharzia and malaria and the ruinous wars of the seventeenth and eighteenth centuries. The colonial administration, too, was very defective. That events rather than climate undermined these communities seems proved by the vigour of smaller groups, which, escaping maladministration and the economic hazards of sugar-planting, and also (lacking strategic importance) the scourge of war, have remained healthy and are increasing in numbers. In the Grand Cayman Islands, 400 miles north-west of Jamaica, in latitude 19° N, and where the annual mean temperature is but little below 27° C (80° F), are 2,000 Whites, descended from settlers who migrated from Jamaica about 200 years ago. The men are mariners and ship-builders. The women, though not working out of doors, are active in their homes. A strict colour-bar has been observed, and there has been no intermarriage with mulattos or Negroes. The sanctity of marriage is rigorously preserved, although husbands are often absent for long periods at sea or in the ports of the mainland. A little inbreeding has happened, but not to noticeable enfeeblement, and recent investigations have shown that physique and intelligence are good. Social standards have been maintained and improved, as the large, well-painted houses reveal to visitors.

A similar community lives and flourishes on the Bay Islands, forty miles off the north coast of Honduras. About half the population of 4,000 is of British stock, which has retained its characteristics for two centuries, notwithstanding that since 1859, when the islands were ceded to the Republic of Honduras, determined attempts have been made to suppress British culture. It speaks well for the vigour of this small British group that success has been won in the dual struggle with a humid tropical climate and an unsympathetic or hostile government. Strict abstention from intermarriage with other racial stocks and a stable livelihood based upon ship-building, trade and growing tropical fruits have laid the foundations for this achievement.

Corroboration is provided in Saba, a mountainous island only five square miles in area, among the Leeward Islands. Originally colonised by the Dutch early in the seventeenth century, it was held by the English for two periods during the Anglo-Dutch Wars, during which the mother tongue was changed, although Holland has exercised sovereignty continuously since 1682. At about that time, Negro slaves were introduced; but the resultant economy may be described as farming rather than planting, for the holdings were small, and the slaves owned by a white proprietor rarely numbered more than ten. It is thought that masters and slaves worked side by side on the land. Later, many Sabans took to a seafaring life in sailing ships. Till late in the last century, the white settlers in Saba refrained from miscegenation, and remained vigorous. Father Labat, who visited the island in 1701, wrote afterwards in terms of lavish praise for its prosperity and welfare. Raynal, eighty years later, was equally impressed. Fifty European families with 150 slaves then grew garden produce and cotton. He commented that the European stock had remained purer than elsewhere in the Caribbean region, and observed that the women, especially, had remarkably fresh complexions. But in the mid-eighteenth century the slaves were freed and later the sailing ship became obsolete. Many men left the island permanently, taking their wives and obtaining economic advancement by becoming ships' officers or officials in steamship companies or harbour boards in the USA or the larger ports of the Caribbean. Thus they proved that their stock had remained vigorous; but their departure sapped the community remaining in Saba, which is dying out in several villages, and is now somewhat enfeebled in another. At Windwardside and Hellsgate, however, White farmers are still established, and perform almost incredible feats of exertion in tilling and carrying crops on steeply sloping land. Their children are healthy, and respond to education as well as comparable groups in Europe. Adult women seemed somewhat enervated to Dr A. Grenfell Price, who attributed this condition to a sedentary indoor life, which necessitates long hours of lace-making by the light of oil lamps.

The Grand Cayman Islands[1], Bay Islands and Saba are all relatively free from tropical diseases, including two which are most prevalent and debilitating: hookworm and malaria. Thus they offer some evidence supporting the view that failures of other tropical settlements by northern Europeans have been caused by disease or social conditions rather than climate. Moreover, in all three, Whites and Negroes live side by side; but the former, though employing the latter, have avoided physical and moral mutation by engaging in vigorous manual work and refraining from intermarrying. How regrettable that these successes should be on so limited a scale! Yet it would be ignoring realities to suggest that these lessons from the smaller West Indian islands are applicable to the greater problems of Africa. It should also be observed that climatically all these islands are exceptional. They are swept throughout the year by the Trade Winds, which, blowing steadily, naturally ventilate the houses and cool the sweating skins of outdoor and indoor workers. This is but one of many tropical climates, and these maritime, equable, windy characteristics do not widely prevail in low latitudes.

The American achievement in the Panama Canal Zone is less convincing. It has proved that in a most disease-infested, fully equatorial climate, modern sanitation and hygiene can keep a White population healthy and efficient. More germane to the question before us: many of these Whites, engaged in strenuous manual work, including even labour in foundries, continue with unimpaired health for many years. They bring up their families in the Zone, and some men of the second generation are apparently as capable of vigorous work as their parents. But Americans began to live here only in 1905. Sixty years is too short a period in which to judge the permanence of a settlement. Moreover, the economic

[1] This restricted discussion of acclimatisation ignores recent Caribbean developments, especially of tourism.

base of the American community is extremely artificial. Thanks to the ships which pass through the Canal from all parts of the world, an unusually varied diet is available. Also, vacations are commonly spent in the United States. Americans in Panama do not perform unskilled work out of doors, and coloured servants are usually employed in houses, to the detriment of the American women, who are often under-exercised through lack of muscular work. Thus, at Panama, the community is not well balanced and has a very unusual, artificial economic base; but, nevertheless, it is working, it is healthy and has every prospect of being permanent.

Queensland is a remarkable and at the same time a much-studied example of European penetration into the tropics. The coastal districts, which receive moderately heavy rains, chiefly in summer, were settled from several ports (Brisbane, Bundaberg, Rockhampton, Mackay and Cairns) by sugar-planters, after 1860, who introduced labourers from Polynesia and China. Except for a limited, land-owning class, the White population was under-mined and demoralised by the competition of peoples accustomed to lower standards. From about 1885, the 'White Australia' policy was gradually enforced, but it was not until the First World War that the last of the Polynesians ('Kanakas') were finally repatriated.

Meanwhile, the sugar industry, strongly supported by bounties and tariffs, continued to flourish, although it had been pro-phesied that it would disappear through lack of labour. Fresh immigrants from Britain, Australians and a small number of Italians have, aided by a more efficient organisation of planting, milling and refining, contrived to maintain production and ensure a reasonable standard of living. A rigorous medical investigation in 1924 revealed that the White population of Queensland was quite normal. Men, women and children were as healthy as their fellow-countrymen of the temperate south. Men were able to per-form arduous outdoor work, such as cutting cane or unloading ships, without ill-effects. Women, particularly those who did housework, were healthy, although it must be admitted that some doctors believe that women in Queensland age more quickly than their southern sisters. This might well be remedied by better town-planning, for at several ports houses are huddled in hollows close to the harbours instead of being situated upon headlands or the open coast and thus better exposed to the Trade Winds. Houses better adapted to the tropics, with netted windows, external kitchens and thermally insulated roofs (instead of corrugated iron) would also be beneficial, by improving the housewife's working conditions.

The sugar-planting districts are, however, marginal to the tropics. Maryborough and Bundaberg are actually south of the Tropic of Capricorn, whilst Rockhampton is situated almost on the Tropic. Only the Burdekin valley, Cairns and Cooktown are fully tropical, having mean monthly temperatures throughout the year above 18° C (64° F). Thus, in general, the people of Queensland live in a climate with distinct seasonal contrasts, and only the months of the southern hemisphere summer are truly hot, by having mean temperatures above 27 °C (80° F). In June and July the mean temperatures are nearly 10° C (15° F) less. The plateaux of north-central Queensland offer a similar climate, in the hinterland of Cairns and Townsville, where a sparse population is engaged in cattle-rearing. Again, the temperature of the coolest month is below 18° C (65° F). Moreover, the summits of the coast ranges rise above 900m (3,000 ft), and provide sites for hill stations close to the principal sugar-producing districts. People of all classes can gain relief from the greatest heat in December and January. The boarding schools attended by children of wealthier parents are also situated at altitudes exceeding 450m (1,500 ft), and where mean temperatures in all months are lower by at least 3° C (5° F).

It has also been observed that workers engaged in the heaviest manual labour, especially cane-cutting, tend to leave this occupation, and frequently the province, after an average period of about eight years. And in the extreme north, around the fully tropical Cairns and Cooktown, the requirements of sugar-growing have been satisfied only by immigrant Italians since the last Kanakas left. Beyond dispute, Queensland has been successfully settled by a community mainly of British descent. But it is equally clear that the principal populated areas are marginally tropical, and are seasonally subtropical.

Similar climates prevail over intertropical African plateaux which have been colonised by Britons since effective government began about seventy years ago. In Kenya, Malawi, Zambia and Rhodesia, altitudes of 900m (3,000 ft) and upwards in all the principal areas of permanent settlement reduce the tropical heat, although the Equator passes across Kenya. At Nairobi (latitude 2° S., altitude 1,700m (5,450 ft), the mean annual temperature is 17° C (63° F). At Salisbury (latitude 17° S., altitude 1,500m (4,880

ft), the mean annual temperature is 18° C (65° F). The maintenance of health and vigour is no problem in these territories; but it
has only been proved that northern European peoples can live in
subtropical or warm temperate climates.

The experience of British, French, American and Dutch communities in the Orient remains for discussion. Nowhere have these
nations established balanced communities in south-eastern Asia or
in the East Indies. Living amongst very numerous agricultural
populations, persons of white origin have spent their lives as
government officials, managers of estates or factories or as merchants. They have avoided all forms of manual work, including
domestic work in their homes, and have generally been sojourners
rather than settlers. The Englishman in India, Ceylon or Malaya
has looked forward to retirement 'at home' at the close of his
working life; and in the last seventy-five years (since steamships
quickened the speed of travel between western Europe and the
East) has returned to his native country to recuperate every three
or four years. He has sent his children, from the age of seven or
eight, to schools situated at hill stations or in England, until the age
of eighteen or twenty, partly for fear of the effects of heat during
youth upon adult vitality, and partly to preserve them from alien
influence during formative and impressionable years. In these
artificial conditions, English families have been established in
India and other countries in south-eastern Asia for two or three
generations, without loss of vigour, and the East has gained by the
work of administrators, engineers, merchants and planters who
have been accustomed to the climate and to the indigenous societies from childhood. It is rarely claimed that this is permanent
settlement. The prevailing opinion (but not universal) among
English doctors with experience of the tropical East is that English
stock permanently established in these hot climates, without
periods of leave at hill stations or in England, and including the
years of youth, could not retain its vitality.

A contrary conviction has, however, been affirmed by Dutch
investigators, who have abundant data from the lengthy occupation of Java. Policy and practice there differed from those of the
British in India. Dutchmen going to the East Indies generally
settled there for life, and reared their families in the islands. Until
recently, mortality was not light; but an analysis of statistics to
separate the toll of tropical disease from other causes of death
lends support to the opinion that climate, alone, has no patho-

logical effects. Within the last thirty years, medical investigations, similar to those undertaken by Australian doctors in Queensland, have revealed that persons of Dutch extraction in Batavia have not in any way been physiologically affected by upbringing and residence close to the Equator. These observers stress, like Price, the importance of sobriety, good hygiene, modern sanitation and manual work or energetic exercise to ensure good health.

Thus, as a result of migrations since 1500, northern European peoples have successfully colonised subtropical lands, and are established within the true tropics, but only on the margins, where distinct seasonal fluctuations of temperature are felt. The capacity of northern European races to colonise *equatorial* lands remains unproved, for the successful instances, in the West Indies and Java, are too localised in comparison with the totality of lands lying within 10° of the Equator. Europeans from Mediterranean lands appear to be rather better fitted to tropical climates, for in Puerto Rico, Cuba, Costa Rica and Brazil are healthy and vigorous communities numbering several millions. But again, all these regions are towards the margins of the tropics, and, especially in Brazil, the heat is tempered by altitude. For the most extensive area of white settlement in Brazil, in the state of São Paulo, has an altitude of from 300–900m (1,000–3,000 ft), and in the tropics, an increase of altitude of 1,000 ft reduces mean temperatures—of the day, month or year—by about 2° C (3° F).

BIBLIOGRAPHY

ADOLPHE, E. F., *Physiology of Man in the Desert*, 1947.

BUTZER, K. W., *Environment and Archaeology*, 1964.

BURTON, A. C. and EDHOLM, O. G., *Man in a Cold Environment*, 1955.
Changes of Climate (Proceedings of UNESCO/WMO Symposium, Rome, 1961), *Arid Zone Series*, 20, 1963.

COON, C. S., *The Origin of Races*, 1962.
—*The Living Races of Man*, 1966.

COON, C. S., GARN, S. M. and BIRDSELL, J. B., *Races . . . a Study of the Problems of Race Formation in Man*, 1950.

LOEWY, A. and WITTKOWER, E., *The Pathology of High Altitude Climates*, 1937 (especially ch. 2).

NEWBURGH, M. D. (Ed.), *Physiology of Heat Regulation and the Science of Clothing*, 1949.

PRICE, A. Grenfell, *White Settlers in the Tropics*, 1939.

SHAPLEY, H. (Ed.), *Climatic Change*, 1953.

What is Race?, UNESCO, 1952.

ZEUNER, A. F. E., *Dating the Past*, 4th ed., 1962.

C

3

THE FOUNDATIONS OF THE
HUMAN ECONOMY

Hunting and food-collecting livelihoods

Towards the end of the Pleistocene period, the main continental areas of the globe were occupied by man. As the European and Siberian ice sheets melted, groups migrated northwards until they reached the shores of the Arctic Ocean. After they had gained entrance to the New World, they spread southwards throughout North and South America. Long previously, during the transition from his pre-hominid phase, man had conceived and applied the three fundamental innovations which distinguish him from other animal species: his use of fire, tools and clothing. The basic human need, for food, was satisfied from more diverse sources as man dispersed across the earth. He became omnivorous instead of vegetarian. He preyed upon the animal kingdom and plucked experimentally from every phylum among plants. Hunting and food-collecting tribes surviving until recently exemplified this mode of living.

The Australian aborigines afforded a striking illustration of this intensive, intelligent quest throughout the living environment for sustenance and subsidiary human needs. It is remarkable what was edible in the 'Dead Heart' of Australia. The eggs of emus, crocodiles and tortoises; chrysalises and worms; caterpillars, grasshoppers, crickets, slugs and moths were all collected and consumed. Over 300 plants have been enumerated as sources of their food, from seeds, roots, bulbs, flowers, shoots, buds, leaves or fruits. Kangaroos, opossums, tortoises, frogs, rodents, snakes and many birds were killed and eaten. Fresh-water snails were gathered for food. Tribes living near the coast hunted certain species of whales, as well as sharks and other large fish. They also collected shellfish. The economy of the Guayakis, a primitive people living in South America, in the forests between the rivers Parana and Paraguay, was equally diversified. They hunted numerous birds and beasts with bow and arrow. Also, they gathered the larvae of beetles parasitic to certain palms, with the pulp and flowers of another palm. They also learnt to pick sour oranges from the gardens of abandoned Jesuit colonies, and search for the aphrodisiacal honey of a wasp.

This diversity, whilst perhaps assuring a well-balanced diet, does not guarantee regular meals. Among such peoples, living mainly in warm climates, where food storage is impossible, lean and good times alternate. Orgies and gluttony after good hunting are succeeded by days or weeks of abstinence. Moreover, this dietetic catholicity exists only where lack of knowledge (or lack of resources, as in the arid regions of Australia) hinder a regular food supply. If a few species of game or fish abound, men become especially skilled in trapping, hunting or fishing, and invent specialised weapons. The Plains Indians, living on the prairies of North America before their dispossession by whites, co-operated in surrounding and slaughtering bison. In northern Asia, some Mongoloid peoples chase reindeer at one season, fish for salmon in the estuaries at another, hunt seals and walruses at a third, and during the rest of the year catch marine fish.

Among peoples now vanished from the earth, whose mode of life has been revealed by archaeology, were the cave-dwellers of western Europe during the Aurignacian and Magdalenian periods of the Upper Palaeolithic Age. Using bow, arrow and spear, these peoples obtained their food supplies by hunting the numerous beasts whose bones have been identified in the rubbish accumulated upon cave floors, such as the mammoth, reindeer, bison, musk ox and wild horse. Several of these animals are fierce, large and aggressive. It may be inferred that the ability to kill such formidable quarry was rewarded by an alleviation in the incessant search for food which is the lot of primitive peoples dependent upon smaller animals and gathered vegetable produce. They appear also to have fished for salmon in the enlarged rivers of that period. The frosty winter probably ensured a measure of natural cold storage, relieving the men from incessant hunting. It was perhaps during winter leisure, thus gained, that the remarkable cave-wall drawings were executed. The sedentary or semi-sedentary existence which was thus devised; the great range of implements which were fashioned from bone; the ritual and art which were practised all warn us, in Childe's phrase, 'not to underrate the possibilities of food-gathering as a livelihood'.

The North-West Indians of North America, who survived into the nineteenth century, also exemplify the advantages to be exploited from an abundance of utilisable food and other resources. The sea and the rivers of what is now British Columbia and south ern Alaska are rich in fish, especially salmon. Dense coniferous forests provided the materials for construction and tool-making. Early travellers were astonished by villages of massive timber houses and by intricately-carved totem poles. Dug-out canoes as much as a hundred feet long were elegantly fashioned from cedar. Polished stone and copper were used to fabricate a great range of tools, implements and weapons. Bones, horn, ivory and shells were also used skilfully and artistically. Their hunting and collecting economy could sustain a living standard probably higher than in many peasant communities of the modern world.

Food-collecting peoples rarely, if ever, wandered at will. Men and women might travel widely in search of useful plants, and trudge great distances when hunting. But boundaries were generally set to their movements. Each social group—generally a small number of parents and children—was confined to a recognised tract. To invade the territory of neighbours was an act leading to hostilities. This parcelling-out of territory may be an adjustment of population to resources. It may also arise from a limitation upon the collective capacity of a small group to acquire and apply its understanding of the topography, flora and fauna of a tract of land. We may also remind ourselves that many species of animals and birds recognise food areas exclusively used by mated pairs or groups. Primitive man, in this sphere, was no innovator. He followed the instincts of other species which, like himself, hunted and gathered food from nature.

The extent to which habitations were in fixed locations varied. Food-gathering peoples in tropical jungles could be constantly moving, having hardly any need for shelter. At times of heavy rain, they could spend a few minutes constructing a temporary shelter of small branches and large leaves or palm fronds. Caves were also occupied during rainy seasons. Among the Veddas of

Ceylon, low land near rivers, liable to flood during the rainy season, was then avoided, and the available territory divided so that each group could resort to uplands where movement in the forest is not so restricted in wet weather. Peoples living in colder climates tended to live in one place during the winter, and huts could be occupied for several years. During the summer, a more migratory existence could be adopted, light tents being carried to provide shelter. Alternatively, a form of tent such as the *tipi* of the now vanished Plains Indians might be used throughout the year, and pitched in one place for several months during mid-winter. The large established Indian villages of the British Columbian coast, or the apparently-permanent cave dwellings of the Aurignacians, were exceptional.

It can hardly be said that a network of communications existed among food collectors. Defined, well-beaten tracks can appear only when the population is numerous and sedentary. The search for food caused men and women to wander. They could not keep to a trodden path. Locally, in hilly country, or where fords were few and far apart, the hunter frequented the easiest way when returning from the kill. This was exceptional. The absence of paths or tracks in terrain occupied by primitive peoples—so often the object of surprised comment by travellers—was no more than a consequence of the economy. Also, it was due to the sparsity of the population. The numbers of primitive peoples are very difficult to estimate, and no systematic study of population density in simple economies has ever been made. It has been estimated that the hunters living in Britain during the Upper Palaeolithic period could not have numbered more than a few thousands. There are fewer than 100,000 Eskimos along the lengthy Arctic coast of Greenland, Canada and the Canadian archipelago. One person required many square miles for his support.

The origins of food production

In the Old World, the slow transformation of the wandering hunter into the shepherd or herdsman, the peasant, the townsman and eventually to civilised man began with the domestication of animals: the fourth revolutionary achievement in man's technical progress. Archaeology has revealed that towards the end of the Palaeolithic period, the dog had become man's companion and partner in hunting. Somewhat later, the reindeer and goat were domesticated, almost certainly before the beginnings of cultivation.

The ancestral species of the dog are undoubtedly the wolves and jackals, living wild in early times throughout much of Europe and Asia, excluding the tropical south-east. The several known species can interbreed; and this in part accounts for the great variety of the breeds of domestic dogs. Species of wolves are also native to North America, but none of these was domesticated. In the Old World wolves and jackals were probably first associated with man in hunting, and as scavengers. They would eat offal and scraps of meat on carcases left behind after man had taken all he wanted. Moreover, wolves and jackals are intelligent and social animals. They hunt in packs; and man must have realised the advantages of relying upon wolf-packs to harass prey. The young would first have been tamed. Zeuner states that 'young wolves have been reared in captivity many times'. The social instincts of the species, in the course of training, can be conditioned so that man comes to be regarded not only as a member of the pack, but as its leader. Later, dogs could be bred to accept separation from others of his species, living as individuals in a human group. But for some purposes, such as fox-hunting, dogs still live and hunt in packs.

A means of domesticating the reindeer arose from its craving for salt, which man's urine could satisfy. The animal's nomadic habits, corresponding to those of human hunters, also contributed to its subjugation by man. Decoy-hunting, which has been observed among the Samoyeds and Tunguses of Siberia, was probably the innovation promoting domestication. Young tamed females could be employed to decoy animals from wild herds, and the kill would be the easier. The other stages, enabling reindeer to be milked, ridden and used for traction, were not reached until much later, after cattle had been domesticated.

Evidence of domesticated goats has been found at Jericho, in early Neolithic layers dated between 6000 and 7000 B.C., and in the Belt Cave, near the Caspian Sea, in a late Mesolithic layer dated about 6000 B.C. Zeuner comments that 'the distance between the two sites suggests that the domestication of the goat took place rather earlier than this, since it must have had time to spread'. Hence, he thinks that there may have been 'a late Mesolithic phase of ruminant domestication . . . during which, apart from the dog, the goat was the only animal controlled by man'. The wild ancestral species is the bezoar goat (*Capra aegagrus*), which originally lived in south-western Asia, Arabia excepted, the Aral-Caspian basin and the mountains north-west of India. It may have been the first animal to be milked; and it is possible that herds were reared for this purpose in late Mesolithic times.

Not long afterwards, the sheep was also domesticated in south-west Asia, with the aid of the dog. Three ancestral species have been identified: the mouflon (*Ovis musimon*), originally native to Europe and western Asia; the urial (*O. orientalis*), distributed over west-central Asia; and the argali (*O. ammon*), a larger species found in east-central Asia. There is also the bighorn sheep (*O. canadensis*), living in western North America and eastern Siberia, but never domesticated. The varied domestic breeds are descended chiefly from the mouflon and urial. The former predominates when the animal is reared mainly for meat or milk; the latter when it is reared for wool. In the Belt cave, sheep bones are abundant in the early Neolithic layer, deposited in the sixth millennium B.C. Coon, who excavated this site, believes that sheep were then being kept for meat and skins. Few lambs were then being killed, and it is inferred that the young were kept in order to increase the amount of meat yielded by the flock. Later, however, the proportion of immature bones increases, indicating, possibly, that mature females were being reared to be milked. The Belt cave is not far from steppe lands where the winter is very cold; and it is likely that wool began to be used for clothes instead of skins soon after domestication. Wild sheep moult in patches in spring; and masses of hair and wool can readily be felted to form thick fabric: a craft still practised in west-central Asia.

The beginnings of agriculture followed soon after the domestication of the goat and sheep. This fifth fundamental step in the evolution of the human economy was encouraged by two biogeographical factors. First, about 8000 B.C. the European ice sheets entered upon their final decline, and the last (Würm) of the four Pleistocene glacial periods ended. The climate of central and western Europe changed from sub-Arctic to temperate; and of Mediterranean lands from temperate to subtropical with a summer drought. On the eastern margin of the Mediterranean basin, deserts and semi-deserts became more extensive. Here, in south-west Asia, many rivers ceased to flow in summer, and many more flowed only intermittently even in winter. At that period, man did not know how to utilise underground water, except perhaps in shallow holes dug in the gravels of river beds, and he became dependent upon limited and localised springs, marshes and the few perennial rivers. The need among wild animals to use the same limited sources may have facilitated the domestication of the sheep and goat. One of the sites yielding evidence of early agriculture, at Jarmo in north-eastern Iraq, was then situated in a marshy depression. In the final stages of gathering wild seeds, when vegetation was disappearing or thinning, the denser growth near such sites may have anteceded agriculture. Simple irrigation may also have been used to encourage the growth of seed-producing plants in semi-arid regions. The sickle, also, seems to have been invented to harvest wild grasses in south-west Asia before cultivation began.

The Paiute Indians, living in the Great Basin of the USA, gather, among many other products, bulbs and the seeds of grasses growing close to stream beds. They do not cultivate or sow; but they build dams and divert water in simple channels to places where these plants grow, to increase the yield. Rice cultivation may have a similar origin. The two wild species from which cultivated varieties are derived grow in the hills north-east of India, especially in marshy valley bottoms. Scattering a few ears after gathering to ensure a fresh crop may have been the beginning of the Oriental rice civilisations. The grasses of which the temperate cereals are members tend to grow closely in a suitable habitat and to scatter their ripe seeds in the autumn to perpetuate the species. Nature suggests to the children of nature the notion of sowing. Thus, in the habits of wild species of animals, before domestication, and the manner of growth of certain *Graminae*, we can visualise, archetypically, characteristics of herding and cropping, as well as powerful influences upon human economies. Both before and after domestication, men became increasingly dependent upon a few species in order to gain an assured food supply, and a livelihood less arduous and uncertain than hunting, fishing and gathering wild plants.

The second favouring biogeographical factor during the Neolithic period was the unusual wealth of wild species of plants, ancestral to cultivated varieties, in south-western Asia. According to Vavilov, nearly all the world's cultivated plants were first discovered and used in principal 'centres of origin', of which most are in the Old World and only three occur in the New World (see Fig. 3). Of the Old World centres, three are so close to each other as to overlap. These are (1) the Central Asian, comprising the mountains north-west of India; (2) the Near Eastern, including Asia Minor, Transcaucasia and western Iran; (3) the Mediterranean

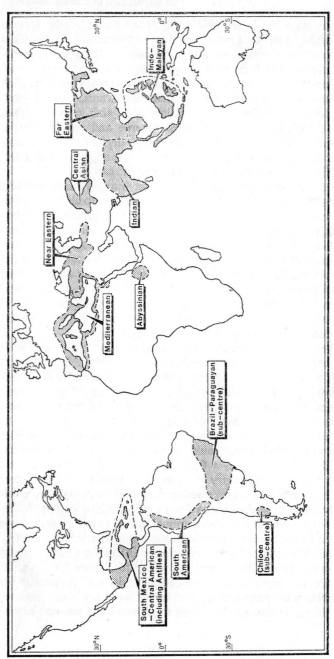

Fig. 3 The centres of origin of cultivated plants (after Vavilov)

littoral, with the lower Nile valley, the interior of the Iberian peninsula, southern France and the southern Balkans. In these three centres of origin, the wild parent species of the most important crops of the Near East and Europe are still growing. These include cereal staples such as wheat, oats and rye; vegetables such as various peas, beans, lentils, radishes, turnips, carrots, beet, cabbages, artichokes, celery, onion, leek and lettuce; fodder plants, including clovers, vetches, lucerne and alfalfa; cotton, sesame and flax; and, finally, numerous fruits and nuts, including pistachio, apricot, pear, almond, grape vine, apple, walnut, hazel nut, fig, pomegranate, cherry, olive and the carob.

The Neolithic agricultural revolution brought many of these plants into cultivation. Man taught himself how to clear and cultivate land, and how to sow, weed and reap. He adopted a sedentary mode of life near his cultivated land. The art of polishing and grinding stone was also invented at this time, enabling him to use fine-grained volcanic and metamorphic rocks for tools, weapons and vessels. Pottery-making, spinning and weaving were not long in appearing, to add to man's range of utensils, clothing and furnishings. And 'the most important step in the exploitation of the animal world' (in Zeuner's opinion) followed, when cattle were domesticated during the fifth millennium B.C.

The species from which domesticated cattle are descended is the aurochs (*Bos primigenius*), which until the Neolithic revolution lived wild in Europe, western Asia and northern Africa. Zeuner believed that wild cattle were still hunted during the earliest agricultural phase; but man then found himself in a dilemma, because cattle acquired the habit of crop-robbing. Domestication was chosen as a more advantageous course than extermination. For the domesticated animal could yield milk, hides and dung (the last useful for fertilising, as a fuel and as an ingredient of plaster). Meat became a secondary consideration. It was not long before cattle began to be used for traction, for primitive ploughs were certainly being used during the fourth millennium B.C. The availability of a strong domesticated animal trained to pull seems to have been a factor predisposing the invention of wheeled transport.

The pig was tamed and domesticated in the Near East at about the same time as cattle, and according to Zeuner for a similar reason. The pig's omnivorous eating habits and propensity for grubbing must have enabled him to lay waste fields and gardens. But the pig is also productive of much meat and fat, and can be reared either in an enclosure or in herds roaming for food in wood-lands, forests or scrub.

As the Neolithic age attained its climax, the plateaux of Anatolia and Iran, and the Fertile Crescent, became dotted with villages composed of timber-framed, plastered and thatched houses. In the tilled fields around, the western cereals were being grown as the principal source of food, and, on a smaller scale, many familiar Western vegetables, fodder crops, fruits, fibres and oil-seeds were being produced. Dogs, sheep, goats, cattle and pigs were all reared.

The desiccation of the region after 8000 B.C. had been turned to advantage. For if man had not domesticated animals and taught himself how to grow crops, his numbers would have declined. The expanding desert and the summer drought would have reduced the numbers of game animals and hence the earlier basis of human subsistence. But the innovating genius of the Neolithic Age enabled the food supply and hence the population to expand. The agrarian and pastoral basis of both the Western and Islamic civilisations had been created.

Moreover, the first cultivators took advantage of sparser vegetation. Their stone, wood and bone tools would hardly permit them to clear forest. But where the mountain forests merged into piedmont steppes, trees became more widely spaced, and a culti-vator could clear bushes and grass mainly by fire. Fire, again, could be used to clear reeds along the banks of marshes and rivers, that would be dry in summer and could be cultivated in winter or spring, protected by low embankments and watered by ditches: in short, the most elementary form of the irrigation systems slowly elaborated in Egypt and Mesopotamia.

The selection of land suitable for cultivation was among the early lessons to be self-taught by the collector of wild grain who was pondering how he could become a producer. The decreasing rainfall of the Near East during the Neolithic period must have prompted him to see the advantages of deeper soils and of fields along the margins of marshes and perennial rivers, where the sub-soil would remain moist even when rainfall was capricious. His simple wooden implements prompted him to choose lighter soils free from stones. Fertility was probably judged at the beginning of agriculture by observing the growth of wild plants. Close, flourish-ing plants (especially of the species being cultivated) could be taken as an indication that farming would be successful. On clearing, trash and brushwood would be burnt; though it would not be immediately realised that the ashes enhanced fertility.

But how could fertility be maintained? For all cropping exhausts the soil. Natural vegetation normally forms part of a slowly-operating cycle of fertility. Plant residues restore nutrients that are being abstracted by living plants. But usually this cycle operates slowly and throughout a substantial depth. Most crops are shallow-rooted, and demand great amounts of nutrients, often during a short period. The only natural soils storing substantial amounts of nutrients are the dark-coloured soils of temperate grassland, known to pedologists as black and chestnut earths. These receive the residues—roots, stems and leaves—of a dense annual growth of grass, which accumulate as humus in a climatic régime characterised by light rainfall and cold winters (and hence of partially-inhibited decomposition and no leaching). Such soils have been identified locally in the Near East in regions inhabited by Neolithic farmers, e.g. in north-eastern Iraq, and may be included among the environmental assets favouring the invention and spread of cultivation.

The value of animal manure was doubtless discovered early, for domestic animals tethered overnight near villages would fertilise land that would be later planted to vegetables, fruits or grain, and the superior yield would soon be obvious. This effect would, however, be lacking on land at a greater distance from a village; and generally it would become understood that yields would decline when cropping was repeated on the same piece of land. Hence, temporary cropping would soon become the rule. Fresh land would be cleared annually, or at least every few years. After some years, when all suitable land within a convenient distance of villages had been used, the experiment of cultivating afresh land abandoned a long time ago would be tried. Thereby the principle of bush fallowing to restore fertility would be put into practice. The natural vegetation and soil partially recover after cropping; but before the former attains maturity, the regrowth is again destroyed to make way for further cultivation. Such land rotation or shifting cultivation—essentially, the selection of land most suitable for the crops being grown, and its periodical cultivation—is characteristic of primitive agriculture wherever it survives today in simpler societies, whose mode of living enables us to visualise the more readily the activities of the first farmers of the Neolithic Age.

From the Neolithic revolution to the Great Age of Discovery

To what extent were the bases of livelihood among the Neolithic peoples of the Near East—crop-growing and animal-rearing—adopted generally by mankind afterwards? How may we
account for the regional diversity of economies existing in the
world at the dawn of the modern age, and revealed to science by
the discoveries and expeditions of the past four and a half
centuries?

The Neolithic revolution took place in the heart of the Old
World. Hence, its principles could become widely known by
diffusion. By the third millennium B.C. a settled agrarian economy
had been founded in the lower Indus valley. Not long afterwards,
villages of cultivators became numerous in northern China.
Although the basic cereals of the Near East, notably wheat and
barley were important, especially in the Indus valley, the latent resources of the Indian and Far Eastern centres of origin of cultivated plants were soon brought into the fields. Thus, buckwheat
was among the earliest of crops grown in northern China; and
sesame has been found at Mohenjo-daro and Harappa in the Indus
valley. Rice, the high-yielding cereal of moist, hot summers, came
into cultivation during the second millennium B.C. in northern
India, and soon spread into China. Gradually, the agrarian features of the Monsoon Lands appeared. Cultivation also began in
the Malay Archipelago, and brought its fruits, tubers and spices
into production.

Essential agrarian features of the major Old World civilisations
therefore arise from the centres of origin of cultivated plants with
which they either coincide or are in close proximity, in conjunction
with the extended range of important cultivated plants (already
noted as a result of the invention of agriculture). Trade between
the Mediterranean world and the Asiatic civilisations was well-
organised both by land and sea by the Roman period, and led to
the introduction of the mulberry tree (and the silkworm), rice,
sugar, and citrus fruits into the Near East and the Byzantine world.
The later Malay migration across the Indian Ocean took the coconut, the clove, rice, the banana and yams to Madagascar and
Africa, with important consequences (see p. 171).

Only a few additions to the list of domesticated animals were
made after the Neolithic period. The horse was domesticated in
central Asia (Turkestan) and the camel in western and south-

western Asia. Since these regions already had the goat, sheep and cattle, these newcomers to the range of animals reared by man widened the basis of pastoral life. Other favourable conditions existed in the extensive steppes, semi-deserts, and mountain ranges too rugged for cultivation, but with upper slopes eminently suitable for grazing cattle, sheep and goats in summer, especially when forests had been cleared. Hence, in western Asia, nomadic and semi-nomadic pastoralism has been a means of subsistence and the basis of social life for millennia. Thence, pastoralism spread into the drier savannas and semi-deserts of Africa.

India, China and the Malay archipelago, however, lie largely outside the natural range of the domesticated animals of western Asia, with the exception of the pig, which originally lived wild in China, and since domestication has remained the most important source of meat to the Chinese. The camel, horse, sheep and goat do not flourish in the Monsoon Lands proper. They keep to the drier north-western fringes of India and China. The humped or zebu variety of cattle, which probably originated in India, however, is numerous throughout the subcontinent; and is also present in much of China, to which it was brought after domestication. But the basic local cultivated plants of the Monsoon Lands have their counterpart in two domesticated indigenous animals: the buffalo and the elephant. The former, whose habitat is swampy ground, is still at home when marshes are converted into rice-fields, and provides the tractive effort needed for ploughing muddy land. The buffalo is thus as closely associated with rice in the Monsoon Lands as are cattle with the temperate cereals of western Asia and Europe.

The Indian elephant survived locally in south-western Asia (Syria) until the historic period. The related African species was represented by a small variety in northern Africa. Domestication took place both in India and northern Africa; but breeding has not been continued in the west, where the species became extinct during the later Roman period. The Indian elephant in India, how-ever, continued to be used in war until the end of the Moghul period; and is still employed in road construction, timber-extrac-tion and ceremonially. The African species still lives wild in Africa, south of the Sahara.

The number of domesticated animal species therefore remains small, and nearly all were brought under man's control in pre-historic times. Other species have been and are tamed or kept in captivity; but this is not domestication, which implies complete control of breeding and a primary economic purpose in rearing. It has been asserted that the power to domesticate now seems to be lost. Only primitive man, living with the beasts upon whom he came to depend, taught the sheep, goat, ox and horse to do his bidding.

Galton argued, not without cogency, that all species capable of domestication had been brought under human control. He believed that primitive man had experimented widely, and had achieved all that was possible in this field. In ancient Egypt, the gazelle and antelope were kept captive and were much admired. May we infer that some inherent characteristics prevented their domestication? On the other hand, we must remember that the caribou of North America is very closely related to the reindeer of Europe and Asia. One has not been domesticated; the other has. Why should not some of the mammals of the African savanna be domesticated as readily as the horse or goat? A greater variety of domestic animals would certainly enhance the productivity of the Tropics. It can at least be argued that man has been somewhat selective in his choice for domestication, and that the present range of domesticated animals arises from a particular conjunction of circumstances in the societies of Europe and western Asia at the close of the Great Ice Age. The rearing in captivity of fur-bearing animals such as the mink, chinchilla and silver fox is perhaps a renewal of domestication. So also are the experiments in rearing the musk-ox recently at the University of Alaska, primarily for its wool. This enterprise has the further aim of providing a livelihood in the Arctic for Eskimos (see p. 25).

Zeuner, however, came to a somewhat different conclusion from his more recent study. He thought that the conditions of life created by the Neolithic revolution inhibited further domestication.

As soon as man adopted the Neolithic settled mode of life, restrictions of mobility, space and climate imposed themselves upon him which made it increasingly difficult to try out new species. Moreover, once a sufficient number of species had been domesticated to satisfy the needs of human life, providing man with food and raw material, nothing was to be gained from undertaking the difficult task of reducing additional species to a state of domestication. It is economic considerations as a rule, therefore, that prevent further experiment.

In the New World until A.D. 1492, the human economy developed independently. The original area wherein wild plants were

cultivated was Mexico, Central America and the western cordillera
of South America as far as about latitude 40° S. Here, in the pre-
Columbian age, and quite independently of the Old World, was
cultivated an array of plants quite equal in importance to those
known to Neolithic peoples in the Near East so much earlier. Two
basic food plants must first be recognised: maize and the potato.
A wild species of the former has not been discovered, and the
present cultivated varieties are thought to have arisen by hybridi-
sation in Central America. By the Great Age of Discovery maize
was cultivated from the Great Lakes to La Plata. The potato,
originally a plant of the high Andes, was until the sixteenth century confined to the cool mountain zones of Peru, Ecuador and
southern Colombia. Tobacco, most probably native to the dense
tropical forests of eastern Peru and Bolivia, and doubtless originally cultivated there, had spread almost as widely as maize by the
time Europeans set foot upon the shores of the Caribbean. The
cacao (cocoa) tree was known both to the Aztecs and Mayas. The
quinoa was grown in Peru for its seeds. The sweet potato, arrow-
root and the manioc, all native to South or Central America, were
important sources of food to the aborigines of the Andean region
and the Antilles. Among the many fruit-bearing plants two—
tomato and pineapple—were later to acquire greatly increased
significance. And the toiling serfs under Incan despotism forgot
their hardships with the aid of coca leaves, from a plant which
grows wild on the eastern slopes of the Peruvian Andes. Jerusalem
artichokes, vanilla, sea-island cotton, and cayenne or Guinea pepper
were also first cultivated by the peoples of the New World before
Columbus crossed the Atlantic Ocean. Two mammals—the llama
and the alpaca—were domesticated, and also the turkey (*Meleagris
gallapavo*).

The types and distribution of economies in A.D. 1500

The world map of economies at the beginning of the Great Age of
Discovery (fig. 4) reflects the expansion of agriculture and animal-
rearing in both the Old and New Worlds. In the former, the most
advanced agrarian economies were located in Europe, producing
mainly the crops and domestic animals basic to the Neolithic
revolution in the Near East, and in the Monsoon Lands, utilising
mainly rice and other indigenous plants, as well as the buffalo.
Pastoral societies dominated the drier interior lands of both
Eurasia and Africa. Simpler forms of cultivation prevailed in the

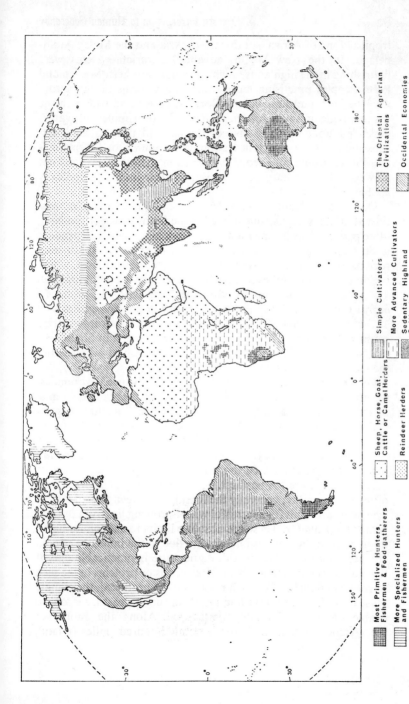

Fig. 4 The economies of mankind in A.D. 1500

Most Primitive Hunters, Fishermen & Food-gatherers

More Specialized Hunters and Fishermen

Sheep, Horse, Goat, Cattle or Camel Herders

Reindeer Herders

Simple Cultivators

More Advanced Cultivators

Sedentary Highland Cultivators

The Oriental Agrarian Civilizations

Occidental Economies

tropical zone of Africa, south-eastern Asia and the Malay Archipelago. In the New World, advanced agrarian systems were
flourishing in the highlands of what are now southern Mexico and
Peru. Peoples practising more rudimentary forms of agriculture
were to be found in southern North America and widely in the
warmer zone of South America. Generally, the simpler cultivators
depended upon hunting and collecting wild produce for part-
subsistence. They also relied upon land rotation or shifting cultivation to ensure an adequate yield from their sowings; and not
all were fully sedentary, for they shifted their homes periodically
as they did their fields.

Despite the advantages of agriculture and the rearing of domesticated animals, eight millennia after the innovations of the Neolithic period of the Near East mankind remained partly dependent
upon hunting and collecting. Moreover, in extensive continental
regions, only simple forms of cultivation had been adopted, which
in some areas did not even sustain a sedentary form of rural life.
The urban life which appeared in the Near East, at Jericho, as
early as 7000 B.C., had spread throughout Europe, and across Asia
as far as China and Japan; but had not penetrated into Africa
south of the Sudan. Nor had towns been founded in Siberia. In
the New World, the only societies that had evolved urban settlements were restricted to Mexico and Peru.

Of the limitations to the spread of more advanced economies,
we may select three as outstanding: first, the geographical limits
to cultivation; secondly, the extent to which humanity has remained, like plants and animals, subject to bio-geographical laws
of distribution, and, thirdly, the effects of disease.

The poleward limits to the cultivation of important crops are
shown in many atlases. Of the temperate cereals, certain types of
barley and rye are the hardiest. These can rarely be grown north
of the 60th parallel; generally the limit lies between 50 and 60° N.
The poleward limit for successful wheat-growing lies from 3° to 5°
nearer the Equator. These are absolute limits to economies based
upon cultivation, and, ultimately, are due to the influence of cold
climates upon the plant world. Agriculture is practicable only if
the plants accumulating carbohydrates, oils or proteins in the seed
or root will flourish. For such reserves to be produced, the climate
must be sufficiently warm and moist, during at least a season, to
enable starch to be rapidly synthesised. Along the shores of
the Arctic Ocean, and for several hundred miles inland,

there are but a few weeks of warm weather intervening between winters nine or ten months long. Neither the trees of the northern forests, nor the humbler plants of the tundra, provide food assimilable by man. Only small berries and rare edible roots are to be gathered, providing but a supplement to a diet which, mainly, must come from other sources. It should be added that the effective limit of agriculture is considerably south of the absolute limits. The northern coniferous forests have nowhere been extensively replaced by cropped land. In the greater part of eastern Siberia, the subsoil is permanently frozen; in Europe and North America, the recent glaciation has left innumerable small marshes and thin, stony soils. Even deeper soils are acid and infertile. Moreover, cultivation of the temperate cereals is normally associated with domestic animals, especially cattle, and for the latter, winter maintenance is very difficult. In Canada, recent successful farming within the northern forests in the clay belt of Ontario is based partly upon the lavish use of silage and substantial buildings in which animals are stall-fed in winter. In Norway, the rather older cattle-breeding, with ancillary grain-growing, is possible in a region where the climate is unusually equable for so northern a latitude.

Certain mosses of the tundra are, however, assimilable by larger mammals, such as the reindeer and caribou. The former, as already noted, was domesticated by the Lapps in northern Europe and by the Tungus in Siberia. Pastoralism is thus not precluded from the lands beyond the limits of grain-growing. In North America, where the domestication of animals, and cultivation, came later, the northern part of the continent, within the northern forests and barren lands or tundra, was occupied by hunters and fishermen, practising rather specialised economies.

The bio-geographical factor was analysed by Alfred Russell Wallace, contemporary and co-discoverer with Charles Darwin of modern theory of evolution, who collated the increasingly precise knowledge of the world's fauna and flora then being rapidly amassed by exploring naturalists, and showed how geographical and geological changes had influenced the distribution of animals and plants. He pointed out that the equatorial forests of South America, Africa and the East Indies had so long been separated from each other that their similarity of appearance concealed great floristic differences. Isolation in similar environments fosters parallel evolution. The several types of vegetation comprising plants adapted to heat and moisture, or to drought, appear as a result of natural selection in the climatic regions of land masses; but families, genera and species are different. But to isolation, in this sense, must be added remoteness from the theatres in which new forms of life appear. Advanced and recently-evolved families of plants and animals, capable of withstanding a considerable environmental range, and often, by the mechanisms of seed dispersal, or speed of locomotion, able to migrate for long distances, have nevertheless incompletely colonised the world.

As an obstacle which could not be passed, the sea is foremost. The islands of the world are characterised by their limited, peculiar and more primitive associations of plants and animals. In this respect Australia is the most remarkable of all the continents. Its geological evolution has preserved its isolation from the rest of the Old World since the end of the Mesozoic era, and thus no mammal is native to it. Marsupials and monotremes consorted with flightless birds in forests of strangely unfamiliar appearance, to astonish the first European explorers. Remoteness, accordingly, not only engenders peculiarity but also archaism. In the wider spaces of the greater land masses, environments are multiplied. Variability and mutation readily produce new species, the more so because migration mingles species and intensifies competition. Moreover—and this Wallace underestimated, for the geological and climatological study of the Quaternary era was only just beginning in his day— many discontinuities in distribution have been caused by the frequently-changing pattern of terrestrial environments in recent geological time. Many species of plants and animals, forced to migrate by the sudden onset of a more rigorous climate, could not survive elsewhere, when confronted with new competitors. Thus, today, even species of birds, having the mastery of air and distance, may be confined to distinct and widely separated regions of the earth.

Man has also been subject to these laws. The principal races of modern man appeared in widely separated regions of the Old World, and, initially, inherited physical traits derived from the already diverse strains of hominids (see Chapter 2). The occupation of the Old World, and later the New, brought many groups into a relative isolation in which further differentiation was promoted. But the limitations to man's mobility have been decreased by his technical innovations, and over much of the Old World interbreeding has more recently arrested the tendency for new races to appear. A substantial proportion of the human race is now of decidedly mixed ancestry. But the Pygmies, the Bushmen, the Ainu and the Andaman islanders remain to remind us that the human species, under certain conditions, might have proliferated new breeds, varieties, races and ultimately species. If the Australian aborigines had remained isolated from the rest of mankind for a million years instead of a few thousand, there would have arisen, not an Australian race of man, but a distinct species. Economy is often associated with race, and new modes of livelihood, such as the spread of agriculture into Europe, have been often carried afar by movements of people. Intercourse alone can widely diffuse not only knowledge of new arts but also useful species of plants. But, again, there are limitations, of which the geographical is not the least significant. Knowledge of agriculture, domestic animals and the art of using metals had not reached the Australian continent before its discovery by Europeans. Similarly, the use of the plough was confined to the Mediterranean, by the broad wastes of the Sahara, until the European penetration into the Negro world. To the sea and the desert, as isolating factors, we may add tropical and equatorial rain forests, especially when combined with mountainous terrain.

Tierra del Fuego is without question the remotest part of the human habitat, from the original home of mankind in the warmer parts of the Old World, by the only route available to primitive man, through north-eastern Asia and the whole length of the two Americas. To the huge distances to be traversed must be added the desert barrier of Patagonia, the forested southern Andes and the stormy moat of the Magellan Straits. Slowly, migrating hunters and food gatherers made their way thither, adapting economy to changing resources, and always maintaining a pure subsistence economy, by living entirely from the land they occupied. Those who reached the extremity of the continent were, until visited by Magellan and his successors during the age of oceanic exploration, in unconscious confinement and totally separated from the social advances of their own continent, quite apart from those of the Old World. Hermit peoples, aloof from the rest of humanity, subsisting upon hunting or gathered shellfish, they were debarred from intercourse with neighbours by which exchange of goods, and, more important, of ideas, might have been achieved. It is true that Tierra del Fuego is beyond the Antarctic limit of cultivation for any useful plant known in the Americas before the Age of Discovery; but this absolute limit was not the most critical factor.

For, farther north, in what is now the Pampas of Argentina, over a plain which is now one of the world's granaries and stockyards, the aboriginal inhabitants lived by hunting until the nineteenth century. For the inability of the Alacaluf and Yamana to practise agriculture is less significant than the failure to invent tools and weapons which would widen the scope of hunting or fishing, to provide adequate clothing and shelter in one of the bleakest regions of the earth. Apart from the change of diet, they lived as if their island were tropical. They plucked shellfish from the shore instead of fruit from trees.

In south-western Africa, and now largely confined to desert or semi-desert, are the Bushmen, who contrive, much more ingeniously than the Fuegians, to wrest a living by hunting and gathering from plants in a dry and largely waterless country. By stature they are to be grouped with the smaller races of mankind. They are rarely more than five feet tall, and they lack the thick, everted lips of the Negroes. By these characteristics, and their tight, peppercorn curly hair, they appear to be related to the Negrito peoples of Malaya and the western Pacific, suggesting that all are relatively archaic, and have been preserved only by their remoteness and isolation from extinction or absorption by the more numerous and physically stronger races which have occupied most of the Old World. They are unique in their tendency, especially among women, to steatopygy, or the accumulation of fat in the buttocks. They wander far in families in search of game and vegetable produce when rain is more likely to occur, during the summer of the southern hemisphere (October to April). But in the drier months they camp in larger groups nearer the rare permanent water-holes, to which they, as well as their game, are then bound. Uniting, the men then stalk the larger animals, especially species of antelope, such as the kudu, duiken and steenbok. Their economy is more elaborate than that of the Fuegians. Their knowledge of the topography of vast areas, of the habits of animals and the technique of hunting has been admiringly described by many ethnologists.

It may perhaps be thought that the aridity of their country debars any alleviation of their hardships by the introduction of domestic animals or any form of cultivation. But, until the eighteenth century, they inhabited a far larger area in South Africa. Remains of their encampments, and their burials, have been investigated by archaeologists at several places in the Veld. The

Bushmen have been confined to their present terrain by the southward expansion of Bantu peoples, who had not reached the Cape
of Good Hope at the time of the first Dutch colonisation, and by
the Boers, who have displaced them in order to practise a pastoral
economy in the north-western part of Cape Province. The survival
and confinement today of the Bushmen in the Kalahari Desert
are due to the fact that stronger pastoral and agricultural peoples
have no use for land which will not support their sheep or cattle.
But a few centuries ago the Bushmen hunted in lands well suited to
pastoralism or agriculture. They appear, in fact, never to have
had knowledge of even purely African cultivated plants, e.g.
millets and peas; although they gather the fruit of a wild
species of 'melon' (*Citrullus vulgaris*); and the non-exigent millets
could certainly be cultivated by the intermittent watercourses of
the semi-desert. Bushmen cave art and weapons have suggested
to more than one ethnologist a parallel with the later Palaeolithic
cultures of western Europe. Thus, by isolation in a corner of the
Old World, a race and an economy have been preserved which
have long been replaced elsewhere.

The Australian aborigines, till the settlement at Port Jackson in
1788, lived by hunting, fishing and food-gathering throughout the
continent. Today, they are confined to the arid interior and to the
tropical forests of Arnhem Land. To reach Australia, their ancestors must have crossed the sea from the Malay Archipelago, perhaps during a maximum phase of the Würm glaciation, when
the sea level was lowered and the straits narrowed, particularly
between Cape Yorke and New Guinea. They may therefore have
already ceased to need boats, if they entered Australia dry-shod
along a broad land bridge uniting New Guinea with the larger
island. They have since had little to gain by learning or re-learning
navigation in a land where rivers are shallow and variable, and
coasts are surf-beaten.

The imperceptible rise of the sea level, during a period lasting
perhaps 15,000 years, was unnoticed by peoples living from the
land; and their increasing isolation from the rest of mankind un-
realised. The aborigines of Tasmania, also, may have reached
their homeland on foot, for Bass Strait is nowhere more than 600
feet deep, which was the probable minimum sea level at the time
the continental ice sheets were claiming their maximum tribute
from the oceans. But here, the restriction to a comparatively small
island, with adjacent islets, may have stimulated attempts to

navigate the sea, for remains thought to be of boats have been discovered on small islands in the Bass Strait. But, apparently, intercourse by sea with the mainland, if ever established, was not maintained, for the Tasmanians, who were exterminated during the first half-century of the British settlement, were not seafarers when first known to Europeans. At the time of the Dutch discovery of Australia, the littoral tribes of the Arafura Sea and the Gulf of Carpentaria had acquired the art of canoeing along the coast and in tidal estuaries; but it seems likely that this was a recently-acquired skill, due to renewed intercourse with the island world to the north, the connection having been established by Malays rather than Australians. Thus, isolated in an extremity of the habitable world, they continued to practise a Palaeolithic culture, using stone, wood and bone for their weapons and implements, in ignorance of metal, cultivation and the domestication of animals, weaving, pottery and building. The absence of mammals in their homeland may have inhibited domestication and pastoralism; but it seems unlikely that there is no Australian species of plant worth cultivating. Indeed, in Queensland, the seeds of wild grasses were gathered in the autumn, without any attempt being made to increase the yield by artificial means. Thus they neither cultivated nor kept animals in the plains and hills of New South Wales and Victoria, where today millions of sheep graze, wheat grows in profusion, the vine flourishes, and towns, villages, farmhouses, roads, railways, mines and factories have been established.

Fuegians, Bushmen and Australian aborigines remained as exemplars of the first human economy because of geographical isolation from more elaborate techniques and forms of social organisation which were evolving elsewhere. To sheer distance was added such formidable obstacles as the sea, ice, the immensity of northern forests and the deserts of Patagonia. The economies of certain other peoples suggest that distance may be less important than impediments to free movement, on foot, to pack animals, vehicles or small boats. For the mountainous larger islands of the Malay Archipelago, and the interior of Malaya, are thickly clad with equatorial forest. The Semang and Sakai tribes of Malaya, the hill folk of Sumatra and Borneo and New Guinea could creep only slowly and with difficulty through the gloomy labyrinth of trees, fallen trunks, climbing plants and undergrowth. They constantly wandered but never travelled far. If they were more skilful in the art of penetrating and living in what, to Chinese or Europeans, is a fearsome, mysterious and repellent wilderness, they have nevertheless remained largely isolated from the far-reaching social developments of the adjacent Asiatic mainland. By navigation Mongoloids, and, later, emigrants from India and China, reached the shores of this island-world, and established permanent settlements based upon rice cultivation. Almost everywhere, this agricultural economy is confined to coastal lowlands, although in Java, exceptionally, it extends much more widely. Thus, on plains accessible from the coast, where forest can be cleared to permit a permanent, irrigated and intensive rice cultivation, hunting and food gathering have been replaced by agrarian modes of life. In a few hilly or mountainous districts, the expedient of terracing, or (in New Guinea), building soil-retaining fences, has also permitted the cultivation of crops differing from those of the littoral to become the basis of food production. Generally, however, the forest reigns unchallenged. To inaccessibility engendered by the rank vegetation has been added the difficulty of navigating even simple craft upstream against swift currents and frequent cataracts.

In the Amazon lowlands of Brazil, the equatorial forest, here called the selvas, is continuous for a thousand miles, east to west, and north to south. It is traversed by magnificent navigable rivers. Ocean-going steamers can ascend the main river for a thousand miles from the sea. But ships glide between unbroken green walls: there is never a glade, or a distant view, except along straight reaches of the river itself. Yet this means of communication is barely used; the river ports are no more than a row of shacks, and but a trickle of trade is borne by the greatest system of navigable rivers in the world. Even if the Amazon lowlands possess the superb navigable rivers that the interior of Borneo lacks, they avail nothing. They link only the small riverain villages of whites and half-castes, who obtain produce from the forest. But to the indigenous peoples, the rivers are natural wonders, and, occasionally, sources of fish. The aborigines, in fact, remain in the depths of the forest, as far from the rivers as possible, and isolated from their neighbours, whom they see very rarely, for either peaceful or hostile purposes. Even before the advent of Europeans, there is nothing to suggest that the natives made use of these rivers for intercourse. Perhaps the fact that the *navigable* Amazon and its tributaries are coincidental with the equatorial forest deprived water transport of utility, because exchange between regions producing different commodities could not be achieved. The gorges

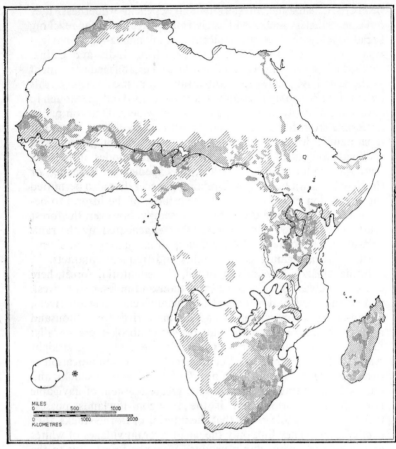

Fig. 5 Cattle and the Tsetse fly in Africa

* Tsetse-infected area. Shading denotes location and density of
cattle.

and rapids of the mountains were interposed to bar them from
trafficking with the only people in the continent practising a more
advanced economy—the Incas—and thus they were as effectively
imprisoned in the labyrinthine forest as the primitive folk of the
East Indies. The greater rivers rather were barriers to hunting and
the search for fruits, and thus the community houses in which
several Amazonian peoples dwell are quite inaccessible except to the

native who is skilled in finding a way where the inexperienced would be helpless. Thus isolated, they have continued to live by a simple economy and form self-sufficing small groups. They are, it is true, not pure hunters and food gatherers, for they produce manioc and other crops. Also, they build houses and make use of a variety of weapons and implements. But they have been effectively immured by the all-pervasive forest. In Amazonia, as in the Congo basin and most of the East Indian islands, the forest admitted many simpler societies to a kind of monastic seclusion, which debarred from association with the rest of mankind.

The effects of disease are exemplified most strikingly in Africa, where species of the *Glossina* genus of flies (tsetse) are the vectors of the trypanosome, a micro-organism causing sleeping sickness in man and a similar fatal disease in cattle. Trypanosomes live in the bloodstream of many African mammals. The tsetse fly flourishes in the forested, humid regions of the continent. Bovine trypanosomiasis has therefore been an insurmountable barrier to the spread of cattle or buffalo into those regions of Africa most suited (by reason of higher rainfall) to agriculture (see Fig. 5). Agriculture, notwithstanding, is the basis of society; but in a restricted, not very productive, form. Lack of milk frequently causes malnutrition among young children.

The principal later inventions

Food production was the last precursory step towards the civilisations of the modern world. What were the principal intermediate steps? Man's powers of invention, exercised over such a long period, have produced an extraordinary complexity of devices, material and social, sustaining the present fabric of human existence. Which inventions since the Neolithic period have been the most crucial? Which rival the discovery of fire, clothing and tools, or the much later domestication of animals and the beginnings of cultivation, in the potency and profundity of their effects upon the human economy? By these criteria, the two most fundamental inventions since the Neolithic period are the discovery of metals and the use of inanimate motive power.

It is as difficult to visualise the exact beginning of the use of metals as it is of the domestication of animals. Gold and copper were being used towards the end of the Neolithic period in the Near East. Gold, occurring in its metallic state, often in river gravels, was initially a gathered resource rather than an extracted metal. So also was copper when first used, which was certainly found, if rarely, in its native state in the Near East. Most pre-historians regard the invention of bronze as crucial. This happened about 4000 B.C. The knowledge that the addition of a small proportion—about a tenth—of tin to copper in the fused state produced a harder alloy than either of the constituent metals could only have been discovered by experimentation, amounting to a new application of that very early natural agency utilised by man: fire. Not only did the use of bronze stimulate trade in copper and tin throughout Europe and western Asia, but it encouraged further search for useful minerals. As an outcome, about 1400 years later, iron came into use in Anatolia. Since iron ore is more abundant than copper and tin, metal could now replace stone, wood and bone in the manufacture of tools and weapons.

Inanimate motive power was first used before the discovery of bronze, for a representation of a boat with a square sail of late predynastic date (during the fourth millennium B.C.) has been found in Egypt. This early use of the wind to supplement the human-powered oar in propelling ships greatly promoted inter-course between the regions bordering the Mediterranean Sea, and thereby fostered the early progress of both the Oriental and European civilisations. But on land, man relied upon his own muscles, or upon his domestic animals—cattle, horses, asses, mules and camels—in agriculture, manufacture, construction and transport, until much later. A new application of wind power arose in the Middle Ages, in either Iran or China: for the date and place of origin of the windmill are obscure. The invention had, however, reached western Europe by the twelfth century A.D. Somewhat earlier, in the late Roman period (perhaps about the fifth century A.D.), the water mill was invented. Though restricted to corn-grinding, and later to pumping, these inanimate sources of mechanical power on land foreshadowed its more general use during the Industrial Revolution. Mechanical energy in the most advanced Western countries is now the foundation of manu-facturing, production, agriculture, transport and domestic life (see Chapter 4).

BIBLIOGRAPHY

CANDOLLE, A. L. P. P. de, *The Origin of Cultivated Plants*, 1864.

CHILDE, V. G., *Man Makes Himself*, 1941 and later eds.

DAVIES, W. and SKIDMORE, C. L., *Tropical Pastures*, 1966.

FORDE, C. D., *Habitat, Economy and Society*, 1934 and later eds.

GOUROU, P. (translated Laborde, E. D.), *The Tropical World*, 3rd ed., 1961.

GUYOT, L., *Origine des plantes cultivées*, 3rd ed., 1964.

HAUDRICOURT, A. G. and HEDIN, L., *L'homme et les plantes cultivées*, 1943.

VAVILOV, N. I. (translated Chester, K. S.), *Origin, Variation, Immunity and Breeding of Cultivated Plants*, 1951.

ZEUNER, A. F. E., *A History of Domesticated Animals*, 1963.

4

THE MAJOR HUMAN SOCIETIES

Some secular characteristics of life in the Near East

South-west Asia is composed of isthmuses and peninsulas. The Persian Gulf and the Red Sea approach the eastern basin of the Mediterranean. The Black and Caspian Seas interrupt the continuity of the Eurasian landmass, thus separating Asia Minor and western Iran from the Russian lowlands. The sea is accessible from almost the entire region, for it penetrates most remarkably into the Old World landmass.

The land is mainly mountain and plateau: the former dominating in the north, the latter in the south. Since the end of the Great Ice Age it has been a dry region, and its aridity on the whole increases southwards. Only the northern mountain ranges receive considerable rainfall, confined mainly to the winter months, and falling as snow at higher altitudes. Here only are forests, mainly of oak. Elsewhere, the natural vegetation is mainly steppe or semi-desert, which merges into absolute desert in the interior of south-eastern Arabia and central Iran. South-west Asia is the central segment in the dry zone of the Old World that extends from the west coast of Africa to Mongolia.

The mainly White or Caucasian peoples inhabiting the region have practised characteristic forms of farming including pastoralism for the last ten thousand years. Archaeology and the representations of daily life in the bas-reliefs and wall paintings of Egypt show that the basic foods since the Neolithic era have been obtained from the temperate cereals, fruits and vegetables found in the largely coincident centres of origin of cultivated plants. These are grown not only intensively where water can be brought by irrigation, but also extensively upon lands receiving 20 cm (8 in) or more of rainfall during the winter season, although here the range of crops is smaller. Many villages in northern Iraq, Anatolia and on the Iranian plateau grow little but wheat and barley.

Permanent cropping has always been conjoined with animal husbandry in the Levant and south-west Asia. The produce of animals has not only been consumed to supplement the yield from crops; but animals have been employed to lighten human toil. The earliest pictorial representations of Egyptian agriculture reveal the ox-drawn plough performing the heaviest tasks of cultivation; and it was already a tradition in Old Testament times that 'the ox treadeth out the corn'.

But animal-rearing is not confined to the cattle, goats, horses and asses kept by the scattered sedentary cultivators. Pastoralism is all-pervasive and assumes two main forms. The first is montane, and is based mainly upon sheep and goats. In summer, when snows have melted, there is good grazing at high altitudes. In winter, the light rainfall at lower altitudes renews foliage and brings forth herbs and annual grasses. Hence there is a seasonal rhythm in the movements of the pastoralists and their flocks from lower to higher altitudes and back again. This is generally known by the French term *transhumance*. The second type of pastoralism prevails in drier and hotter lands, especially in Arabia. This is camel nomadism—the *grande nomadisme* of French writers. Camel nomads may migrate hundreds of miles in the course of the year, and rarely remain long in one place. Their movements are dictated by the availability of water and pasture. Frequently they oscillate between winter and summer pastures. Thus the Ruwela beduin of Syria spend the winter in the desert, and move in summer towards the coastal mountains and valleys of the Levant (see Fig. 6).

The rôle of Egypt and Mesopotamia as the seats of the earliest civilisations cannot be underestimated. The advances in polity accompanying the rise of irrigated agriculture were doubtless fostered by the need for a determinate authority to construct and maintain irrigation works. The lay-out of ditches and the construction of embankments—essentially works of civil engineering —necessitate calculation, for the successful irrigator must know how large a ditch is needed to irrigate a specified area of land.

Where land is permanently cultivated, inheritance, judicial process and taxation demand survey and mensuration. Mechanics, mathematics and government based upon written law and procedure accordingly had their origins in the riverain civilisations of the Near East, and astronomy in the need for an accurate calendar to regulate the annual cycle of agricultural operations when it was realised that greater efficiency could be assured by correctly anticipating the annual flood. The ease with which stars, planets, the sun and moon can be observed in almost cloudless regions—perhaps combined with the fact that in Mesopotamia it is pleasanter to spend the night out of doors than indoors in summer—contributed to the birth of astronomy. With the need for the civil functions of government were also combined the military; for the crops of sedentary peoples are readily raided by marauding pastoralists or hunters. Internecine warfare between the separate villages of cultivators in Egypt and Mesopotamia preceded a unification in the former from within, and imposed upon the latter from without. We do not know—and can only suspect—that dissensions regarding the use of water and land may have fomented internal hostilities. Alternatively, the vision of a more populous, united Egypt or Sumeria, by the exercise of authority over land and water, may have fired the ambitions of the first kings over these lands.

But the piedmont oasis, watered by rivers descending from the mountains, is a *leit-motif* of the geography. It is most significant that the oldest town so far discovered by archaeologists—Jericho—which was flourishing in the seventh millennium B.C., stands in the dry Jordan valley where the perennial Wadi el-Qilt leaves the rugged wilderness of Judaea. The never-failing water of this stream is derived from a resurgence in the massive limestones of the Judaean plateau, which, honeycombed by fissures, caverns and tunnels, provides a vast natural underground storage reservoir for the winter rains. Jericho is not alone as an oasis dependent upon large springs. Damascus, almost as ancient, depends upon

---

Fig. 6 Regional and transect diagrams depicting land use in the
Near East

This diagrammatic sketch map and section typifies the relief, hydrography, settlements and land use (both agricultural and pastoral) for much of Iran, Turkey, Syria and northern Iraq. (In winter, pastoral movements are reversed.)

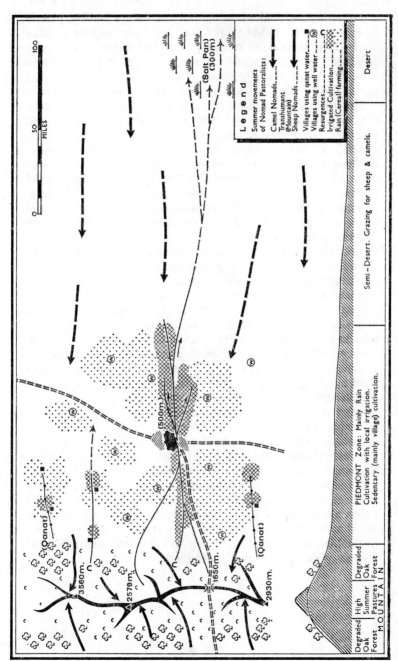

Fig. 6

a similar supply. And where natural sources are lacking, human invention and effort has availed. In Iran, from early times, adits driven into porous formations at the foot of mountains have canalised the water needed for gardens, villages and towns. From Iran, this device—usually known by its Persian name *qanat*—has spread far and wide in south-western Asia and adjoining lands.

Moreover, pack and riding animals, especially horses and camels, can readily traverse steppe and semi-desert. Not only could exchanges arise between sedentary people and pastoral nomads, but trade could be promoted between more distant places, thanks to the revictualling possible *en route* at the piedmont oasis towns and villages. This general freedom of movement is not interrupted by the mountains, for there are many passes in Anatolia and Iran. It is notable that the first large states to bring extensive territories under a single authority in Iran, Anatolia (the Hittite), and in Assyria, were created in these largely open regions across which the movement of caravans and armed forces was little impeded by natural obstacles. (Early Egypt and Sumeria were small and comparatively localised by the alluvial plains upon which their populations were concentrated.)

Ease of movement and exchange within the region could assume a new function after sedentary societies had spread widely to the west in Europe and in India (later in China) to the east. Southwest Asia became and remained a region of transit between Europe and the remoter Orient. This middleman's rôle was stimulated by navigation on those nurseries of mariners—the enclosed Mediterranean and Red Seas—recorded by Egyptian history from at least the third millennium B.C. Finds of objects traded by Phoenicians during the second millennium B.C. reveal that their operations extended throughout the Mediterranean lands, along the east African coast and as far into Asia as western India, Afghanistan and Turkestan. When, towards the end of the first millennium B.C., the Roman empire had become firmly established in the eastern Mediterranean basin, there was regular trade with China along the Silk Road through central Asia; and ships also sailed across the Arabian Sea from the straits of Bab el-Mandeb to the Malabar coast of India, relying upon the monsoonal wind reversal which by then was understood.

Dar el-Islam

Schmitthenner's longer title for this major human group—the Oriental or Islamic society—is perhaps more acceptable in Germany than in the English-speaking world, where the Orient includes India and the Far East as well as those lands of south-western Asia and northern Africa where Islam was born and matured. Nevertheless, it is important to recognise that Islamic society in its formative phases did not make a complete rupture with the past. Certainly, Mohammed and the early Caliphs were social innovators; but they built upon foundations laid long before in the Neolithic and Bronze Ages. Islam, in the lands of its birth, is the successor to the earliest civilisations. This fact logically justifies its place in this chapter after the general consideration just accorded to the conditions of living in the ancient world of the Near East. In short, we proceed to later phases of historical and social evolution in the region where civilised communities first emerged, before turning to other major societies of earlier and later maturation.

Islam integrated local societies already long established in the Near East: oasis cultivators, peasant grain farmers, nomad pastoralists (who also provided man and animal power for caravans), sailors on the Mediterranean Sea and Indian Ocean, urban merchants and craftsmen. Mohammed was a merchant before he became a prophet, for Mecca in his lifetime was a commercial city engaged in the traffic between the south-eastern Mediterranean littoral and southern Arabia. In his person, therefore, he symbolised the world rôle of the Near East. The monotheism he proclaimed replaced beliefs and cults of local and tribal deities by a common faith, which, once accepted, brought all men into a universal brotherhood. The sense of unity was reinforced by the prayer ritual, during which all devout Muslims turn towards Mecca five times daily. To dogma and worship was superadded pilgrimage to Mecca, which, enjoined upon believers as one of the Five Pillars of the Faith, has preserved and strengthened Islamic unity for thirteen centuries. Significantly, the Pilgrimage has been inseparable from trade; for those journeying to Mecca have brought spices, carpets and jewellery to sell *en route* and thus to pay their expenses. And, as will be shown later, trade has been an important means of extending the Faith.

The hold of Islam upon the populations of far-flung lands was reinforced during its formative period (from the seventh to ninth centuries A.D.) by the astonishing success of Arab armies, which brought all the lands from Iberia to Persia under the Caliphate. The use of Arabic as both the sacred language and the medium of government caused it to prevail throughout much of south-west Asia (where it displaced cognate Semitic tongues), and widely in northern Africa. We may fairly regard these Arab-speaking lands as the core of the Islamic world. Here, in the chief cities, Muslim law and polity were formulated in the great codes of leading jurists. Though the Arab Caliphate disintegrated towards the end of the Middle Ages, a great part of Islam was again united under the government of the Ottoman Turks, whose sultans became Caliphs in the sixteenth century. The sense of unity among Muslims is derived not only from common doctrines and social customs but from the tradition of a common polity. Lands inhabited by Muslims are one homeland: *Dar el-Islam*.

Islam has, however, not been immune from sectarianism; and many Muslims do not follow the orthodox (Sunni) dogmas professed in Egypt, the Levant and Turkey. Berber tribes in north-western Africa not only speak their own languages, but are addicted to cults of local saints, with which are associated fairs and religious festivals. The Wahabite, Senussi and Mahdist sects in Arabia, Libya and Sudan, all of recent origin, combine doctrinal dissent with political aims that may be regarded as the Islamic equivalent of nationalism or self-determination. Arab rule in Persia was imposed upon an ancient civilisation, which was transformed but not extinguished. The Shiite heterodoxy proved particularly congenial to the Persian mind, and its adoption was undoubtedly a kind of ethnic self-determination. During the sixteenth century, when Persia was struggling to regain her autonomy under the Safavids, and her chief enemy was orthodox (Sunni) Turkey, conformity to Shiite tenets was enforced throughout the country.

Apart from these shades of heterodoxy among Muslims, Christians and Jews under Muslim law have had the status of protected communities (*dhimmi*) arising from the respect given to their teachings by the Prophet Mohammed himself, who realised that his own doctrines were partly of Christian and Jewish origin. The separate status of these non-Muslims was reinforced by their economic functions. In most of the Ottoman empire, Armenians were bankers and craftsmen, whilst commerce was largely in the hands of Greeks. In Egypt, most of the Government accountants and clerks were Copts. Rather exceptionally, other Christians are found in rural districts, especially in Lebanon and in Middle Egypt.

The nature of Islamic society strongly influenced the plan and buildings of the Muslim city (see fig. 7). At the heart is the chief or congregational mosque, which is essentially a large open courtyard in which a large concourse can meet for the noon prayers on Friday and to hear the weekly sermon. Close to this mosque is the bazaar or *suq*, in which trades are segregated, some in specially built halls. Here also are the *khàns* for the accommodation of visiting merchants, their animals and wares. Residential quarters, mainly Muslim, are provided with many smaller mosques and baths (*hammam*). There are, however, enclaves occupied by Jews and Christians, readily located by their synagogues and churches. The street-mesh is labyrinthine. Even the main streets are narrow and winding. Many houses are accessible only from alleys and *cul-de-sacs*. Houses often meet over vaulted stretches of streets. They are usually built around courtyards, and at ground level present externally only a blank wall and a door. The first floor, however, commonly reveals an overhanging screened balcony, forming part of the women's quarters. Such narrow streets were quite convenient in communities accustomed to go about daily errands on foot, and in which animal transport was also used, but they exclude the use of vehicles. Also, cities could be compact, and thus economise both in building town walls and in increasing military effectiveness by reducing the total length to be defended in relation to the population.

Islam made an equally strong impression upon the countryside. Its prohibition of pork and wine causes pig-rearing and viticulture to be absent from Muslim lands, except locally where Christian farmers survive. And the fact that the armies of both Arabs and Turks were recruited from nomadic tribes gave a prestige and an impetus to nomadism that in many places restricted cultivation. Where Islam overran earlier civilisations, it revolutionised both country and town. Nowhere was this change more profound than along the southern and eastern littoral of the Mediterranean sea, where the Arab armies occupied the Byzantine provinces of Africa, Egypt and Palestine. Byzantine farming was based essentially upon cropping; both annual and perennial (the latter including the vine, olive and fig). Water and soil conservation were practised, which included terracing of steep slopes, irrigation from springs and rivers and the construction of cisterns. The irruption of Arab nomads still retaining tribal grouping into these Byzantine provinces, and the later incursions of nomadic Turks into Anatolia and Asia Minor, led to a decrease in the extent of cultivated land, some of which reverted to grazing. There was also abandonment of viticulture and pig-rearing, as the rural population was converted to Islam. Some towns were also abandoned, and where ruins have been preserved, e.g. at Jerash and Leptis Magna, we can see readily how the Romans planned and built their cities. At Jerusalem, Damascus and Aleppo, the Islamic street plan, houses and public buildings have been fitted into the framework of the Roman street plan.

The south-eastern Mediterranean littoral is, however, the western humid margin to the dry lands of south-western Asia in which Islam had its origin. Earlier, it had occupied most of the Iberian peninsula. The Ottoman Turks, too, overran the Balkans, much of the Danube basin and the south Russian steppe. Why did Islam fail to retain these European lands? Earlier, the Arabs had converted the Levant and North Africa, apart from small minorities. The Turks, too, converted the majority in Anatolia. The question readily arises but the answer is not easily reached. There is some truth to be gleaned by reflecting upon the simple observation that Islam broadly corresponds with the dry lands of the Old World. The nomad could readily penetrate and migrate within this zone and constrict cultivation to his advantage. He could also dominate communications by his monopoly of caravan traffic. The Turks, Seljuk and Ottoman, could effect a pastoral colonisation of Anatolia, and Islamise the reduced sedentary population. But in the Balkans, half-forested and half-cleared, nomadic pastoralism could find only a local foothold.

In the drier savannas of northern Africa, Muslim Berber and Arab nomads could again dominate scattered, localised cultivators, as far south as the higher, denser savanna and the limit of the tsetse fly. Merchants and teachers, crossing the Sahara by the caravan routes operated by the same nomads, could found a string of Islamic states from the Senegal to the Blue Nile. In India, Islamisation was mainly in the north-west, in Punjab and Sind, where, until the modern irrigation works, cultivation was restricted. But generally the subcontinent is closely cultivated and

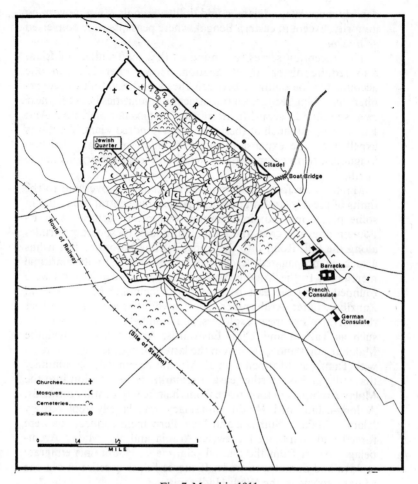

Churches _____ †
Mosques _____ C
Cemeteries _____ ⌒
Baths _____ ⊛

0   ¼   ½   1
M I L E

Jewish Quarter

River

Citadel

Boat Bridge

Tigris

Barracks

French Consulate

German Consulate

Route of Railway

(Site of Station)

Fig. 7 Mosul in 1911

This plan, based upon a German survey, depicts a typical Turkish
provincial city on the eve of modern changes, yet not fully occupying
the space within the medieval walls. The consulates and the railway
in course of construction were heralds of twentieth-century suburbs.

densely populated. Islam could infiltrate only as a governing minority, except in eastern Bengal, where peasants were converted *en masse*.

This exception serves to remind us that the frontiers of Islam also require historical explanation. How, otherwise, can one account for the contrast between Iberia and Anatolia? Geographers have long recognised fundamental similarities between these two subhumid, semi-Mediterranean peninsular-plateaux. And Islam occupied much of Iberia for seven hundred years. Yet it was expelled by the expansion and consolidation of the Christian kingdoms, from comparatively small and localised origins in the north.

Mainly, therefore, the expansion of Islam was overland to the limits of the dry lands in northern Africa and central Asia; and in some places into adjoining humid regions. In central Asia its domain does not cross the Pamirs, although its sphere protrudes along the Silk Road into the upper Hwang-ho basin. But it has also been propagated across the Indian Ocean, by its maritime merchants. In the Middle Ages, a number of Islamic ports were founded along the east African coast, including Mombasa and Zanzibar. Later, Arab traders penetrated into the interior, before the arrival of European explorers, and founded other trading posts, such as Tabora and Ujiji. Eastwards, Arab ships reached the Malabar ports and Ceylon. On the latter island, they intermarried with Tamils and formed a small Muslim commercial community that still persists. Farther east, a remarkable penetration into the Malay Archipelago took place from the fifteenth century onwards. A long-established Hindu supremacy was largely replaced by Islam in Malaya, Sumatra and Java. Permanent connections were forged and maintained between Arabia and the Malay Archipelago. Apart from the annual pilgrimage, Hadhramis emigrate to Java and Sumatra to trade. If successful, they retire in old age to oasis towns in the Wadi Hadhramaut.

The frontier of Islam therefore brings it face to face with Europe in the west, Negroid Africa to the south, India to the south-east, the USSR to the north, and China to the north-east. Its sphere therefore is interwoven with those of the other major societies surrounding it. The resultant interaction could form a study by itself. On the Mediterranean frontier, Turkey, Lebanon and Egypt have been strongly stimulated by the European economic system. Istanbul, Beirut and Cairo have grown rapidly

and are now mainly westernised. Egypt and Turkey have undergone agrarian and industrial revolutions. In Africa, however,
some Muslim pastoral tribes have changed from camel to cattle
nomadism, and also engage in African hoe cultivation. Clearly,
their way of life has become partly African. In India, in contact
with Hinduism, Muslims have in general been scattered as a
minority: a governing minority during the Moghul period and in
the Muslim states during the British period. But in the north-west,
the Sikhs profess doctrines first expressed in the sixteenth century,
which synthesise Muslim and Hindu beliefs. Amritsar is the
Sikhs' holy city. The basis of both Islamic and Hindu society has
been, and still largely is, religious. Hence, the outstanding characteristic of an intermediate society is also religious.

Despite the changes wrought by legal reforms in the sacred law
of Islam (the *Shari'a*) and a decline in religious observance,
Muslims still regard themselves as a universal brotherhood. The
teaching of the Koran in schools, and Islamic history, together
with the continuing popularity of the Pilgrimage, serve to maintain Islamic identity. So also has the achievement of independence from the colonial powers between which much of Islam was
divided forty years ago. But there is no political or economic
unity. The Arab countries forming the core of Islam are members
of a political league; but other Islamic countries align themselves
in other ways. Pakistan and Malaya remain within the Commonwealth. Turkey is a member of NATO. This fragmentation and
diversity of external policies arises partly from population distribution and geographical incoherence within the Islamic region.
Although the greater and contiguous part of Islam falls within the
Dry Zone of the Old World, Muslim populations are scattered in
local concentrations separated by empty expanses of desert or
high mountain. And the Muslims of the Malay Archipelago are
separated from their co-religionists by the whole width of the
Indian Ocean.

The sailing *dhow* has not been entirely displaced by the steamship
in the Red Sea and Persian Gulf. But the caravan has disappeared
from the Sahara and the Near East, although camels, horses,
mules and asses are widely used for local transport in rural areas.
Motor trucks and cars travel far on unsurfaced roads and on frequently quite unmade tracks in the most arid parts. Arabia is now
traversed by motor roads. The rôle of the Near East as a transit
region was mainly fulfilled for almost a century (1869–1967) by the

Suez Canal, which, however, is now (1969) indefinitely closed. Much air traffic between Europe and the Orient still crosses the lands between the Mediterranean Sea and the Indian Ocean. Cairo, Beirut, Ankara, Teheran and Bahrein are important nodes of international civil flying.

Until recently, economic advances in Muslim countries were restricted and unequal. Industrialisation had hardly begun. The most prosperous countries sold agricultural products and some minerals, e.g. rubber and tin (Malaya), sugar, coffee and tea (Java), jute and wheat (Pakistan), cotton (Egypt and Sudan), olive oil (Tunisia), and wine (Algeria). In the last thirty-five years most Arab countries and Iran have been enriched by petroleum.

The proportion of urban population remains low, despite the characterising and ubiquitous presence of towns, many of historic renown. Egypt has more than a third of its population in towns; but this figure is misleading, because many places listed as towns in census reports are simply hypertrophied villages. More generally, the proportion of urban population in Muslim countries is only from one-tenth to one-fifth. Most larger towns have expanded, Westernised quarters, with commercial, administrative or industrial functions. Some suburbs are often disfigured by shack towns, *bidonvilles* or the 'one-night' homes of Turkish squatters: for neither the State nor private enterprise has been capable of providing homes for more than a small fraction of urban manual workers.

Agrarian improvement in many countries is laggard, despite the success of local schemes, already mentioned, in providing export earnings. There is a tendency for cultivation to replace pasture along the margin of semi-deserts—for instance, in Syria and northern Sudan. Much of the cultivated land in West Pakistan has been reclaimed from near-desert since about 1880, when the first of the modern Indus valley irrigation schemes was constructed. The cotton grown near the Blue Nile in northern Sudan, on the Gezira and Manaqil Schemes, occupies land that was previously used only by pastoral nomads or hoe cultivators. But countries like Algeria, Sudan (away from these comparatively restricted Schemes) and Iran have millions of near-subsistence farmers and numerous pastoral nomads whose use of natural grazing is usually non-conservative, and who often have the increase of flocks and herds as their prime aim rather than the production of meat, milk, wool and hides. Technical, financial and social obstacles to progress are great; but serious remedial attempts are also being made, notably in Iran, where oil revenues are being applied to convert illiterate share-cropping tenants into literate peasant proprietors, to create the rural institutions required if the countryside is to become prosperous, and to provide a market for new industries.

Population is increasing fairly rapidly. Algeria, Tunisia, Morocco, Egypt and Pakistan face population problems arising from shortage of land and backward agriculture. Turkey has surplus manpower, which partly finds employment after emigration (mainly temporary) into western Europe, especially West Germany.

The Western economy: its origins and progress

Compared with Hindu and Sinic civilisations, the Western has undergone not only a more complex evolution but also, and to a considerable degree concomitantly, has revealed a tendency to territorial expansion which, in the past three centuries, has changed the geography of the world. But in western and central Europe, civilisation was slow to take root. In its latest and most characteristic phase, it has established itself in environments, such as the cool, temperate, deciduous forest and the temperate grasslands, which previously had not proved capable of supporting dense populations. Until the end of the Middle Ages, the thin population of these regions north of the Alps was backward compared with the ancient riverain communities of the Near East and the Mediterranean coastlands. The older and most fundamental elements of the western economy were introduced to Europe from the Levant. Not till the Neolithic Revolution had been completed, and the cultivation of temperate cereals, the rearing of the ox, sheep and goat, the manufacture of pottery, weaving and building were well established in the Near East, did small villages of settlers begin to appear on the shores of the Mediterranean and sporadically along the middle Danube, in France and Britain, superseding the long-practised Mesolithic hunting and collecting. Later, when bronze and other metals were being worked, and villages by the Euphrates and Nile grew into cities, conditions of living changed but slowly in the West. Till society became much more developed in Mediterranean lands, and later in many parts of central and western Europe, cropping was limited, domestic

animals were of equal importance, and hunting remained a necessary source of sustenance. When population was extremely small
and sparse, cattle and sheep could browse widely for suitable
herbage in the forested terrain, finding grass in glades and where,
on heathy land, trees grew less readily. Cultivation, for long, was in
temporary clearings where undergrowth was destroyed by burning and trees killed by ringing. But the removal of close-growing
oak trees was for long unachievable. Thus the elements of sedentary life, although known from intercourse with the Near East
(especially by reason of the search for bronze, tin and gold which
was widely prosecuted after the utility of these metals had been
demonstrated), could not be effectively applied in the West, and
productivity was lower. Mesopotamia and Egypt were advantaged
by the conjunction of alluvial plains with an annual summer flood.
The latter renewed fertility and enabled irrigation to be practised
without the aid of elaborate mechanical devices or large works of
civil engineering. Thus the effort to clear reeds and, perhaps, some
timber, was justified, because the land was not only extremely
productive; but it retained its fertility by a non-human agency. In
the forested lands to the west, not only was land more difficult to
clear, but cultivation brought a smaller return and could not be
permanent. In short, knowledge of cereal cultivation, alone, could
not enable the people of Europe to equal in production those of
the Levant. Means to conquer the forest, to enhance and maintain
the fertility of the soil were also needed. These requirements were
not satisfied till much later.

The use of iron, probably first discovered by the Hittites in Asia
Minor about 1500 B.C., soon spread widely in the Levant. This
metal, and the domestication of the horse, caused turmoil throughout the Levant and the grasslands of eastern Europe. By 1000 B.C.
Aryan-speaking peoples were overrunning the forested lands of
Europe, and were infiltrating into Italy and Greece. By 900 B.C.
iron-working was active in the Alps at Hallstadt. The scale of the
operations reveals clearly that weapons and tools were more
readily available than in the Bronze Age, for iron is a commoner
ore than copper or tin, and, when properly treated, is more dur-
able. Tools to fell trees and grub roots were now readily obtained.
Thus it was towards the end of the first millennium B.C., during
the spread of the La Tène or Iron Age B culture in western and
central Europe, that oak forest was extensively felled to make
room for cultivation.

Meanwhile, important developments had been going on in Mediterranean lands. The keeled ship, known in Mesopotamia about 3000 B.C., was introduced to the Inland Sea, where, at first plied by oars and fitted with a small square sail, it served the purposes of maritime trade between Crete, Hissarlik (or Troy, on the Dardanelles), Egypt and Syria. About 2400 B.C., as the search for bronze intensified, sea-going ships sailed regularly not only in the western Mediterranean, but also along the Atlantic shores of Spain and France, to link Britain to the Continent. Thus for more than 4,000 years, maritime trade has been the warp in the fabric of the western economy. Now water transport is the most economical way to carry persons and goods. It may not be the speediest; but it costs less per ton-mile. This relative cheapness has been maintained since the Industrial Revolution, for the steamship is cheaper than the train. (This fact is the secret of sea-power, in the military sense. It enables armies to be sustained at distances far greater from a base than is possible when communications run across lands.)

In the West, from the beginning, there were cities and even states which were entirely dependent upon sea-borne intercourse. The Phœnician cities of Tyre and Sidon, built upon rocky islands or peninsulas, and Crete in Minoan times (though this island is large enough to have provided food for the small population of those days), may be regarded as the earliest examples. Later, the cities of the Greek homeland, notably Athens, intensifying trade with the colonies scattered along the littorals of the Mediterranean and Black Seas, discovered that the amount of food which could be produced from the very restricted cultivable land on that mountainous peninsula was insufficient for their population. A mercantile relationship, similar to that subsisting between Britain and her overseas empire during 1850–1914, was accordingly devised. Athens imported grain from the Black Sea colonies and North Africa, dispatching in return 'manufactured' goods, such as cloth and fine metal work, produced by numerous slaves huddled in the city's workshops. Rome, when the imperial system reached its zenith, unified the Mediterranean lands. The main shipping routes were as arterial in their function as the roads. Rome imported grain from Egypt, North Africa, France and Spain to feed its swarming population.

Equally important were the advances in agricultural economy during the classical civilisation. The early Greeks were pastoralists rather than cultivators (to judge from the allusions in the epic poems of Homer), and the small-scale farming of Latium was but a prototype of later systems. In the Mediterranean lands, extensive plains are rare, and much hilly ground must be tilled. The soil is rarely fertile, so that the problems both of erosion and the maintenance of fertility are pressing. As population increased, any form of shifting cultivation became impracticable. The solution was discovered in the combination of trees and shrubs with field crops; in terracing slopes; in the use of leguminous crops, and in fallowing. Thus the Mediterranean economy was perfected. The knowledge and methods of organisation thus established have remained in the European tradition. Among the most useful trees native to the evergreen sclerophyllous forest is the olive, which bears a dark-green fruit rich in edible oil. It flourishes on rocky slopes (for its roots abhor stagnant water) and is such a valuable source of food that it is grown almost everywhere. On sloping land well-mantled with soil, it is accompanied by other crops. Here, stone retaining walls are commonly built to prevent erosion and to allow the land to be levelled for cultivation. Then the vine may be trained over the dry-stone walls, and grain sown on the terraces between the olive trees, whose sparse shade does not inhibit growth beneath. In viticulture, and in the cultivation of the almond and other fruits, pruning, fertilising and selection as the basis of improved varieties are understood. Thus horticulture is wedded to agriculture. To preserve soil fertility when cropping is continuous, leguminous crops, such as beans, clover or lucerne, are alternated with wheat or barley. Or again, the land may be fallowed for a year, and used for pasture, where sheep can find nourishment during the colder season, before ascending the mountains to their summer grazing lands. Their droppings, and humus derived from the decay of grasses and other annuals when the land was again ploughed, renew fertility, and grain can again be sown successfully.

New agrarian institutions accompanied these technical advances, enabling agricultural production to satisfy the needs of the Roman economy. In southern Italy, the peasantry was displaced, and large estates created by amalgamating farms, which were operated as units by a slave-labour force, chiefly for grain production. This institution, modified in the course of centuries, has persisted until today. South of Rome, the land is still largely held in great estates called *latifundia*. In southern France, Roman legionaries were granted land to clear and cultivate by the labour of servile Gauls. Here, at the French Revolution, the large estates were broken up, and the agricultural unit again became the peasant holding. In the Mediterranean lands in classical times, then, a monoculture on large holdings became firmly established, to provide bulk supplies of a uniform product which was handled by a large-scale commercial organisation. It co-existed with the smaller holding, where a greater variety of crops was grown, largely for subsistence, but also to provide small saleable surpluses of olive oil, wine, grain and animal products. Such smaller holdings have in the course of time evolved into the *métayage* tenure, which is common today in Italy and is slowly disappearing from the *Midi* of France. This, in its simplest form, is a co-partnership between 'owner', who provides land, fixed and movable capital and seed, and 'farmer' who provides labour and stock in return for a share of the produce. In Spain, during Moorish rule, and afterwards more widely, flood-plains and river deltas were irrigated, so that full advantage could be taken of the hot summers.

The Mediterranean economy is thus a combination of grain growing, horticulture and sylviculture, symbolised by the three principal economic plants—wheat, the vine and the olive. Stock rearing is subordinate, for the fierce heat and drought of summer parch all pastures. Cattle are not numerous. Goats and sheep are more common, for they can walk farther for fodder without suffering. The former, under the control of a goatherd, browse in the scrub which has replaced the original forest, and, in collaboration with the fire-wood cutter and the charcoal-burner, prevent full regeneration of the original vegetation. Sheep, in large flocks, alternate between high mountain pastures in summer and fallow land or coastal marshes in winter. Commerce and political organisation have long sustained a rich urban life. To the Greeks and Romans, civilisation was synonymous with life in cities.

Whilst this economy was reaching its maturity, during the most halcyon days of Rome, the forests of central and western Europe were little changed. The Gauls, the Teutonic tribes of Germany, the Britons, the Slavonic tribes farther east were scattered in small communities, each isolated from its neighbour by uncleared woodland. Only their tribal, fortified capitals approximated to towns. In the general scattering of population through forested country, these peoples resembled many African tribes before the European penetration into that continent during the nineteenth century. It should not be supposed that the woodland was untouched, although it was largely uncleared. Iron had been known for nearly a thousand years, and timber could thus be used for building huts, making stockades and implements. But these peoples were pastoralists and hunters. Grain they grew only in patches, in partial clearings. Where Roman colonists had established *villae*, in France and southern Britain, more effective clearance was undertaken, and regular cropping, based upon the use of leguminous crops, manure and fallowing, was practised, together with an animal husbandry. But in the turmoil and migrations of peoples from Germany which followed the breakdown of the Empire, the *villae* were destroyed. In France, some survived, to continue the tradition of a rational husbandry; but the forests regained their hold upon many Roman clearings. The renewal of felling, and the final conquest of the forest, were the achievements of the Teutonic peoples who settled in northern France, Britain and western Germany. Before the Imperial defences were breached along the Rhine, the Teutonic tribes had become more numerous, and had been admitted as settlers in eastern France. The cattle-rearing and hunting economy was failing; and more attention had to be given to grain-growing, in a region where soils are frequently wet and heavy, and of only moderate fertility. Realising that adequate cultivation is the key to a good crop, the Germanic peoples used a larger and more robust plough, which, however, required a team of oxen—usually four—to draw it through the soil. The oxen required guiding—and doubtless goading—and the clumsy plough needed one or two men to keep it in its path. Ploughing thus became a co-operative effort. Four men, each contributing an ox, commonly worked together in England in Anglo-Saxon times. Permanent villages became established, and the land around was divided into the open fields and strips which have so often been described by writers on mediaeval history. As population increased, the fields were extended, and the forest gradually felled. But not till the end of the Middle Ages was the clearance completed. On the open fields, a two- or three-course rotation was practised, comprising a winter crop (grain), a spring crop (grain or a leguminous crop) and fallow. The fallow period, during which cattle and sheep were pastured on the arable land, enabled fertility to be restored. In eastern France and western Germany, the distribution of land in strips around the village has persisted until today, although co-operative ploughing has ceased, since the adoption of horse traction and more efficient types of ploughs, harrows and drills. In England, surviving open fields were abolished during the Agrarian Revolution, and enclosed fields, grouped in farms, were substituted. But compact villages remain in the Midlands to remind us of the now-vanished open field communities of which they were the nuclei. The enclosure movement in England was not the only changing element in the older agrarian economy, for there is great diversity in rural settlements, the manner of holding land and the products now being raised from the land. Fundamentally, however, the farming of western and central Europe combines animal husbandry (the rearing of cattle, sheep and pigs) with cultivation of the land, to produce crops of the western bread grains (wheat, barley, oats and rye), augmented more recently by new leguminous fodder crops, maize and root crops, especially the potato and sugar-beet.

But forest clearance, extension of cultivation and growth of population were gradual. Notwithstanding the technical improvements which promoted forest clearance, the yield of grain, in a cool, temperate climate, was small and uncertain; of animal products likewise. Famine was not infrequent, and social customs, including the celibacy of religious orders and late marriages, ensured that natural increase would be very slow. War and pestilence, such as the Black Death of 1348, not once, but several times, left villages empty and fields untilled. Labour was accordingly scarce, and the introduction of serfdom appears to have had its origin partly in the determination of the ruling classes to use the population to the best advantage. But there was an incentive to economise labour and animals, which found expression in the renewal of invention. The water-mill was beginning to be used in Mediterranean lands about the time the western Roman Empire began to totter, although it is not known where this device originated. But, during the early Middle Ages, the water-mill was introduced throughout western and central Europe. It was, in fact, an integral part of the Feudal System, since mills were generally owned by the lord of the manor, who received a proportion of the flour as a part of his dues.

But in the plains and marshes of western Europe, stream gradients were insufficient to enable water-wheels to operate. New invention was again applied. Windmills began to appear in Germany and Holland during the thirteenth century, whence they were introduced into England and France. The windmill is to be associated with a unique enterprise begun by European peoples towards the end of the Dark Ages. The art of embanking low-lying lands, in order to control the application of water to crops, had been known throughout the Roman Empire, the source of the knowledge being the Levant. Small areas of the Fens, in eastern England, are known to have been embanked and drained by the Romans. For in these cooler latitudes, the removal of excess water is imperative; rather than the application of water to remedy deficiency due to irregular rainfall or drought. Early in the Middle Ages, riverain lands were widely drained in western Europe, mainly to provide meadow, which could be mown to provide for cattle feed in winter. In Holland, where the littoral is below high-water level and the flood level of rivers, very fertile land can be used for meadow and cropping if embanked and ditched, provided that rainfall and seepage can be pumped away. The windmill and the pump can achieve this, and the technique was perfected in Holland towards the close of the Middle Ages. Other inventions paved the way for the expansion of European peoples and the later technological advances. In the fourteenth century, Roger Bacon invented gunpowder, enabling the cannon, and later the musket, to transform warfare. The change from swords to fire-arms would, however, have been less effective had it not happened that the blast furnace, in a rudimentary form, came into use for smelting iron at about the same time, in southern Germany and eastern France.

Printing caused ideas to ferment. The mariner's compass and improvements in ship design, first introduced by the Portuguese, at length brought the western European peoples to the beginnings of their transoceanic expansion.

The expansion of Europe

The Portuguese, Spanish, English, French and Dutch mariners who crossed the Atlantic and circumnavigated the Cape of Good Hope from 1492 onwards were not the first ocean navigators. Viking ships had been sailed and rowed to Iceland, Greenland and 'Vinland' five centuries earlier. Malays had crossed the Indian Ocean and the large canoes of Polynesian peoples had been extending the bounds of human settlement in the island world of the Pacific. Mariners from Arabia and India had been crossing the Indian Ocean, north of the Equator, for at least a millennium.

Western European countries were nevertheless operating on a

wider—in fact a global—scale and were exploiting a particular geographical advantage which they all shared. They were profiting by their situation at the centre of the land hemisphere, where products from all the continents could be assembled. Transhipment across the isthmus of Panama began in the early years of Spanish rule. Later, railways and the Panama Canal have rendered more effective the commercial ties between the eastern Pacific coastlands and western Europe. The Suez Canal performed the same function for the Indian Ocean. A reciprocal relationship took form between Europe and transoceanic territories. From Europe, colonists have implanted both the material and non-material elements of Western culture in the Americas, Africa and Australia. Europe itself has received new products, and its own economy has been transformed by the introduction of new plants and the demand for manufactured goods by oversea traders and colonists (fig. 8).

Redistribution of cultivated plants after 1500

Before the sixteenth century, European agriculture was still fundamentally based upon the plants and animals first domesticated in the Near East in prehistoric times. It had received, however, certain additions through the mediumship of regular trade between the ancient West and East, none of which profoundly altered the general characteristics of the European economy, except in the Mediterranean lands of Europe, where rice, citrus fruits, the mulberry and sugar-cane, all introduced from the Monsoon Lands in classical times, were important additions to the older cultivated plants. Tobacco has arrived more recently.

North of the Alps, since A.D. 1500, maize and the potato have spread widely. Contributing more substantially to basic foodstuffs than the plants brought earlier to the Mediterranean, these two prolific sources of carbohydrates have, concomitantly, profoundly modified the agrarian life of many countries in western and central Europe. Maize is now grown from north-western Spain to the mouth of the Danube. In the fertile plains of the Garonne, northern Italy, the middle Danube and Wallachia it is as important as wheat. In the valleys and mountain-girt basins of the Balkans it is the basic cereal.

Deffontaines showed how the adoption of maize, in the lowlands between Bordeaux and Toulouse, revolutionised the rural economy.

Maize took the place of corn in the diet of the peasant. It is difficult to ascertain when it was introduced ... but it only acquired importance from the beginning of the 18th century. The success of maize was entirely due to the small man. Considered to be fodder, it was not subject to the *dîme*, nor did it enter into *métayage* leases; it was acceptable to all. ... Its yield in grain was greater than that of corn—more than three times greater; in all, thanks to rapid ripening after the growing period lasting only 70–80 days, it did not occupy the land so long. ... Moreover, it became the cleaning crop *par excellence*; the 'strong lands', which were difficult to crop because the fertility encouraged weeds, were completely conquered. On the flood plain of the Garonne, where spring floods imperilled the yield from corn, maize, sown in May, triumphed completely.

He continued by emphasising the value of maize as a source of food for man, cattle and poultry.

The plains of northern Italy remarkably exemplify the results of progressive agricultural improvement. Roman husbandry, described by Virgil in his *Georgics*, sought to rear cattle, sheep and pigs, and to grow the western cereals and fruits, such as wheat, barley, the vine and the apple. The introduction of the mulberry, the silkworm and rice from the Orient did not bring great changes at once, because of the disturbances during the Dark Ages; but, during the Italian Renaissance, the variety and abundance of products from the land helped to foster the luxury which was so admired by the rest of Europe. The finest manufactured goods were wrought from silk, wool and leather. Rice stimulated the Italians to drain extensive marshlands and to control their turbulent rivers, which were prone to overflow after heavy rainfall on the environing mountains, and when winter snows melted in spring. It is no coincidence that Italians largely created the branches of applied mathematics dealing with fluids. For nearly a century they have generated electrical power from their mountain waterfalls and lakes. Italian engineers have won distinction in this branch of technology. This competence in drainage and irrigation

---

Fig. 8 The dispersion of wheat and cacao

1–2 Present areas of wheat and cacao; 3 Range of wild ancestors of wheat; 4–5 Migration routes of wheat and cacao; 6–7 Dates of introducing wheat and cacao into new areas of cultivation. Criollo and forastero are two species of wild cacao, which originally grew, respectively, in Central America and northern South America.

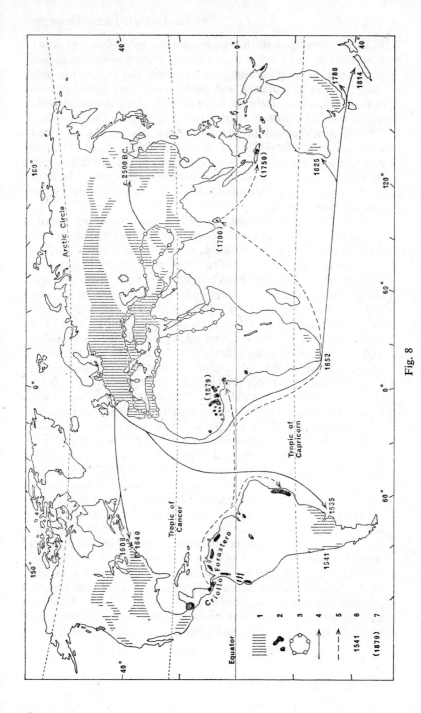

Fig. 8

in turn encouraged further improvements in husbandry. Away
from the coast and main rivers, soils are more porous and do not
permit the flooding necessary for successful rice cultivation. But
meadows can be irrigated, and maize, which would yield uncert-
ainly if dependent solely upon the rainfall, is much more prolific
when watered regularly from rivers and canals. The introduction of a succession of new cultivated plants has provided
stimuli, and has provided the means by which one of the most
complex and intensive agricultural systems of the world has been
developed. A social and economic dynamism has gained impetus
by the acceptance of cultivated plants from the Levant, the Orient
and the New World.

In north-western Europe, the potato has proved an equally
potent influence in the social economy since it became known towards the end of the sixteenth century. More productive of carbohydrates in bulk than any other crop grown in cool temperate
latitudes, it has enabled many regions to sustain denser populations. Thus Ireland, a pastoral country till modern times, was
conquered and 'planted' by English and Scots in the sixteenth and
seventeenth centuries, who dispossessed the native Irish. The
latter either settled upon boggy land, unsuitable for arable farming, or in the hills at altitudes where the climate and thin soils
minimised the value to the ascendant class. Others remained on
the lands which were once their ancestors' as tenants at will, giving
labour in return for the right to build a cabin of turf or stones and
to till a small plot. On the bogs or hills, and as tenants, the native
Irish were sustained by the potato. The malice of Cromwell's
troopers, harrying, cattle-killing and crop-burning, could not
destroy tubers beneath the soil. Thus the oppressed realised the
value of the potato compared with cattle and grain. It was discovered that on small plots of an acre or so (called *conacres* when
let by a Protestant farmer to his Irish dependants) enough potatoes
could be grown to feed a family for a year. Where the Protestant
immigrants did not actually displace the Irish, for instance on the
poorer lands of the west, farms became much subdivided, when
several sons inherited a father's holding; and again, it was potato-
growing which enabled an increasing population to live on extremely small holdings. Supported by the produce of their minute
patches, the native Irish continued to multiply till by 1840 they
had increased to more than eight millions. Then, in 1845, the
blight destroyed the crop, and a people starved. The old system

could not survive this shock; and, as emigrants streamed to America, the institutions of Ireland were reformed.

Germany's rise to be a great power in the nineteenth century was, in part, based upon agricultural intensification, which enlarged the amount of food produced, especially from the light, sandy lands of the North German lowlands. Here, aided by copious nitrogenous and phosphatic fertilisers (partly produced from the mines at Stassfurt), the potato flourished, and enabled farmers not only to rear more animals—notably pigs—but enabled the German nation to become much more numerous. As in northern Italy, a new crop diversified the economy, increased the population and raised living standards.

During the migrations of European peoples since the close of the Middle Ages, crops and animals of mother countries have been established in other continents, reciprocally to the movements described in foregoing paragraphs. Thus, in Canada, Australia and New Zealand, wheat, oats, cattle, sheep, pigs and temperate fruits have flourished where British or French settlers have reproduced the farming of their native lands (Fig. 8).

The peculiar climate of southern Europe, characterised by summer drought and winter rains, is nowhere as extensive as on the Mediterranean littoral; but where it recurs in other continents, European colonists have been quick to recognise the similarity and have begun to grow plants, which, indigenous or exotic, have long flourished in Spain, Italy and Greece. Thus, in the vale of central Chile, Spaniards divided the land into estates, and, using the labour of subjugated natives, successfully grew wheat, vine and olive brought from Iberia. In California, Cape Colony and southern Australia, British, French and Dutch farmers have introduced the vine and citrus fruits. From these regions, wine, raisins and oranges are largely exported.

Elsewhere, the basic crops and cultivated plants of Europe have been combined with those of the New World in novel cropping schemes. In the warmer, moister, longer summers of the middle west and the 'South' of the USA maize yields abundantly, to supplement wheaten flour in human dietary. It is also used as a fodder crop, for both pigs and young cattle. The 'Corn Belt' is one of the greatest sources of meat in the world, which, from the big 'packing' factories in its cities, distributes to the rest of North America and to Europe. Truly remarkable productivity has ensued by associating maize—of New World provenance—with the

domestic animals of the Old World. More recently, the soya bean
has arrived from the Far East. Farther south, the still hotter and
moister summers promote fungoid diseases in the temperate cereals
and wheat disappears. But maize remains, and joins cotton to be
the chief products of an economy which, in the association of
plants and domestic animals (cattle and pigs), the use of the
plough and the cultivation of flat, sloping and even hilly land in
fields, is fundamentally derived from the European tradition. How
different would be the 'Deep South' if it had been colonised by
Chinese or Tamils, instead of by Europeans and Negroes taught
to employ European methods of cultivation! The broad flood
plain of the Mississippi would be an expanse of rice, in small,
embanked plots separated by irrigation channels; and elsewhere
ribbons of rice would follow the course of every stream. Settlements would accompany this concentration of effort along the
valley bottoms, and the slopes would provide land for subsidiary
crops, or would be used as a source of fuel and compost. Thus the
economy of Europe, based upon cereals and animals first employed in the Near East, retains its characteristics in the New
World, even when adapted to the production of new crops.

The industrial and agrarian revolutions

In another sphere, Indian cottons and Chinese porcelain suggested
new manufactures in countries which were striving to export. It
was in England, foremost in transoceanic commerce during the
eighteenth century, that a series of inventions widened the use of
metals and revolutionised all branches of manufacture by the
introduction of power-driven machinery. The growth of modern
industry from beginnings in England (afterwards, in continental
Europe and North America) is familiar. The productive system
depends upon mechanical power for manufacture, transport, and,
in lesser degree, agriculture. Moreover, the volume of useful
products has been greatly increased only by dint of intense
utilisation, and, in many places, destruction of natural resources.
For whereas in many regions of both the Occident and the Orient
the agrarian economy is perpetual because the soil fertility is permanently maintained—Chinese and French peasants are alike in
achieving this, by very different methods—the introduction of
European methods of cultivation and European domestic animals
into North America, Australia and South Africa has caused losses
not only of fertility, but of the soil itself. Restorative methods are

being applied but slowly, and the loss of potential productivity is serious when human beings are increasing as rapidly as at present. But the soil is not the only sufferer. The coniferous forests of Canada and northern Europe are being rapidly depleted for constructional timber and pulp manufacture. Some coalfields, for instance in Lanarkshire, are virtually worked out. The Occident has accepted the opportunity to build an economy linked by oceanic transport and based upon mechanical power, but only to create new problems, of which the conservation of natural resources is but one.

Oceanic commerce and population distribution

Ocean commerce after the fifteenth century also created a new category of city: the ocean port. The Greek cities around the Mediterranean and the Hanseatic towns were prototypes. The greatest city of North America—New York—is the principal terminus of transatlantic shipping, and owes its continuing pre-eminence to the exchange of goods between the most productive region of the continent—its hinterland—and the rest of the world. On the eastern coast of South America, Rio de Janeiro (the greatest city of Brazil), and two capitals, Montevideo and Buenos Aires, are all ports. Nearly all the other important towns of Brazil, such as Bahia and Pernambuco (São Paulo being the chief exception), are also ports. The best location for towns from which political and economic control can be exercised over the most developed regions of this continent is coastal, because the exchange of goods between these countries and the rest of the western world is more important than internal movements of goods. But the law of city location in these countries is operative also elsewhere, for there are only coastal towns in the Guianas, and also, mainly, in Chile, where the capital, Santiago, is situated only a few miles inland in a longitudinal valley. Caracas and Lima—the latter the seat of Spanish government before the colonists seceded—are both close to the sea, and essential to each are the respective ports of La Guaira and Callao. Maps showing the towns, railways and population of South America reveal clearly how the penetration of the western economy has proceeded inland from numerous points of original settlement along the coasts, and in only a few places, such as the Pampas of Argentina and in the Brazilian states of São Paulo and Minas Gerais, has colonisation extended far inland. The interior is in fact still the domain of primitive peoples and is not more populous than in 1500. The high plateaux of Peru and Bolivia are the only exception; but the greater density of population, and many of the towns, such as Cuzco, already existed during the Incan Period, before the advent of the *conquistadores*.

Australia, even more than South America, has been settled around the periphery, especially along the eastern and southern coasts. Aridity debars even pastoralism in the interior, which was aptly called the 'Dead Heart' of Australia by Gregory. All the state capitals are ports, or, like Perth, have an adjacent outport. In Queensland, as in Brazil, most other towns are also on the littoral. The town sites most valuable to the Commonwealth are harbours so situated as to command routeways leading inland, to hinterlands suitable for agriculture or pastoralism.

The colonisation of the New World and Australia by Western peoples therefore diffused not only cultivated plants and systems of farming but also towns. Because the earliest new settlements were mainly on or near coasts, ocean ports in some countries and even continents still dominate the urban scene. Inland towns may still be smaller and subordinate. However, where continental interiors have been thoroughly settled, especially in North America, inland towns of metropolitan rank have appeared, such as Chicago.

Ocean ports of Western foundation are not confined to the Western world. Commerce with Asiatic peoples was also an objective of Europeans during the Great Age of Discovery. Along the shores of the Indian Ocean are many large ports which were originally founded as European trading centres. In the Indian subcontinent and Burma, these ports gained in importance during the growth of the British empire in India because they were also the bases of political power. Thus Calcutta, Madras and Bombay were the capitals of the three most important provinces of British India. Colombo was the capital of Ceylon and Rangoon of Burma. After trade with China expanded in the nineteenth century, Hong Kong and Shanghai soon grew to the status of world ports.

Urbanisation in the West

The urban community, composed of traders, craftsmen, priests and rulers, has existed in the West from its earliest phases as a civilisation. The very idea of civilised life—as the etymology of the word makes clear—to the Greeks, was equated to the institutions of the city. Greek colonisation on the shores of the Mediterranean and in western Asia (under Alexander and his successors) in its essentials was simply the founding of cities. The Romans adhered to the same principle. Their *colonia* were new towns, often inhabited at the outset by legionary veterans, and linked together by their remarkable system of paved roads. Most older towns of England and France are of Roman foundation, and frequently preserve part of their original street plan, including the alignment of fortifications. The progress of forest clearance during the later Middle Ages in western and central Europe accompanied a growth in population which created a need for more manufactures and markets: hence, for more towns. Kings and greater nobles conferred municipal constitutions by charter to induce people to build and live in towns, often on sites adjoining castles. Somewhat later, as the political map of Europe took shape, capital cities, such as Florence, Venice, Paris, London, Madrid and Berlin, began to outstrip their lesser neighbours in size and grandeur. By the eve of the Industrial Revolution, Europe possessed a stipple of small market towns with a population of a few thousands (or perhaps only a few hundreds in the more sparsely-populated regions), usually located from 16 to 24 km (10 to 15 miles) apart. Thus the majority of the population, living in the countryside, could visit a market town and return home, on foot or on a riding animal, within a day.

The increasing concentration of population in towns, as a consequence of the revolution in industry and transport since 1750, has already been mentioned (Chapter 1, p. 25–6). This process has transformed older Western cities and towns, and has brought into existence many entirely new towns. Provision of mechanical transport by rail and road promoted the growth of residential suburbs around early towns, which are now partly or wholly rebuilt to serve as the commercial cores. Purely symmetrical expansion is, however, unusual. Generally, the railway skirts the old town on one side, and has caused suburban growth to be lopsided, especially if large-scale industry has appeared.

In industrial regions, of which the earliest corresponded with the major coalfields of western Europe and eastern North America, amorphous aggregations of factories and workers' housing grew around and among older market towns and villages. The market towns often expanded and began to specialise in commercial activities related to local industries. Urbanised and industrialised regions were thereby formed, for which Geddes publicised the term conurbation.

A somewhat different type of urban region has arisen from the modern growth of capitals or larger states. In the early twentieth century, London was a comparatively compact metropolis. Its core consisted of the City (corresponding with Roman and medieval London), but given over entirely to commerce, together with the West End, an extension from the ancient royal palace and abbey of Westminster, which was the seat of the central government, and also the focus of entertainment and the luxury trades. All around, to a radius of about 12 to 16 km (8 to 10 miles) from the City, were the mainly residential suburbs. The Thames, below London Bridge, was the Port of London. The whole was knit together by a system of underground and suburban railways, electric trams and omnibuses. Since the war of 1914–18, the former well-defined capital city has become the centre of a metropolitan urbanised region. This change has been wrought by electricity and motor transport. The former has loosened the hold of coalfields upon industry, enabling many factories to be located within or close to the largest market of the country. It has also increased the speed and carrying capacity of the suburban railway. Indeed, many former main lines connecting London with the North Sea or Channel coasts, or with the Midlands, now electrified, have become busy carriers of the daily-journeying office worker to and from his desk. Many new outer suburbs have appeared, which are often expanded villages or small market towns, like Guildford or St Albans. Some are industrial, especially along the shores of the Thames estuary and some of the main railways radiating towards the Midlands. Among the newer features of the metropolitan region are several new satellite towns, of which Letchworth and Welwyn Garden City were the first, succeeded, since 1945, by Stevenage, Harlow, Basildon, Crawley and Hemel Hempstead. These new towns have been designed to provide both industrial and office employment and thereby to reduce congestion in the metropolis proper.

Complementary to London itself, its satellite towns and its outer suburbs, is another type of satellite: the holiday resort, generally located along the coast. Brighton, founded in the late eighteenth century, is the oldest and most famous. Some, such as Folkestone and Bournemouth, are resorted to by the retired as well as by summer holiday-makers. Royal Tunbridge Wells, a small spa founded in the late seventeenth century, is inland and is a residential outer suburb as well as a magnet for those about to retire within the metropolitan region.

Throughout south-eastern England, urban expansion has been in competition with farming and with rural amenity. The 'urban sprawl' that until the Second World War was disfiguring and often destroying very beautiful rural landscapes has now been checked by comprehensive land planning introduced after 1947. The best scenery and exceptionally productive agricultural land are now preserved from urbanisation. Suburbs are kept compact; and new towns are exercises in modern principles of urban planning and design, in which shopping and residential precincts are segregated from transport.

The London metropolitan region is not unique. Many of its features appear in and around Paris, Tokyo and along the eastern seaboard of the United States of America, where an intricate system of new main roads capable of carrying great numbers of fast motor trucks and cars is promoting an expansion of older cities, such as Boston, New York, Philadelphia, Baltimore and Washington, as well as a growth of new outer suburbs and in- dustrial towns. To this metropolitan urban region or tract, Gottman has given the name Megalopolis.

Russian expansion eastwards

But the conquest of the deciduous forests and the oceans, and wresting from Nature the secret of mechanical power, does not end the story of the evolution and geographical expansion of the West. In Poland and central Russia the deciduous forest stretches east- wards, narrowing in the Volga basin till it disappears near Kazan, unable to withstand the increasingly rigorous climate. Here, in the Middle Ages, forest clearance and agricultural settlement were also proceeding. The solid nucleus of the future Russia was the Moscow region, thanks to the exploitation of its nodality by its Grand Dukes, who were not lacking in statecraft. Southwards lay the open steppes, which, extending to the lower and middle Danube basins, were the home of pastoral peoples, governed by the Mongols and the Turks, both militant nomads from the pastoral heart of Asia, who had pressed westwards across these continuous plains to the gates of Vienna. From the sixteenth cen- tury onwards, the Russian tsars advanced southwards and east- wards. No longer compelled to lurk in the forests for fear of the

Tatars, they were able first to gain a foothold on the grasslands, and later to extend their power to the Black Sea. The military superiority over a hitherto invincible cavalry was gained by numbers, artillery and fortifications, about which Peter the Great had been instructed in western Europe. New arsenals in Saint Petersburg were a foundation of the expansion of Russia to the northern and southern seas. But the consolidation of new territories was the task of the peasant.

Agriculture was not unknown in these spacious grasslands. During the earlier Kiev period of the Russian monarchy, and still earlier, when Greek colonies flourished along the shores of the Black Sea, grain was grown along the valleys of the Dnieper and Don. But successive westward migrations of aggressive pastoralists had retarded the work of the plough. Quite late in the Middle Ages, the destructive Mongols caused most Russians to withdraw from Kiev to the Upper Volga. The grasslands were thus largely preserved for the sheep and horse until modern times. But then the military supremacy of a peasant people wrought also an economic revolution in the steppes. Countless new villages were founded, until the Dnieper and Don basins were tilled from source to mouth. By the end of the nineteenth century, little of the steppe, west of the Lower Volga, had not felt the ploughshare.

A similar colonisation of grassland had, meanwhile, been proceeding in the middle Danube basin. The Hungarians, who had established themselves astride the river in the early Middle Ages, were a people of the horse, and despised agriculture. Their subjugation by the Ottoman Turks in the sixteenth century, followed by Austrian campaigns, forcing Turkish power to recede to the Balkans, still further retarded the development of agriculture. But after the peace of Karlowitz (1699), the Hungarian *puszta* was converted from pasture to grainfields. The Hungarians themselves, Germans from the west and Slavs from the south (seeking refuge under a Christian monarch, from Turkish oppression), attracted by land granted in return for military obligations in a frontier region, established themselves in compact and originally fortified villages. Again, power won by a superior army was consolidated by the plough. In the nineteenth century, after railways had been built radiating south-eastwards from Vienna and Budapest, the Hungarian Plain became a granary serving new industrial cities of central Europe.

The Western economy: summary

Europeans have settled closely in the Mediterranean lands, deciduous forest lands and temperate grasslands of their continent. The capacity of the most tractable soils in the forest to maintain artificially-enhanced fertility, and the notable reserves of humus in the grassland soils, have enabled rural populations to increase to densities of the order of 200–250 to the square mile, which is comparable with the population supported by irrigated rice-growing land in India and China. A belt of such dense population has appeared on the map of Europe, extending along the northern edge of the mountain zone, beginning in northern France, and passing through central Belgium, central Germany, southern Poland to the Ukraine. Thus for the first time the population of Europe north of the Alps has become comparable with that of the Ganges valley or the Yangtze-kiang basin. The western cereals have regained equality with rice as a staff of life to the human race. Coincident with this European fertile belt are the coalfields providing much of the fuel and power consumed in industrial processes.

The European economy, then, is based upon a quadruple discovery; first, that temperate grasslands are much more productive when tilled than when pastured; secondly, that a mixed husbandry incorporating a range of crops and domestic animals having, as part of its method, enhanced fertility of soils won from deciduous forest, can support a moderately-dense sedentary population; thirdly, that coal, and increasingly other sources of energy, can be employed as the basis of industrialised society; and, fourthly, that the use of enclosed seas as means of intercourse between economically-complementary regions can be reproduced on the much larger scale of the oceans and continents.

The extraordinarily rapid progress of settlement within the United States after 1815 was the outcome of a realisation, by immigrant European peoples, that the environmental conditions which their ancestors had so laboriously learned to exploit co-existed also in the New World. To the temperate hardwood forests of the Middle Atlantic states and the Ohio valley succeeded the unbroken prairies of the Middle West. The single state of Pennsylvania contains a substantial part of the world's coal reserves. In one hundred and fifty years—instead of a thousand years—a manufacturing and farming belt similar, though somewhat smaller, has come into existence as the counterpart of the European original.

Some aspects of Western institutions

So far, our attention has been confined to economic growth in the West: to the progress of food production in its ecological setting, to the growth of commerce, industry and population, to transcontinental and oceanic expansion, and to urbanisation. We must now consider the correlated evolution of institutions, social and political.

The West shares its hearth—south-west Asia—with Islam, for both must trace their origins to the Neolithic Revolution. Thus the West is unique among the major societies, because its hearth, now within *Dar el-Islam*, lies outside its own core, domain and sphere. Not only did Europe receive the basis of its husbandry and early knowledge of metals from the Near East, but, in addition, the Judaeo-Christian religious belief in monotheism and the equality of man before God: also present, in a somewhat different interpretation, in the tenets of Islam. Toynbee, however, points out that during its evolution, Western civilisation absorbed Scandinavian, Saxon and Celtic cultures.

European languages, with the exception of Basque, Hungarian, Finnish and Latvian, all belong to the Indo-European family. From an origin probably in the steppes of southern Russia or the vicinity of the Caspian Sea they were widely dispersed by warlike horse-riding folk during the Bronze and early Iron Ages, not only within Iran and India (see p. 147–9), but in Europe. Linguistic divergence inevitably followed, for government was still largely tribal and local. Moreover, writing was not adopted in central and western Europe until much later. Some fourteen major languages and a number of minor languages and dialects have thereby arisen. Much later, language became a potent influence in the creation of nations and states, with some exceptions, such as Belgium and Switzerland.

The common grammar and similarities of vocabulary somewhat reduce the difficulty of learning languages of neighbouring countries, and also facilitate the introduction and borrowing of new terms, especially those required by the sciences: the more so, because the works of Classical Greek and Latin authors are the foundation of the Western literary inheritance, knowledge of which is indispensable to the mature Western mind and hence in education. Translation is also made easier, ensuring that the literatures of different modern as well as classical Western languages together form a common treasure. The relationship already existing between Norman-French and Anglo-Saxon aided their fusion and accompanying grammatical simplification, after the Norman conquest. The coincidence that English was the mother tongue of the most successful Western colonising power has enabled it in the past two centuries to become the most widely-spoken world language, and the most important second language where it is not the prevailing language.

The first language of mainland Europe to be written was Classical Greek, and not long afterwards its speakers, under the hammer blows of Persian aggression, were shaped on the anvil of history into the first European nation. Their intellectual and artistic gifts enabled them not only to assimilate the knowledge of Babylon and Egypt but to rise to achievements in literature, including drama, sculpture and architecture that permanently influenced the future of the Western mind. From their talent and zest for rational debate, combined with intense curiosity, extending to Nature as well as Society, arose not only the natural but also social science. Their conviction that man's character is stunted unless he bears responsibility within a representatively-governed state has dominated Western political thought since the Middle Ages. During this period, too, the vocabulary of Classical Greek enriched all living European languages by providing new terms required by modern science.

After the ancient Greeks had passed their climax of achievement, leadership in the West passed to the Romans, whose capacity for military and civil organisation enabled them to conquer and administer an empire that included the entire Mediterranean basin, Gaul (France), Britannia (England and Wales), and Central Europe as far as the Rhine and Danube. Their early history, like that of Athens and other Greek city states, is a record of uneasy, often violent, oscillation between representative and despotic government. As the Empire expanded, representative institutions withered, and the emperor became the supreme legislator, commander and judge, advised by a few chosen counsellors, whose decisions were applied by a numerous trained civil service and army. The Romans conceived the state as a centralised empire, composed of many peoples, tolerant towards religions and customs, provided subjects could reconcile their beliefs and rituals

E

with those of the Roman state religion, knit by good communications on land and sea, with a common official language (Latin), administered from cities having municipal institutions permitting partial self-government to merchants and craftsmen, and with a uniform law taught and practised by specialists. Codified Roman law forms the basis of many modern European legal codes, as well as legal training. In Western history, this imperial type of state, as an alternative to the Greek ideal of self-government, has prevailed for lengthy periods in the annals of many nations. The two co-existed within the British empire. Roman society, however, accepted inequality without criticism. Although, during the second and third centuries, the number of Roman citizens in towns was increased by imperial policy, most of the population, in town and country, lived as slaves. The land was parcelled into estates where the labour force was regarded as capital or property: as little more than animate instruments of production.

While the Empire was still largely inviolate, though beset by aggressive tribes from without and by factions within, it became Christian. From an origin as an obscure Jewish sect in a remote corner of the Empire, in three centuries Christianity gained widespread support at the expense of pagan cults. Moreover, it was a unified and well-organised body already, in many respects, mirroring the state itself, and Constantine's conversion, his liberation of the Church, and its establishment as the state religion by his successors were undoubtedly calculated to underpin the Empire's integrity at an epoch when it was threatened with disruption. The political motive was made even clearer at the Council of Nice at which doctrinal disputes were resolved by the formulation of a uniform expanded version of earlier Christian creeds. The new capital (New Rome) on the Bosphorus was planned as a Christian city, culminating in great churches on the principal heights; and the adaptation by his architects, for ecclesiastical purposes, of Graeco-Roman principles of design for public buildings permanently influenced the urban landscape of the West.

The Constantinian policy was nevertheless only partially successful. Within a century, the western half of the Empire had been invaded and divided between Lombards, Franks, Visigoths, Ostrogoths and Saxons. But in the east, the Empire continued for another thousand years. The deep contrasts between eastern and western Europe arise from these events.

In the East, the empire slowly declined in the face of Islamic aggression; and all of its territories east of the Straits were eventually incorporated in Islam. But the Church had meanwhile evangelised the Slavonic tribes of the Balkans and Russia, among whom political institutions were derived from those of New Rome. The supreme ruler was a caesar (tsar) and the Church was identified with the state. Government was for a long time mainly tribal but later became feudal and eventually bureaucratic. The divergence of the East from the West was aggravated after the Ottoman Turks had overrun the Balkans and the Lower Danube, together with the Black Sea coastlands, in succession to similar earlier inroads by Mongols, causing Russians to withdraw northwards and eastwards into the forested lands of the Upper Volga basin.

In the West, the Church revived the rôle of Rome as a capital. Attempts to re-create an empire—at first under Charlemagne—were unsuccessful. For many centuries, government was mainly local, under hereditary rulers; but eventually nationalism, based upon the main languages, became the basis of most states. In the absence of political unity, the popes of Rome created and maintained an ecclesiastical unity until the sixteenth century, transcending ephemeral frontiers and embracing western, central and northern Europe, by converting the peoples beyond the original Roman frontier as well as Italy and the Iberian peninsula (as it was freed from Muslim rule). The Roman Catholic Church thus welded the peoples under its ecclesiastical rule into a single society by the use of Latin as its language in ritual, communication and administration, and by its influence upon social institutions, notably in its insistence upon monogamous marriage and its monopoly of education. To ensure that its ministrations were universally available, it extended the system of dioceses and subdivided dioceses into parishes, and thereby gave many villages a church as a nucleus, and many towns a cathedral.

In the countryside, the feudal system evolved out of the Roman estates and the settlements of the non-Roman peoples. The lord became responsible for security and justice and was obliged to give military service to his overlord. The population remained servile, and was bound to its villages. As the Middle Ages proceeded, this rural social system was slowly changed by its conversion from a near-subsistence to a partially-commercial economy, and by the growth of the western European state. The central (royal) government took over the full responsibility for military forces, and much, if not all, of the judicial function of lords.

Feudalism declined; and the descendants of feudal lords became landed proprietors. Serfs became tenant farmers or farm-labourers. In some regions, a rural middle class appeared, composed of more substantial tenants and smaller proprietors who farmed their own land. This type of rural society has shaped rural settlement in western Europe, composed as it is of castles or great houses, farmhouses of tenants and smaller proprietors, and cottages of the manual workers, often largely concentrated in villages, but in some regions partly, or wholly, dispersed.

The later Middle Ages witnessed a growth of manufacture and long-distance commerce, especially in the cities of northern Italy, such as Venice, Genoa and Milan, as well as in the Low Countries, stimulated by connections with the Orient through Constantinople and Cairo. The introduction of printing (by cheapening and increasing the production of books) and the discovery of the New World, stirred minds in all countries and generated a reform movement within the Church. Insistence by the reformers upon the individual's duty to understand and intellectually to accept the Christian faith gave an impulse to translate the Bible into vernacular tongues, to education and to learning generally. A further result, after living European languages became the vehicle for the writer, was the strengthening of national sentiment. Protestant churches, rejecting papal authority from Rome, were formed: in some instances, the breaking-away was an act of intensifying nationalism. Rejection of ecclesiastical absolutism was soon followed by dissatisfaction with political absolutism, often, in the early phases, a claim for religious toleration, where rulers had remained Catholic, or, if Protestant, had insisted upon uniformity in doctrine and worship: in other words, a state church.

These issues were first fought out in seventeenth-century England, during the Civil War, which ensured the ascendancy of an elected legislature over the monarchy, and deprived the king of any power in the courts of law. At the same time, England was beginning to participate in oceanic commerce and in colonising newly-discovered lands. Like other western European maritime nations the English aim was to establish and maintain commercial and political connections between metropolitan countries and those which were newly-discovered or newly-attainable by sailing across the oceans. After the examples of Rome and Venice, which had bound scattered dependencies to the seat of authority by sea routes, Portugal sought to create an Empire on the shores of the

Indian Ocean, and Spain on the western shores of the Atlantic. The rivalry of other western European peoples caused these exclusive schemes to break down, and the New World, Africa, Australia and parts of south-eastern Asia became divided between Spain, Portugal, France, Britain and Holland.

The growing middle class in Britain, seeking fresh profitable investment, undertook the commercial exploitation of new inventions, and from about 1750 the industrial revolution started its course. From the Reform Act of 1832, this entrepreneurial class secured the passage of legislation removing restrictions upon capitalistic enterprise and freedom of trade. Hence, by 1850, Britain led the world in industry and commerce. Having, after 1815, obtained the naval supremacy of the oceans by the occupation of strategically-located bases and the sheer number and armament of its warships, it was able to acquire the largest overseas empire, supported by sea power and including temperate lands suitable for settling emigrants from the home country, where population was increasing rapidly.

Somewhat later, similar political and legal changes were initiated on the continent of Europe by the French revolution and the temporary extension of French rule to neighbouring countries under Napoleon. The industrial revolution spread to Belgium and France immediately after 1815 and to Germany from about 1830, fostered by the first railways and the commercial union (*Zollverein*) of that archaically-fragmented country. France (after 1830) and Germany (after 1870), as well as Holland (which had occupied colonies in the Malay Archipelago during its seventeenth-century naval domination of the Indian Ocean), followed Britain's lead in developing overseas dependencies as markets for manufactures and sources of raw materials. By the end of the nineteenth century, western Europe was supreme in commerce, finance, manufacture, and science. New institutions, such as modern banks, exchanges, and the limited liability company; and legal innovations, such as codes of commercial law, provided the milieu in which capitalistic production and trade could flourish. In the sphere of government, besides elaborating the administrative apparatus for controlling commerce, transport and health, and for providing universal education, western European countries devised the means to pacify, police and encourage modern commerce in colonial territories.

Colonial policies, however, differed widely, and the western European colonial legacy should be studied comparatively. Two

broad categories of former colony were distinguished in Chapter 1
(p. 28); the tropical or subtropical, and the temperate. The first
was commercially exploited; the second was occupied by emigrant
settlers. Most of the former colonial empires (though not all)
included both categories of dependency.

In the New World, Central and South America became the chief
component of the Spanish empire, for three hundred years (apart
from Brazil, which was Portuguese). In this immense continental
expanse, the aboriginal population was extremely sparse, except
on the highlands of the northern Andes and on the Mexican
plateau. The Spanish and Portuguese monarchies, untouched by
the Reformation, and with feudal institutions less modified than
in England or Holland, encouraged the Church to christianise the
natives. The state itself suppressed indigenous ritual and worship;
and the Church substituted its own, though not without some
concessions to traditional cults, which in remoter areas are still
practised. The largely agrarian society of Iberia, in which a
privileged aristocracy dominates a poor tenant or labouring class,
was reproduced in the more populous and accessible parts of
Central and South America. In the remoter tropical interior, however, colonial government amounted to little more than a claim to
sovereignty. Aboriginal tribes still live in the rain forests and
savannas, little influenced by the West. On the tropical eastern
coasts, where the aboriginal population was not numerous, and
did not survive the European occupation, Negro slaves were introduced on plantations that were essentially estates growing such
tropical products as cacao and sugar, increasingly consumed in
Europe. The Spanish language (or Portuguese, in Brazil), and
Catholicism therefore prevail in Latin America. Political privilege
based upon ownership of land and European descent still persists
in many countries. The majority of the population is usually of
mixed blood, with Negroes in the ascendant where African slaves
were formerly numerous, as in north-eastern Brazil, and American
Indian stock predominating in the highlands of western South
America and Central America.

The upheaval of the French revolution and the Napoleonic
wars caused the Spanish and Portuguese colonial empires in
South and Central America to secede (1809–26) and to break up
into states based mainly upon former provinces. But the socio-
religious characteristics of the imperialist period were little
changed. The local creoles (the small wealthier class of European

or mainly-European descent) exercised power instead of officials appointed by the Spanish or Portuguese governments. The abolition of slavery by Simon Bolivar (except in Brazil) did not effectively amend the subjugation of the workers on plantations or the cultivators on the estates in the Andean countries. But the cessation of the Spanish trade monopoly opened the ports to the commerce of other western European flags, especially of Britain. Later in the century, emigration from Spain and Italy increased into temperate Argentina and subtropical Brazil, stimulating more rapid economic progress. More recently, the power of the landowning class has been diminished. In Mexico and Cuba the large estates have been expropriated. Large-scale mining enterprises, the rise of Venezuela to world rank in petroleum production and the rise of modern industry in Mexico, Brazil, Argentina, Peru and Chile have increased both the urban middle class and the proletariat, and have created a disequilibrium of political forces. In several countries, the urban middle class, the urban and mining working class, the rural workers or small tenants, and the establishment of landed proprietors (in close alliance with the army officer class and the Church) are in rivalry.

The contrast between Latin and Anglo-America remains great. Temperate North America contained neither the gold and silver, nor the potential for sugar production, that lured the Spanish and Portuguese to the Caribbean, Mexico, Peru and Brazil. Hence, Spanish authority was never effective north of the Gulf of Mexico, except in Florida. When in the sixteenth century the Reformers rejected the Pope's claim to supremacy and incidentally his arrogation of authority to divide the entire New World (as he did in 1492–4) between Spain and Portugal, the challenge by Protestant countries to the Hispanic colonial monopoly was strengthened. English sovereignty was proclaimed over Newfoundland in 1583, and in 1607 agents of an English chartered company founded Virginia. In 1620, the Pilgrim Fathers founded the first of the New England settlements at New Plymouth. Dissenting from the contemporary state Anglican church (established, though Reformed), and claiming liberty to formulate doctrine and worship, these emigrants and their descendants in Massachusetts, Rhode Island, Connecticut, New Hampshire and Vermont took the lead in managing their affairs locally and largely independently of the government in London. They founded a society composed mainly of small farmers, who transplanted the mixed farming of England to the far side of the Atlantic. In Virginia and other colonies farther south, tobacco, sugar and later cotton were grown for export; and African slaves were brought in to provide labour, thereby creating a society similar to that of Latin America. Both the New England and the Southern colonies resisted the attempt by the English government to rule more directly in the eighteenth century, and the Declaration of Independence in 1776 was an epoch in Western history, for the creation of the United States of America reaffirmed and indeed extended the political principles adopted in England during the seventeenth century to the colonial world. The revolt of the American colonies intensified the discontent in France with the *ancien régime* and thus helped to kindle the fire of the French Revolution in 1789. It also helped to provoke the rebellion of the Spanish colonies after 1809 and (by warning Britain that colonial economic progress and self-determination were inseparable) contributed to the devolution of government and eventual break-up of the British and other European colonial empires in the century after 1860. No series of historic events illustrates more clearly the essential unity of Western society than the overthrow or curbing of autocracy and the institution of representative and constitutional government successively in England, the English colonies, France, the Spanish colonies, Canada and Australia.

The constitution adopted in 1787 by the former thirteen colonies is an outstanding landmark in the history of Western institutions. It proclaimed the individual's right to religious and civil liberty, to own property, and to participate in the ultimate control of legislation and government through a universal franchise. To secure these ends, the former colonies entered into a federation in which the powers of government are divided between the centre and the several states. Legislative, judicial and executive functions were separated. With some amendments, none fundamental, the constitution of 1787 has remained the foundation of American society for nearly two centuries.

It survived the attempt by the Southern States in 1860 to perpetuate, by secession, their unwillingness to enfranchise their Negro slaves and thus to extend to their entire population the rights assured by the Constitution. Until then, the contrast between the South, where society was agrarian, and composed of a small landed class dominating slave workers, and the North, composed of small White farmers and an urban commercial class,

had tended to sharpen. After 1783, New England ships were active
in ocean commerce and in whaling. Moreover, by 1860, modern
industry was spreading, and the Middle West was being settled
by the flood of European immigrants, attracted by the free farms
assured by the Homestead Acts. Northern and middle-western
states were clearly following an economic path parallel to
Britain's. After 1864 and the abolition of slavery, the gap between
the universality of civil rights in the North, and their partial
suppression in the South was diminished, though not entirely
eliminated. The supremacy of the institutions first established in
New England was maintained.

Equally remarkably, the constitution proved adequate during
the expansion of the Union from thirteen to fifty states as the
frontiers of settlement were pushed westwards and the population
multiplied from the 4 millions of 1790 to the 197 millions of 1966.
The guarantees of the individual's civil rights: of his participation
in free elections, his equality before the law, his freedom of enterprise and to own property in a continent containing great reserves
of fertile land and minerals, especially coal, petroleum and iron
ore, promoted an altogether unprecedented expansion of both
agricultural and industrial production. The combination of great
wealth, widely diffused, and the maintenance of civil liberties
within a super-power has carried the United States to a position
of leadership among nations, disputed only by Russia and its
satellite states in Eastern Europe, to which we must now turn.

Soviet society

In the past fifty years, Russia has undergone such profound insti-
tutional reform that there is justification for regarding it as a major
society distinct from the West proper. But it must be remembered
that the political and social theory on which the Russian state is
now based originated in the minds of Germans, especially Karl
Marx. Moreover, medieval Russia derived its Church and political
concepts mainly from the eastern Roman Empire, and historical
continuity may be discerned in the perpetuation to the present
time of centralised, authoritarian government. Ivan IV (1558–81),
who first assumed the title of tsar (caesar), believed his dynasty to
be the successor to the imperial line that was overwhelmed at the
fall of Constantinople in 1453. Thereafter, Moscow was given the
figurative title of the 'Third Rome'.

The medieval Russian state ruled by the Dukes of Moscow, and for a time subjected to Tatar domination, was markedly feudal. The peasants, who earlier, in at least some regions, had previously lived as free communities, were reduced to serfdom and bound to the soil. Ownership of the land became vested in the nobles, who, in return, were required to provide military service and local government. After the Russian monarchy had been consolidated, and freedom from the Tatars had been won, the central government created a regular army and a bureaucracy. Under Peter the Great, the state also founded and operated new industries vital to its functions: initially, armament manufacture and shipbuilding; but later, modern transport, including railways. (The construction of the Trans-Siberian railway was the outstanding achievement in this sphere of the nineteenth-century Russian government.)

From the era of the French revolution, there was continual agitation and revolutionary action to substitute constitutional and representative government for feudalism and absolutism. Feudalism was partly abrogated by the freeing of serfs and their conversion into a peasantry after payment of redemption charges (1860–80). But absolutism, supported by the still privileged nobles, held fast. Local assemblies controlling health, education and roads were established in the same period of reform (1855–80); but the nobles were always in a majority. An independent judiciary and municipalities were also created. No representative central assembly ever functioned; although two attempts were made (in 1905 and 1917) to bring one into existence. Meanwhile, emancipated serfs began to migrate from over-populated country districts into towns, where private enterprise was founding modern industries. An urban wage-earning class, institutionally unprotected, became increasingly numerous, and hence sympathetic to socialism.

When the Russian army collapsed after three years of fighting during the War of 1914–18, and the government was impotent, it was the urban workers in the capital (then St Petersburg) who seized power in the revolution of 1917. Not only were the gentry and nobles either killed or expelled, but factories were taken over by workers in the name of the state. The Church, which had steadfastly identified itself with the old order, was disestablished, deprived of most of its wealth, and repressed. For a brief period (1922–27), the land remained in the hands of peasants, who had increased their holdings by dividing farms expropriated from landowners. In a limited way, free commercial enterprise was permitted. But under Stalin, all trade and production was vested in the state. Peasants lost their land and were reorganised into species of rural factories, called collective farms (*kolkhozes*).

Thus in the Soviet Union, the state has become identified with society. The contrast between the bureaucracy and the rest of the population has disappeared, because everybody is a state employee. Within the state, however, and permeating it by its diffusion throughout all organs of government proper, production and commerce, education, the arts and entertainment, is the Communist party, a numerically small *élite* (numbering between 8 and 9 millions in 1961), self-perpetuating and hence oligarchical, but recruited mainly from urban workers and professions, after devotion to Marxism has been proved.

Despite the destruction and hence setbacks to the economy during the First World War (1914–17), the Revolution (1917–22) and the Second World War (1941–45), Soviet Russia has greatly intensified its industrialisation. Society may be classless (in the sense understood to the West), but is graded, and individuals receive remuneration according to responsibility. The governing and directing grade receive considerably higher incomes than the manual workers; but there is no wealthy class. Priority in the allocation of resources has been given to industrialisation, especially the heavy industries, to the armed forces, to space research, and to the provision of the social services of education, health and pensions. The production of goods for consumption, and the provision of housing, especially in the countryside, has always been subordinated to the priority categories in state planning.

This concentration upon the primary economic and social objectives of Soviet Communism has retarded agricultural progress. Although 25 million peasant holdings have been reorganised into 37,000 collective farms and 12,642 state farms, the operating advantages of larger units have been hampered by under-investment. The rural worker's productivity, and hence his income, have remained depressed. But he has the privilege of selling in the free market whatever he chooses to produce on his small private plot.

Fifty years of Soviet Communism are now deeply imprinted upon the land of Russia. Abundance of coal, natural gas, iron ore and petroleum has enabled state-planned industry to establish large units of heavy industry in suitable locations. Many towns, either newly-founded or expanded from an older nucleus, and essentially industrial in character, have now reached the middle range in size ($\frac{1}{2}$–$1\frac{1}{2}$ million), in the industrial regions of central and southern Russia, along the Volga, in the southern Ural mountains, and in western Siberia. It has indeed been a doctrine in Soviet centralised planning that urban hypertrophy should be avoided. Another achievement, possible only in a centralised super-state, is the conversion of the Volga into a series of large artificial lakes, providing the head of water for power generation at the impounding dams.

Soviet urban planning has passed through several stages. Between 1922 and 1941, a number of projects were based upon current new conceptions in Spain (Mata's linear city), France (Le Corbusier's super-block units) and England (the satellite town). The Moscow plan of 1935 anticipated that the population of the capital would be stabilised at about 5 millions, and would live in a compact, approximately circular tract surrounded by a green belt ten miles wide. The existing radial-ring pattern of main roads was to be retained; but the tendency to tentacular expansion was prevented. Three concentric ring roads were provided (one circumferential), also new internal relief roads and three diagonal routes. In the new residential areas on the upland south of the Moskva, the local unit was the group of apartment super-blocks, each provided with its schools, shops and other communal services.

In the reconstruction period since 1945, the Moscow plan has served as the model for many lesser cities; but has been adapted to terrain, future function and what already exists. It has been insisted that plans must be prepared locally, to avoid the mistakes which arose when decisions were all taken centrally. In cities founded during the Middle Ages, care is taken to preserve buildings and other features of architectural, historical and artistic interest.

The physical planning of the countryside was neglected until after 1944. The first important addition to the traditional village had, however, taken place in the 'thirties, when, after the peasants' holdings had been absorbed in the collective farms, tractors were introduced to replace the work previously performed by oxen. Central tractor stations were constructed to serve groups of villages. Later, these stations became centres for technical and political instruction. In the post-war period, plans for *agrogorods* have been prepared. These settlements are large villages, or small towns, with an agrarian economic basis and a population of the order of 5,000. Selected older villages are expanded and provided with shopping centres, schools, playing fields and clubs. The storehouses, machine sheds, animal houses and offices required for large-scale farming are concentrated upon a single site adjoining the residential area. Such rural towns fulfil the aim, frequently expressed from about 1925 onwards, that the gulf between the town and the country in the Communist society should be diminished.

Another post-war tendency contributes to the same result, and incidentally lessens the divergence between Soviet Russia and the rest of the Western world. Both in villages and towns, families are now encouraged to build and to own their homes. Doubtless this policy was adopted partly to maximise the national effort in making good the destruction caused by the Nazi invasion; but it also provides a means by which those earning higher incomes can tangibly enjoy higher living standards. Hence, in the suburbs of Soviet cities, as well as in the villages, the owner-occupier is now well-represented. It is interesting to speculate upon the extent to which this departure in the direction of permitting private property (from the extremer forms of Marxist Communism enforced during the 'thirties) is strengthening current criticism of Party policy.

The political support and aid given by the USSR to independence movements in the colonial empires of other European powers contrasts markedly with the continuance of Russian rule over the non-Russians within the former Tsarist empire, which (as has already been noted above, p. 28) has been retained almost intact. Indeed, Soviet policy since 1945 in Central Europe and the Middle East is wholly consistent with the steady expansionist aims of Tsarist Russia during the nineteenth century. Some Tsarist conquests or annexations along the Baltic, in Poland and Rumania were relinquished at the Treaty of Brest-Litovsk in 1917. These, however, were all regained (with the exception of Finland) in 1945. In addition, the USSR maintains a military occupation of Poland, Eastern Germany, Czechoslovakia and Hungary. These countries, with Rumania, are subordinated to Russia by the Warsaw Treaty. In Asia the territories, inherited from the Tsarist period have been retained in their entirety, and the Mongolian People's Republic (formerly Outer Mongolia) is within the Soviet sphere of interest. Its economic advance has been planned in the Soviet manner.

In 1959, Russians comprised 55 per cent of the total population of the USSR. With the closely-related Slavonic Ukrainians and Byelorussians, they accounted for three-quarters (76 per cent) of the 209 millions within the Soviet state. Non-Russian minorities thus accounted for a quarter of all Soviet citizens. Among these, the Turkic group (8 per cent) was largest; but Armenian, Georgian, Finnish, Lettish, Latvian, Lithuanian and Mongol groups all contributed to the total non-Russian population exceeding 50 million. There are more Jews in the USSR than in any other country; and there may be more Jews in Moscow than in New York.

Throughout the USSR power remains as centralised in the capital as it was under the Tsars. It is true that the form of the Union is an association of separate republics representative of the chief national groups, including the Byelorussians, the Ukrainians, the Georgians, the Uzbeks, etc. Minor ethnic groups have the status of 'autonomous regions'. Hence, the political map of Russia, both in Europe and Asia, has been redrawn. But the substance of power remains in Moscow. In the former Turkestan, Islam has received the same treatment as the Church in Russia, Georgia and Armenia. Muslim religious endowments have been expropriated by the State, and religious instruction to the young is prohibited. Thus an Islamic Russian dependency, which under the Tsars had religious autonomy, has been secularised and subjected to Marxist economic and social planning.

The Hindu society

The reform and re-emergence of Hindu society in the nineteenth and twentieth centuries constitutes a cardinal event of this age, all the more remarkable because the recovery of its autonomy follows a millennial struggle against non-Hindu social and religious systems seeking to gain ascendancy both from within and without. For Buddhism, especially in the age of Asoka (third century B.C.), threatened to eliminate Hinduism; but from the fifth to the eighth centuries A.D. was gradually overcome. Almost immediately, Islamic armies conquered Sind; and from the eleventh century swept into the Gangetic plain: the very cradle of Hinduism. By the fifteenth century, Muslim armies were conquering the Deccan. Northern India therefore had eight or nine centuries of Islamic rule. The centre and south had between four and five centuries. Yet Islamisation only occurred in the Indus basin (Sind, Punjab and Kashmir) and in part of Bengal. Elsewhere, only the ruling class and its servitors, amounting to about one tenth of the population, became Muslim. No sooner did the last Islamic dynasty—

the Moghul—become enfeebled in the eighteenth century than India was conquered by the British, and Hindus were governed and confronted by a self-confident, leading Western nation. Yet the century of Britain's supremacy in India (1818–1918) coincided with the modern Hindu reformation (partly by the infusion of Western ideas), which ultimately won for it the prize of autonomy.

Pakistan is external to India, when India is defined as the land of the Hindu society. Islamic West Pakistan is typical of the dry zone of the Old World, and includes its characteristically arid plains and plateaux, from which rise more humid, cooler mountains. The geographical nature and affinities of West Pakistan were obscured during the British period, when the gap between the Himalayas and the Thar Desert, just west of Delhi, was too close to the Gangetic plain to be a satisfactory frontier of India, for the martial Sikhs were just beyond, and the Afghans (who had acquired the habit of periodically sacking Delhi) not much farther afield. British military power therefore subjugated the peoples of the Indus plains and pushed the frontier westwards as far as the eastern mountain ranges of Afghanistan. It then became easy to think of the Indian Empire as a subcontinental natural unit, isolated from the rest of Asia and bounded by the Himalayas and the flanking ranges to the north-west and north-east. Moreover the incorporation of the Indus plains into British India was soon followed by the creation of the Indian railway system, and the construction of great irrigation works in Punjab, later also in Sind, which converted thinly-peopled provinces, as much pastoral as agricultural, into immense irrigated tracts producing large volumes of wheat and cotton for export. The peopling of Punjab after this economic revolution included many Sikhs and Hindus, who came not only as farmers but also as traders and officials, and who tended to dominate in newer towns, especially in Karachi. By the close of the British period, then, Sind, Punjab and some enclaves ruled by native princes were well-integrated with the rest of the Indian Empire.

At the same time, Muslims in India were engaged in a similar effort of reform by synthesising tradition—in their instance, Islamic tradition—with Western ideas. Their leading thinkers, especially Syed Ahmed, attracted attention in the Levantine Muslim circles engrossed with the problem of Islam's position in the modern world. By 1933, when the Muslim League was founded, Muslims in the Indian Empire had become convinced of their need for autonomy equally with the Hindus. Hence, in 1947, they insisted upon partition, and separate statehood for both the Indus basin and Muslim East Bengal. Partition was accompanied by exchange of populations. In the west, some 6 million Hindus and Sikhs moved into the new India, and their place was taken by $6\frac{1}{4}$ million Muslims. From the new East Pakistan, between 1948 and 1950, 4 million Hindus left and about 1 million Muslims entered. Proportionately, East Pakistan retains a larger Hindu element than West Pakistan; and as an enclave within India, detached from the main contiguous territories of Islamic states, is anomalous.

Both East and West Pakistan are now well detached from India; and their identification with the rest of Islam has been the clearer since 1955, when they entered into a political alliance with Iran and Turkey.

It is an over-simplification to assert that the Indian Republic consists of the Ganges-Brahmaputra lowlands and the plateau of Peninsular India. Although the southern frontier of Nepal follows the foot of the Himalayan ranges (or the northern edge of the Ganges plain), both to the west and the east, territory administered by India advances into regions that are both mountainous and non-Hindu. To the west, India rules Muslim Kashmir; to the east, the Buddhists of Sikkim, Bhutan and the outlying districts of Assam. Not far away, on the opposite side of the Brahmaputra valley, are the Nagas who live on the hills through which the frontier with Burma is traced. Moreover, the boundary claimed by the Indian Empire and subsequently by the Republic is now disputed by China. Like imperial India, the new republic has chronic frontier problems, intensified by its own intransigence in Kashmir, and by the absorption of Tibet in the new China, thus eliminating this buffer-state. The Himalayas may be a natural frontier zone; but the location of a natural boundary to India within it is debated. Moreover, East Pakistan extends almost to the foot of the mountains, and leaves only a narrow corridor for communications between Assam and the rest of India.

But mainly, the land of India is plain, plateau and hill. Of the plains, the largest is the Indo-Gangetic; for in the Partition, India obtained not only part of the Sutlej basin, but also, in the east, mainly in Assam, part of the lower Brahmaputra valley. The core, however, is the Ganges plain, which is also the focus of Hinduism. From the watershed west of Delhi to the head of the delta is about

800 miles, and it is from 100 to 200 miles wide. Smaller plains of deltaic origin also recur along the Bay of Bengal coast, and expand in the far south. But most of India is plateau or hill. Geologically, it is a smaller and more diversified Africa; and, like Africa, essentially an extensive plateau composed of ancient crystalline rocks (the Deccan). Generally, this plateau slopes eastwards, and its principal rivers drain into the Bay of Bengal, thus forming the deltas already mentioned. Towards the Arabian Sea is an abrupt, rectilinear escarpment, called the Western Ghats, which in the south culminated in the Nilgiri hills at nearly 9,000 feet. Towards the north, the hinterland of the Ghats is overlain by an extensive lava plateau (the Deccan trap). Northwards, the plateau is separated from the Gangetic plain by hill ranges, known as the Vindhyan and Satpura ranges in the west, and as the hills of Chota Nagpur and Rajmahal farther east. As will be shown later, this belt of uplands has exercised a divisive function in Indian history and society.

India, in its entirety from Simla to Cape Comorin, is within the climatic domain of the Asian monsoons, and is tropical. The extreme north has a cooler season in January and February, with light showers, whilst the Deccan is dry, and the extreme south, exceptionally, is rather rainy. Every part of the country is tormented by intense heat between March and June. Then, in late June or July, the south-west Monsoon 'bursts' and the main rainy season follows, lasting from three to five months. Rainfall distribution is, however, rather uneven. The southern interior Deccan, Rajasthan and the Upper Ganges plain often receive only niggardly amounts; but along the western Ghats, in Bengal and Assam, prolonged torrential downpours are frequent. The capriciousness of the summer monsoon is notorious. Regions of light or moderate mean rainfall may suffer acute deficiency, or, more occasionally, abundance or damaging excess. Towards the end of the rainy season, cyclones may develop in the Bay of Bengal, and if they reach Bengal or Orissa, may cause widespread destruction.

Survivors from the sparse aboriginal population of pre-agricultural hunters and collectors still exist, especially in Chota Nagpur. They are affiliated to the Negrito remnants of the Malay Archipelago, and to the Australoids of Ceylon and Australia. But Indians mainly are descended from immigrants who entered the country from the west, probably through what is now Baluchistan, during the third millennium B.C. These folk were Caucasoids,

akin to the Mediterranean race (see p. 56). Slight of build, of light
brown complexion in the north and darker in the south, they dispersed throughout the subcontinent during the next two thousand years immediately preceding the dawn of the historic era in
India.

They brought the arts of the Neolithic and Chalcolithic cultures.
They knew how to plough and to rear domesticated animals. In
the Indus valley, they soon succeeded in founding cities similar to
those already existing in Mesopotamia, in which civilised life
flourished from about 2300 until about 1750 B.C.; but withered
away, possibly from natural causes (according to Wheeler), and a
coup de grâce, perhaps at the hands of the Aryans (see p. 147–8).

Of more important and enduring consequences was their work,
of which archaeology so far has provided only scanty record, in
the heart of the subcontinent. They adapted themselves to the
tropical climate and the potentially cultivable plants of the Indian
centre of origin. To them credit must be given for bringing rice
into cultivation. They imitated the natural conditions in which
this swamp grass flourishes by clearing parts of the Ganges plain
and the northern plateau of its forests, cultivating their fields with
ox-drawn ploughs, embanking plots to retain the heavy monsoonal rainfall and thereby artificially to ensure that during growth the
young plant stands in shallow water. As they improved their
practice, they domesticated the buffalo, whose swamp-loving
habits made him even more suitable for traction than the ox.
Excavation of early village sites in the crescent between Patna
and Poona has revealed that rice was a foodstuff by 1800 B.C.
They had accomplished perhaps the greatest single achievement
in the whole history of agriculture; for rice, cultivated essentially
by this method, and diffused throughout Monsoon Asia, is now
the cereal staple for a third of the human race. Throughout the
Peninsula, they sought level or gently-sloping valleys and plains
where soils were deeper. From this agricultural revolution and
racial dispersal arises the geographical distribution of population
in India today. The greatest densities are located on the Gangetic
plain and the deltas of the Coromandel coast. When Alexander
the Great ushered in the historic age in India by his invasion from
the west, he discovered that India was already the most populous
country on earth.

But the Peninsula is in general undulating or hilly; and in relation to its total area, deltas and valley-bottoms are not extensive.

Moreover, on the Deccan, rainfall is often light and uncertain. Here, to provide the moisture needed by rice, reservoirs (tanks) were constructed, at least as early as the first millennium B.C. Earthen dams were thrown across minor valleys; and the impounded water was led in channels to levelled and embanked terraces below.

Rice, however, is not the sole crop of Indian agriculture, although it is the most important. Complementary cereals are grown in conjunction with it, for the twofold purpose of double-cropping and utilising land not suitable for rice. The chief among these ancillary crops are the millets: *Sorghum vulgare* (common or sorghum millet); *Pennisetum typhoïdeum* (bulrush millet) and *Eleusine coracana* (finger millet), of which two, possibly all three, were growing wild in India before the beginning of cultivation by man. These may be sown after the rice has been harvested, and find sufficient moisture from the closing showers of the retreating Monsoon. In the hillier regions of the Deccan, and especially upon the lava (trap) plateau, they displace rice entirely, and are grown both during the Monsoon proper and the first few months of the ensuing dry season (for the clay soils borne by the trap are very retentive of moisture).

These basic cereals, with wheat grown in the western Ganges plain as a cool season crop with the aid of the occasional showers, some pulses, oilseeds, sugar cane, fibre crops (especially cotton), with the trees and plants of the tropical vegetable garden and orchard, and grown thus on the plains and plateau, have displaced the original forests of India, completely over the plains, and generally over the plateau except where the surface is rugged and hilly. Throughout the length and breadth of this vast cultivated tract (more than 1·1M sq km (300,000 sq miles)) are the villages which since the age of initial clearing and settlement have been the homes of Indian farmers and their families.

What else did these early immigrants bring to India besides the technical basis of the Indian economy? First, the Dravidian language family, still spoken in southern India. Secondly, they brought a polytheism in which the principal gods and goddesses personified male and female attributes. But whilst these early Dravidians were still dispersing southwards, Aryans began to enter from the northwest (about 1500 B.C.), and initially settled in the Punjab. These were fair-skinned people, speaking an ancient language of the Indo-European family related to old Persian. They worshipped nature gods and lived upon both animals and crops. They were fond of hunting, were skilled in the use of iron and generally in handicrafts. They were ruled by kings, councils and assemblies.

In time, these Aryans migrated into the Upper Ganges plain; and from their conflicts with the darker-skinned Dravidian speakers and their fusion with them sprang Hindu society, which by the beginning of the historic era had acquired its hierarchy of four castes—priests, warriors, merchants and farmers—and was worshipping gods of Dravidian rather than Aryan character. In northern India to this day higher castes are lighter-skinned; for one of the rigorously-applied tenets of Hindu law is endogamy within each caste. Hinduism continued to evolve during succeeding centuries to the beginning of the Muslim invasions, to a considerable extent by the acceptance of Buddhist and Jainist principles (which were reforming religions claiming to reveal purer truth than the complex ritualism of Hinduism). Both enjoin reverence for life and non-violence (*ahimsa*); and these principles were adopted by Hinduism, which abandoned animal sacrifice and became vegetarian. Early marriages and unrestrained procreation also became customary; for despite the already large population, there was still unused land, particularly in the south.

Throughout this lengthy evolution, the heart of Hinduism remained in the Ganges plain. Benares became the most holy city where pilgrims flock for the meritorious purificatory rituals (see Fig. 9). Not far away is Patna, capital of Hindu states embracing much of northern India and part of the south from the third century B.C. to the fourth century A.D. After about 500 B.C., intercourse with Persia increased, and stimulated political organisation in the Ganges plain. This trend culminated after the foundation of a Hellenistic state to the north-west by Alexander the Great. Under Asoka, the first large truly Indian state expanded to include much of the north and centre of the subcontinent. Later, whilst India became politically much subdivided (particularly during the Indian feudal period from the fifth century A.D. until the Muslim invasions), Hinduism permeated the entire country. In absorbing nearly all the aboriginal tribes of the plateaux and hills, the fifth main group of Hindu society, the out-castes or exterior castes came into their appointed place, allowed the barest of livelihoods by performing the most menial and degrading tasks. Concomitantly, Indo-Aryan languages continued to displace Dravidian; but not completely. Some languages of this latter family survive, in the Krishna river basin and farther south. Their continued use was aided by the rise of small medieval states in which Tamil was the language of government and writing.

The expansion of Indo-Aryan speech also promoted divergence. Differing tongues, descended from the language of the Aryan immigrants, inevitably emerged. Today, in the western and central portions of the Ganges plain, and the northern slope of the plateau, Hindi is spoken. Farther east, Bihari, Bengali and Assamese prevail; farther west, Kashmiri, Punjabi and Sindi; to the south, Gujarati, Rajasthani, Marathi and Oriya. In all, some eleven major Indo-Aryan languages are depicted on the linguistic map of India. In addition, Sinhalese is current in Ceylon. In the south are four chief Dravidian languages: Tamil, Telugu, Mayalayam and Kannada. As a state, the Indian Union is quite unique in its linguistic diversity. Its fifteen major languages each prevail over a discrete area; and the numbers speaking each correspond with the population of many smaller or medium-sized states. It offers an interesting parallel and a contrast with Europe, where Christendom, speaking about the same number of languages, nearly all of the Indo-European (or Aryan) family, has yet become divided between independent states.

The Islamic conquest, like the Aryan, came from the northwest. The Upper Ganges plain, again, was the seat of power exercised over almost all India by the Moghuls at the climax of their glory in the sixteenth and seventeenth centuries from their capitals at Delhi or Agra. Though subordinated, Hinduism held its ground. Under Akbar and Aurangzeb, Hindus rose to be among the highest officials of the state. Some were rajahs and others commanded armies. Muslims held the reins of power; but in partnership with Hindus. Apart from toleration, mutual understanding and co-operation, how could the miracles of architecture at Delhi, Agra and elsewhere, which synthesise Muslim and Hindu art, have been designed and built? The legacy of the Muslim period is not confined to buildings and cities; for the Moghul system of administration became the foundation of British rule when the greater part of India was conquered between 1750 and 1850. And the Moghuls left a *lingua franca* in the shape of the Urdu so widely spoken in northern India.

It was therefore no new experience for Hindu society to be subjugated by an alien conqueror, whose language, religion and mode of government were utterly dissimilar from the Hindu. Once the

British, like the Muslims preceding them, had shown clearly that Hinduism would be respected and tolerated, Indians began, early in the nineteenth century, to accommodate themselves once again to non-Indian masters. From the position of junior partners in government they were able eventually to take over the country, and thereby to bring into existence an independent Hindu-ruled India for the first time in some 800 years.

Hinduism was able to undermine British rule and eventually to supersede it because the British *raj*, unlike the Muslim, was not a theocracy. Under the Moghuls, Hinduism and Islam assumed the rôles of junior and senior partners, and no more, because the institutions and laws of each were sacred and immutable. But British rule in India was secular, and indeed adapted itself not only to Hinduism but also evolved in accordance with the trends in other British dependencies and in western Europe during the nineteenth century. Hindus could retain their personal law—the very essence of Hinduism—and at the same time accept the new British laws relating to crime, public order and commerce, introduced to restore the security of life and property that had dis-

---

Fig. 9 Banaras, India

This anciently-founded city epitomises Indian history and society. The *raison d'être* of the sacred city proper is ritual bathing in the holy Ganges. Hence, *ghats* (flights of stone steps), backed by many Hindu temples, extend along the west bank for two miles. Adjoining are the suburbs, especially Jaitpura and Adampura, founded after the Muslim invasions of northern India had begun, in which are concentrated most of the mosques. The British period saw the addition of missions, schools and local government buildings to this twin Hindu-Muslim city. The British also gave Banaras the status of a district capital, whose importance arose partly from the bridge carrying the Grand Trunk Road from Calcutta to Delhi across the river. Later, the railway followed the same route. Large outer suburbs were built for civil servants, the garrison and the railway staff. Modern Indian nationalism is symbolised by the Hindu University. Ramnagar was the seat of a princeling. Closely cultivated land of the middle Ganges plain, dotted with villages of varying size, extends in all directions from the suburban limits.

Palaces of notabilities are located by initials:
  RB   Raja of Barhar
  RA   Raja of Amethi
  MB   Maharaja of Benaras

I denotes an iron foundry; CS a cotton and silk factory.

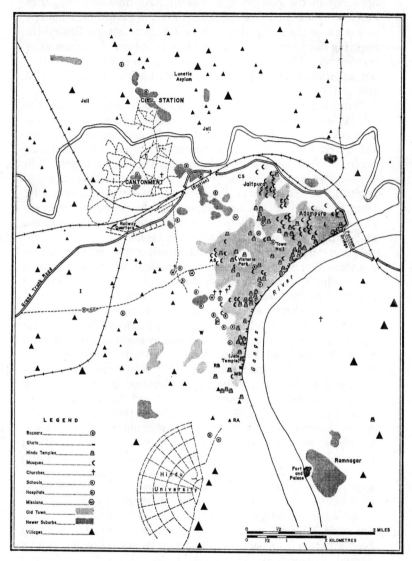

LEGEND

Bazaars..................................(b)
Ghats.....................................
Hindu Temples...............▣
Mosques...........................(
Churches..........................†
Schools..............................(s)
Hospitals..........................(⊗)
Missions............................(m)
Old Town............................
Newer Suburbs................
Villages..............................▲

Fig. 9

appeared in the post-Moghul anarchy. As time went on, they accepted considerable modifications even in Hindu personal law as a result of the interpreting rôle of British courts, particularly in applying the doctrine of equality before the law. The synthesis of Hindu and British law is perhaps the most remarkable adaptation within Hindu institutions and the greatest achievement of British rule in India.

Hindus could also learn English, which besides being the official language after 1835 was the medium of instruction in the new schools then being founded and in new universities from 1857. Here they also imbibed liberalism, and left to swell the new professional middle class which later became the main element in the Indian Congress. English became and remained the language of politics as well as higher education and government. Eventually, when the state itself became Indian, and the princely states were absorbed, the new constitution created a secular republic of India, and retained English as its official language.

Hindu society also underwent considerable transformation economically. Free Trade was applied to India, beginning with the abolition of internal transit dues in 1835. Calcutta, Bombay and Madras were already important ports as well as the principal centres of British power. From them the railways radiated inland and so brought the Indian railways system into existence. On the railways, in these modern ports, as well as at the railway-junction towns such as Allahabad and Nagpur, caste barriers were weakened. Later, Indian industries, especially textile and metal-working, were modernised. Ahmadabad clustered around its cotton mills, and Jamshedpur alongside its iron and steel mills.

But India remains essentially rural. Some three-quarters of the population still live in villages. The village indeed mirrors Hindu society, as it always has (see Fig. 10). Commonly, its inhabitants include landowners, peasants, labourers, craftsmen, traders and untouchables, belonging to their appropriate castes, and usually segregated in different quarters. They worship in several temples, each ministering mainly to one or several castes, and dedicated to a particular god or gods in the Hindu pantheon. Often, too, there are some Muslims, and a mosque. But agriculture has for long been suffering from pernicious anaemia. Its gravest weakness is its animal husbandry, or rather lack of it. Not only is the cow sacred; but the Hindu reverence for life causes breeding to be wholly uncontrolled. No fodder crops are produced, and the far too numerous cattle, male and female, subsist mainly on stubble, waste land or the scrub separating cultivated land (where it exists). The cows produce minimal milk; bullocks, it is true, draw light ploughs and carts; cattle hides are perhaps their greatest contribution to farm income. Some manure is used as fertiliser; but much more must be used as fuel, where wood is unavailable in the densely-populated plains. Cropping, when agriculture was being introduced into India, was indeed an achievement of the first order; but is dismally backward in the age of scientific agriculture. Small and fragmented land holdings compel the farmer to grow mainly food crops by primitive methods, and the return is far below world averages. Taxes and the moneylender in addition deprive him of any hope of buying fertiliser, improved implements and seeds, or to diversify crops.

Rapid population growth since about the turn of last century is gravely worsening the situation. The railway system abolished famine for half a century, by permitting the government to transport grain to regions in which crops had failed. Extension of medical services to villages (mainly by dispensaries) also reduced mortality. But the Hindu injunction to procreate remained. Despite serious attempts to improve farming, India is being overwhelmed by the multiplication of its own population. Most ominously, famine has reappeared (1965–7) in Bihar, Orissa and Madhya Pradesh. The government's belated efforts to induce acceptance of family planning is commendable; but cannot ensure an equilibrium between population and food production for many years.

The administration of British India was shared between the central and provincial governments. In the new constitutions introduced in 1919 and 1935 to enable Indians to participate, provincial as well as a central assemblies existed. When independent India was being legally shaped, therefore, a constitution was adopted in which the British provinces, modified by absorption, amalgamation and addition of the old native states, became the new states of the federal Indian Republic. Meanwhile, education had been widely provided, in the primary and secondary school through the medium of local languages. Not surprisingly, there was a demand to reorganise provincial boundaries to correspond with the principal languages. Linguistic rivalry has subsequently strengthened provincialism and weakened the central government. It has also weakened higher education by introducing Indian languages instead of English as the medium of teaching in colleges and universities.

One of the most acute controversies concerns the anomalous position of English as an official language of the central government. Hindi, as the Indo-Aryan tongue spoken by the largest number, and readily learned by those whose mother tongue is cognate, has strong advocates as a replacement for English. But this move is strenuously opposed in the south, where educated Madrasis not only pride themselves on their fluency in English but have rejected Congress candidates at the last general election (1967) in favour of those committed to retaining English as an official language.

The question therefore arises as to whether Delhi is the best capital for the Republic. It is so excentrically located. It was adopted by the British when they abolished the Moghul empire and substituted their own. There was additional justification in its convenient proximity (but not so close as to be dangerous) to the sensitive north-west frontier. But although Kashmir is the successor to the old north-west frontier problem, the centrifugal tendency of the regions is an even greater threat to the state. Could not the temptation to secession be better countered from a more centrally-located capital in a province outside the Hindi-speaking area? A site near Nagpur might well be appropriate for a new federal capital. It would be analogous to Madrid, which, likewise, is located in the sparsely-peopled heart of Spain, equidistant from the regionally-conscious coastal provinces. But at present India could not afford the expense.

In the 1950s, India had attained to a deserved position of leader-

---

Fig. 10 The village of Aminbhavi, Deccan plateau, India (after Deshpande)

Caste segregation, and the relegation to the periphery of the lowest castes, are well shown. The population at the date of the survey (about 1950) was 4,100.

1	Lingayats	7	Muslims
2	Talwars	8	Hindu temples
3	Jains	9	Mosque
4	Brahmins	10	Wells
5	Shepherds	11	Schools
6	Harijans	12	Shops

VP Village Panchayat; D Dispensary; PO Post Office.

Deshpande (Brahmin) and Desai (Jain) are the principal landowners.

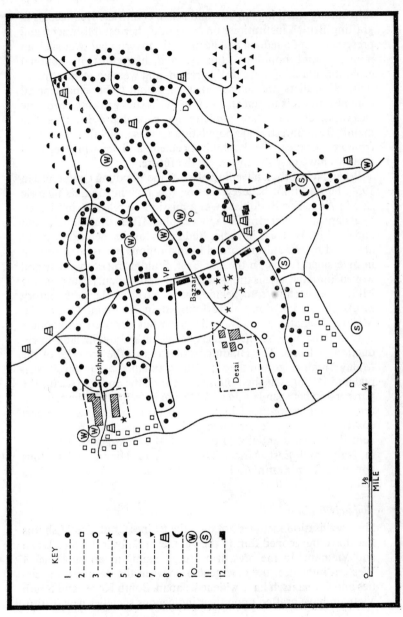

Fig. 10

ship among emerging African and Asian countries. Her success in grafting British institutions on to Hindu; her establishment and preservation of a federal and democratic government over such an immense and populous country, and her effort in national economic planning were justly praised, and were an inspiration to political leaders in emancipated or about-to-be emancipated colonies. But it is undeniable that in the 'sixties growing economic weakness, despite 'plans' and foreign capital provision, arising mainly from unrestrained population increase, inability to resolve frontier disputes, the Kashmir problem and growing regional rivalries have cast shadows over the future.

When Nehru took a leading place at the Bandung conference in 1956, he no doubt believed that he was reviving India's historic rôle in Asia. For Buddhism was a missionary religion, implanted by its apostles in central Asia, Mongolia, Tibet, Burma, Thailand and Ceylon. Whereas in India, Buddhism lost its identity by being absorbed by Hinduism, abroad its institutions persisted, although in diversified forms. In the Far East, Buddhism became a strand woven into the civilisations of China and Japan. Later, in the Middle Ages (but from beginnings as early as the first century A.D.), Hindu kingdoms were founded in Vietnam, Cambodia, Malaya, Sumatra and Java. Hinduism has survived unmodified only in Bali; but elsewhere it has been overlaid by the later introduction of Islam. The Hindu contribution to the societies of the Malay Archipelago and the adjoining mainland has, however, been real and lasting. On the opposite shore of the Indian Ocean, the partnership between Hindu and Muslim in India after the eleventh century was reproduced in the Arab ports of the African east coast. When the interior came under European control, Indians contributed substantially to commercial development, especially in Natal and East Africa. The sphere of Hindu society thus stretches from South Africa to Japan, and from the Sutlej to Bali.

Sinic civilisation

Sinic civilisation includes not only the Chinese, but also offshoots that have burgeoned during the ages, especially in Korea, Japan and Vietnam. In the present century, mainly as an outcome of Western influence, the divergences between the peripheral societies and China itself have widened. Japan, South Korea and South Vietnam have grafted upon their indigenous societies new institutions brought from western Europe and the United States of America, as invisible cargo in the ships of maritime nations fulfilling their destiny since the Great Age of Discovery.

In China itself, for three-quarters of a century (1840–1917), the uncertainty and turmoil caused by the decadence of the Manchu dynasty were a bitter consequence of the acquisitive penetration of the maritime powers and imperial Russia. Fifty years of disintegration followed from the rivalry between Chinese liberal republicanism, Chinese communism and Japanese imperialism. The climax was the Japanese invasion and occupation from 1937 until 1945. In 1949, Communists became masters, at first in alliance with Soviet Russia, but since 1961 in independence and seclusion. It is certain that national life is being remodelled. Industries, towns, the countryside and society itself are being transformed. The exact extent of the changes, and their regional variations are, however, obscure. Very few foreign observers have been admitted into China since 1949, and official Chinese statements are strongly propagandist. From these pronouncements, it is clear that the government's policy is a revolution quite as cataclysmal as the Russian. But how far the fundamental conservatism of Chinese society has been overturned and superseded is only partly known.

The climate of China proper is temperate in the north and subtropical in the south. It is also monsoonal; and most rain falls during the hot summer, brought by steady south-easterly winds from the Pacific Ocean. During the winter, north-westerly winds prevail, which are especially cold, dry and strong in the north. Since the country extends from latitude 20° N to latitude 40° N, the contrast is great between the north, where the summer is short and the winter severe, and the south, where the year is warm or hot apart from a cool season. There is also a relief contrast between north and south. The former consists of plateaux and the North China plain, both mantled by the yellow, fertile loess, borne and deposited during the Pleistocene period by the north-westerly winds from Mongolia. The south, drained by the Yangtze-kiang and the Si-kiang, is a land of hills and broad valleys. The Yangtze also traverses two extensive lake basins as it flows from the Tibetan mountains to the sea.

It was in the north, originally a steppe, rather than in the forested south, that Chinese society had its hearth. During the third millennium B.C., Neolithic cultivators took advantage of the fertile soil and scanty woodland. Remains of their villages have been found in the Hwang-ho basin north of the Tsinling Shan. Fragments of pottery, similar to the ware then being made in the Near East, prove that the axial land route across central Asia (later to be known as the Silk Road) was already being used. At this early period, wheat was still unknown; but by the middle of the next millennium, a flourishing Bronze Age society, based upon both wheat and millet, had acquired the resources and the capacity to build walled towns. By the first millennium B.C. iron had been introduced, irrigation was being widely practised, and a feudal society had arisen. From fortified towns provided with granaries, local despots lorded over the cultivating serfs around. It was in this age that some feudal rulers began to colonise the south, thus initiating the persistent sinification of first the Yangtze basin and then the Si-kiang valley. The south has thus been the main direction of Chinese expansion.

In the course of time, the Yangtze basin became the geographical core of China. Within its watershed live at least 250 million human beings; and it thus supports a larger population than any other river basin. Its main trunk and chief tributaries are thronged with shipping. At every confluence is a great city. The plains extending away from its banks are intensively cultivated, and are irrigated by an intricate system of canals and dotted with villages. Where tributary valleys narrow, the slopes above the valley-floor are painstakingly terraced, and watered by channels following contours. From the Sung period (A.D. 960–1279), during which Mongol aggression caused considerable southward migration, the North has been economically subsidiary to the centre, and at times almost parasitic. This shift of the regional centre of gravity in China is comparable with the accession of population and wealth in central and Western Europe when in modern times the Mediterranean lands were in decline.

The Si-kiang basin and the south-eastern littoral (somewhat inaccessible across the forested mountains of Wuyi Shan), may be regarded as the Sinic domain. Yunnan, the Malay Archipelago (into which the Chinese have been migrating by sea for at least a millennium), Japan, Korea, Tibet and Sinkiang, may be included within its sphere.

Wheat and most species of millet do not flourish in the hot, moist summers of southern China; and rice, using buffaloes for ploughing, became the basis of farming. This crop was of Indian provenance, and must have come to China across the densely-

forested and rugged mountain ranges between Yunnan and
Assam. Despite its difficulties, this route was for long used by
traders; but its relative importance decreased after sea voyaging
had begun. India's botanical gifts to China did not cease in the
prehistoric period, for cotton, now the most important Chinese
textile, arrived about the 12th century A.D. What is indigenous
about Chinese agriculture is not so much its crops (for in addition
to its two chief cereals and other crops received overland, tobacco,
the sweet potato, maize and ground nuts came by sea from the
New World after the Great Age of Discovery), but their adaptation to an intensive cropping system, in which hand cultivation,
water control, the use of human waste, and double- or triple-
cropping ensured higher yields than anywhere else in the world
before the age of scientific agriculture.

Chinese writing had already been invented before the Feudal
Age, and a literate civil service existed within each state. Moreover, there was no regular priesthood. In the sixth century B.C.,
Confucius, who was an official in a small state, Lu, in the Shantung
peninsula, clarified current ethics and social theory. He saw the
family as a microcosm of society; and enjoined correct conduct
between members of the family as the basis of all social relationships. The state was simply an extension of the family. It has been
pointed out that the only Chinese word for society is a compound
formed from the two words for the state (*Kuo*) and the family
(*Chia*).

Confucianism was not alone in an age of perplexity. It was a
middle way between the mystical Taoism, which has survived as a
relief for the Chinese from the artificiality and disillusionment of
civilised life; and legalism, which glorified the despotic ruler. The
latter temporarily triumphed when feudalism was abolished in the
third century B.C., and China was unified and centralised under a
despot, who administered the country through a bureaucracy and
used forced labour on a vast scale to construct new irrigation
works and to bring new land into cultivation. In the succeeding
reaction, the Han dynasty was founded

Confucianism then became permanently established as the state
religion, and Chinese peasant society became stabilised in the form
which it retained until the present century. The individual was
bound within a web of reciprocal duties and obligations, primarily
within the large family, headed by the senior male, which also included married sons, their wives and children. Serfdom had dis-

appeared with feudalism, and the economic basis of the family became the small farm, worked by its members, averaging 3–9 ha. (8–20 acres) in area in the north, and $\frac{1}{2}$–1$\frac{1}{2}$ ha. (2–4 acres) in the south. Holdings were usually fragmented, and were often partly or wholly rented. (Both clans and village temples—see below—owned land and were sustained by the rents from letting.) There was a landlord class that included mandarins, but their estates rarely exceeded 300 acres. On the whole, until the modern population expansion began in the seventeenth century, great inequalities in land ownership (and hence of wealth) did not exist. Neither was land hunger general or lasting, though Chinese records reveal that it did occur temporarily and locally.

The family was, however, bound to other related families in a clan, which might be widely distributed over the country, as a result of the colonisation process. And clans might also embrace whole villages, especially in the south, where village names are often clan names. The large family, then, existed within the intersecting circles of the clan and the village community. The perpetual solidarity of the clan was symbolised by ritual performed during meetings of representatives at ancestral halls or temples, located at a clan settlement. The village had a temple dedicated to a deified warrior or statesman, serving also as a community centre.

Traditional Chinese architecture is adapted to social needs and aspirations (see Fig. 11). Because the large family is the social cell, the home is enclosed within a brick wall and is composed of separate rectangular rooms, usually one-storeyed except in some large towns, opening on to square or rectangular interior court-

---

Fig. 11 Plan and elevation of a middle-class home in Peking before 1949 (after Boyd)

1 Main Courtyard	8 Grandmother's Bedroom
2 Servants' Courtyard	9 Study
3 Small Private or Subsidiary Courtyards	10 Older Children's Suite
	11 Married Son's Suite
4 Domestic Rooms	12 Servants' Suites
5 Kitchen	13 Entrance Porch
6 Main Living and Reception Room	14 Porch leading into Main Courtyard
7 Grandfather's (Head of Household) Bedroom	15 Store Rooms
	16 Watchman's Room

A Verandahs; B Movable Screens with Doors and Windows; C Pillars

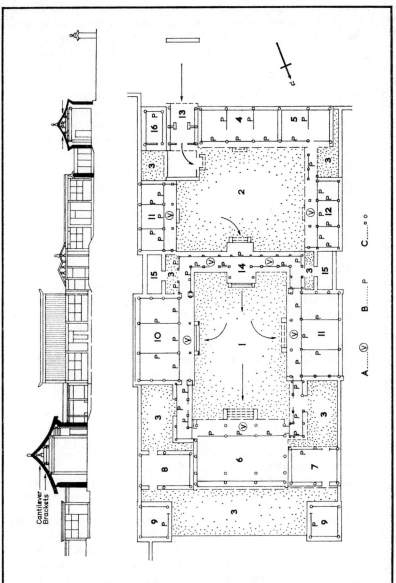

Cantilever
Brackets

A ..... Ⓥ   B ..... P   C ..... □ o

Fig. 11

yards. All except the poorest homes have, however, a decorative porch or doorway. Wood is normally used for the structure and the roof is supported by pillars, beams and bracket-clusters facilitating the design of the characteristic, refined, concavely-curved roofs. The use of partitions for inner walls permits apartments to become verandahs opening on to the courtyards (except in the north in winter). Even here, the windows, of translucent paper, can be rolled up and put away during the summer. The home then is an architectural unity; but partly open to the sky. Such houses can be enlarged by adding further courtyards, proportioned to those already existing. Wealthy families also append pleasure gardens; although some trees or shrubs are normally planted in courtyards.

Town planning has also been practised for at least two thousand five hundred years. Chinese walled market towns are square, and have reticulated street plans. Their capital cities, of which the finest examples are Peking and Hangchow (the latter as described by Marco Polo) were composite but were also based upon a reticulated street plan combined with a north-south main avenue culminating in the palace itself, located to the north at Peking and to the south at Hangchow. At Peking, the Imperial City formed a square within the older or 'Inner City'; and within this square was the still smaller palace or 'Forbidden City'. The north-south axial way, five miles long, bisected all three cities, and the porches, fortified gateways, and courtyards along it, with flanking buildings, all in studied proportion, form one of the world's finest and most impressive monumental architectural compositions.

The whole city was itself a work of art. . . . It . . . was deliberately based upon a previous plan which had been based upon a preceding one and so on. It was, as it were, a collective rather than an individual work of art, and the strict limitations of the Chinese system, and the constant application of a few principles . . . far from being disadvantages, were part of the means by which the Chinese city achieved its high degree of harmony and artistic unity.   (A. Boyd.)

In architecture, as in agriculture, imported elements have been fused with the essentially indigenous features. The pagoda is an example. Its origin is Indian, and it was brought to China by the missionaries who extended the Buddhist faith to central and eastern Asia from the first century B.C., so successfully that by the seventh century A.D., China was a predominantly Buddhist country.

The revival of Confucianism during the Sung dynasty somewhat weakened the Buddhist hold; but until 1949, Buddhist temples were still ubiquitous, and most Chinese believed that Buddhism was one of the three ways to truth, alongside Confucianism and Taoism. The pagoda is an adaptation of the *stupa* or *dagaba* (in which holy relics are preserved), and the towered, tiered Indian temple (the *sikhara*). In China, the pagoda is more tower-like, and less massive than Indian temples. Also, it is often constructed in timber, although brick and stone may be used. Exterior decoration is mainly geometrical, and images are usually placed inside, often on different floors. The external tiers of sculptured figures so characteristic of Indian temples were not copied by the Chinese.

Another Indian construction diffused into China is the ceremonial gateway. The most celebrated example is the five-arched marble entrance to the Ming emperors' tombs near Peking, built between 1522 and 1566. Such arches are also incorporated in the architectural schemes of axial avenues in capital and other important cities.

Until 1911, the state was simply an aggregation of families, clans and villages, largely managing their own affairs. Its main functions were public order and defence, symbolised by the Great Wall, built from the third to the first century B.C. to protect the country from nomad invaders, for the north-western frontier was the most vulnerable from the beginning of Chinese history until the arrival of British naval power in the Pacific. The state also maintained communications by an excellent system of roads and such great works as the Grand Canal (completed in the thirteenth century A.D.). It executed and controlled major drainage and irrigation works. It regulated commerce, issued money and provided famine relief from its granaries. But these functions touched the lives of the rural masses only indirectly, and the state's effectiveness depended mainly upon the abilities of emperors and their immediate entourage of mandarins. The Mongol, Manchu and Japanese invasions, as well as periods of civil war and local anarchy, happened when rulers were effete. China's decline during the closing phase of the Manchu dynasty was all the greater because of a racialist policy of treating the Chinese as an inferior people.

Evidently republican and, even more so, Communist China has been redefining the rôle of the state. There had been earlier attempts. The Sung emperor Shun Tsang (A.D. 1068–85) formed a

F*

militia to guard the frontier against the Mongols and tried to ameliorate the conditions of the rural poor by granting state loans on the security of the harvest. Much more recently, the Republican government tried to provide agricultural credit from a state bank. Neither of these or other measures to widen the functions of the state interfered with the traditional form of Chinese society. But since 1949 landlords have been expropriated and their estates have been redistributed among the peasants. Fragmented holdings have been consolidated. The large family has been weakened since new holdings have been allocated to the small family consisting of parents and their children. At the same time, freedom of enterprise in farming has been ended by the creation of village collectives, subordinated to communes composed of from fifty to a hundred villages. To a large extent, cultivation and cropping are supervised, and the peasant receives a share of produce and proceeds of sale, determined less by the market than by the commune. Clearly, such changes must have undermined the economic basis of the clan, and the village temple as a centre of traditional community life.

Much effort has been expended upon the improvement of transport, especially of railways. Older lines in the north have been extended to Urumchi in Dzungaria and Ulan Bator in the Mongolian People's Republic. Another new line has been built across Szechuan and will eventually reach Liuchow on the Si-kiang. In addition to these new main lines, built by the central government, local authorities are engaged in building branch lines.

Modern industries have been expanded. The output of coal is now of the order of 500 million tons (this can only be an approximate figure) per annum. Greatly increased amounts of iron, steel, textiles and cement are being produced. At the same time, traditional crafts have been reorganised by collectivisation.

Negroid Africa

Unlike the other four major societies of ancient origin and maturation, Negroid Africa has not yet emerged from its formative stage. It has attained self-consciousness and self-determination only in the present century. Earlier, it had been isolated from the rest of mankind. Only after the opening of the continent to the world in the nineteenth century did it enter within the ambit of the major societies.

Composed of the independent Negroid peoples of Africa, Negroid Africa occupies a continental tract that may be roughly defined by the southern edge of the Sahara Desert (at about 18° N) and the southern tropic (of Capricorn, at 23½° S). Along its northern margin (the Sudan zone) it is in contact with Islam. The Sudan, then, is a transitional zone, and belongs to the sphere of each. In the south, Negroid Africa merges with the sphere of both Western and Hindu societies. In Rhodesia and Angola, settled European communities have intruded north of the Tropic into Negroid Africa, from disputed southern Africa.

The home of the Negroid society is essentially a plateau. Its mean altitude is between 300m (1,000 ft) and 600m (2,000 ft) in the centre, north and west; but towards the eastern and southern coasts its surface rises to between 600m (2,000 ft) and 1,500m (5,000 ft) above the sea. Its edges are generally formed by abruptly-descending escarpments overlooking narrow coastal plains. Characteristically, this topographical wall facing the sea is the more formidable because immediately inland is a belt of highland rising above the general level of the plateau. In other words, there is usually a broad rim to the interior plateau. Often the coastal scarp is broken and rugged.

Over much of the plateau surface ancient crystalline rocks (plutonic, metamorphic and volcanic) outcrop, known to geologists as the Basement Complex. Prolonged erosion has worn down earlier mountains to monotonous, gently undulating peneplanes, occasionally diversified by isolated, irregular hills (known as *inselberge*) standing above the general level because locally rocks are more resistant to chemical weathering. The surviving 'roots' of vanished mountain ranges include some mineralised zones now producing for the world market. Through gentle downwarping during several geological periods, some shallow basins have become covered by nearly horizontal sediments, clearly exemplified by the Congo and middle Nile basins. Here the relief is even more featureless than upon the Basement Complex outcrops. The Southern Clay Plain of Sudan must be one of the world's largest true plains.

The subdued relief of the African plateau is to be attributed to its prolonged quiescence (for hundreds of millions of years) during which it has been free from the rupturing, folding and differential uplifting present in other landmasses. However, east and northeast Africa, exceptionally, are traversed by the Great Rift valleys, which for long distances are deep, narrow trenches, bordered by steep, often precipitous escarpments, formed by recent earth movements and locally occupied by lakes, fresh and salt. Nearby are mountains or higher plateaux, mainly composed of recently-erupted lavas. The Ethiopian highlands, rising to between 2,100m (7,000 ft) and 4,000m (15,000 ft) above sea level, are the largest. The Kenya highlands and the Ruwenzori mountains are as high, but smaller.

Related to these features of geology and relief are aspects of climate, hydrography, natural vegetation and soils that together impart marked peculiarities to Africa, considered as a home of man. Since the extremities of this continent are at latitudes 37° N and 35° S, it is bisected by the Equator. Hence, it is mostly subject to a tropical climate without a cool season. Between about 5° N and S, rain falls throughout the year, the total being greater towards the west than in East Africa. Polewards, a dry season alternates with a rainy, and becomes more pronounced as distance increases from the Equator. In this zone, then, seasonal contrasts are emphatic, but arise from the occurrence of rainfall or of drought, rather than from change of temperature. Between about 10° N and about 18° S the rainfall is only locally less than 100cm (40 in), and widely exceeds 200cm (80 in). This regular climatic zonation (and gradual climatic transitions) arise from the absence or mountainous barriers to air movement. The Trade Winds can blow freely over the plateau. The scattered highlands of east and north-east Africa, however, have cooler and wetter subtropical or even temperate montane climates. The intervening plateaux are, however, generally drier than usual for the latitude.

The interior run-off flows into rivers which (owing to the tendency of the plateau rim to be uplifted) converge into a few main trunks discharging into the sea. Not only are the river systems few but their courses are interrupted by rapids or waterfalls where they leave the interior for the coastal plains. Hence, most of the interior drainage of tropical Africa is concentrated into the Senegal, Niger, Nile, Congo, Zambesi and Limpopo; and of these, only the first-named is freely navigable far inland. The great African rivers therefore do not offer ingress into the interior. Thus they contrast markedly with those of other continents (except Australia). Moreover, African coasts are for long stretches harbourless and surf-beaten. Nowhere is there any encouragement to a sea-faring life, except in the Red Sea and along the East coast.

The moderate or heavy rainfall also brings forth an abundant tropical vegetation, which assumes the form of rain forest where the annual total exceeds about 180cm (70 in), and high savanna (composed of woodland and tall grass) where the rainfall is between 85cm (35 in) and 170cm (70 in). On the outer (poleward) margins of the high savanna, the vegetation degenerates into short grass and scattered thorny bushes, especially north of the Equator in the Sudan zone. It should also be noticed that tropical rain forest does not stretch uninterruptedly across the continent in the vicinity of the Equator. An unforested corridor in East Africa connects the northern with the southern savanna belt.

Soils in tropical Africa do not contain any reserve of fertility. Their poverty in plant nutrients arises partly from the parent rocks from which their mineral fractions are derived by chemical decomposition. These rocks as a rule contain only very small amounts of potassium, calcium, magnesium and phosphorus. Outcrops of volcanic rocks (chiefly in East Africa) are, however, somewhat less deficient in these minerals. Although the close, often dense, vegetation cover is continually providing dead plant tissue, the heat and moisture cause very rapid decomposition, and the heavy rainfall leaches the final products from the soil. Hence, the nitrogen content is also small. Such tropical soils are usually red, clayey and slightly acid in reaction. The natural vegetation is able to flourish because its growth is continuous (except during the dry season), and root systems, often deeply-penetrating, can absorb required nutrients as soon as they are produced. The plants therefore consume the income of nutrients in the soil as soon as it is available. None is accumulated. In general, therefore, the natural vegetation is in equilibrium not only with the climate but also with the soil.

An exception, however, occurs where the alternation of well-marked dry and wet seasons at a certain stage in soil evolution causes a crust to form that does not soften during rain. Such crusts can be shown to have a concentration of iron and aluminium compounds. Not surprisingly, they inhibit plant growth.

When the interior of Africa was first reached by European explorers in the mid-nineteenth century, the generally thin population was composed of tribes practising rudimentary hoe cultivation, and mainly without domestic animals, because of the prevalence of trypanosomiasis (see p. 91). In the drier savanna, however, cattle-herding supported some tribes, sometimes in conjunction with cultivation. The plough was not used, even by cattle-owners. The wheel was also unknown. In the absence of money and means of transport (apart from human porterage), trade was almost non-existent except near the west coast, the Zambesi valley, and in the Sudan zone, for gold, ivory and slaves. Generally, African tribes existed at a subsistence level. There were no towns, although the government of large tribes was often conducted from expanded villages containing impressive and elaborate compounds of the paramount chief and his ministers. Such tribal confederations were not lasting, and seldom very extensive. Enduring large states like those of the European and Oriental civilisations, knit together by land and sea communications, dotted with historic cities and administered by literate officials never existed in Africa, except in the Sudan zone during the later Middle Ages as an outcome of Islamic enterprise across the Sahara. Away from this Islamic fringe in the Sudan and along the East African coast writing was unknown. Implements, ornaments, clothing and weapons were made chiefly of wood, bone or skins. Iron was, however, smelted from surface ore deposits by methods resembling those employed in Europe before the introduction of the blast furnace in the fifteenth century. Knives, spear-blades, axe-heads and hoes were all fabricated from this metal. Copper and bronze were not generally known, for there was never a Bronze Age in Africa. African peoples passed from stone to iron without any intermediate stage. Pottery was either not made or was rudimentary. The use of wood and grass was, however, advanced, both technically and aesthetically.

These features of African society are all the more remarkable if we remember its relative proximity to the ancient civilisations of the Old World, between which intercourse had been active since at least the second millennium B.C. In the mid-latitude zones, migration and trade by land and sea seem to have been much easier than in a tropical interior. In Africa, south of the Sudan, there were migrations and the diffusion of knowledge, especially of iron and of new cultivated plants, but little internal or external trade, even where the means of ingress existed, as in the Nile basin of southern Sudan. Although Africa was the cradle of mankind (to judge from its abundance of pre-hominid remains), and northern African peoples in what is now the Sahara Desert were relatively advanced during the later Palaeolithic and the Neolithic periods, its humid tropical lands lagged behind the mid-latitude belt of the Old World, after the Saharan barrier was interposed by desiccation, the disappearance of the plant cover, and the dispersal of its animal and human populations.

Two, or possibly three, distinct races occupied Africa, south of the Sahara, before about 1000 B.C. Most of southern and eastern Africa was thinly populated by a race of which the present surviving remnants are the Bushmen of south-west Africa. Second, in the Congo rain forests dwelt the ancestors of surviving Pygmy Negrilloes. Both of these races lived by hunting and collecting, were nomadic, still culturally in the Stone Age, and were lacking tribal organisation. Third, in the rain forest of West Africa and the adjoining savanna, were the true Negroes. Their adaptation to a fully-tropical humid climate has already been described (see p. 46); in addition they appear to have acquired some tolerance towards malaria infections. For the blood characteristics of the West African indigenous population indicate a defence mechanism capable of resisting this parasite. African adults also may have a measure of immunity from other tropical parasites and bacilli, gained by surviving infections in youth. But there is much mortality among infants unable to survive infection, and many adult Africans suffer ill-health from parasites which their bodies cannot eliminate. At this early period, the Negroes were not metal-using; but they may have begun to cultivate some of the cereals native to the Sudan and savanna zones of central Africa, such as millets and *fonio*. But mainly they must have been hunters and collectors of wild vegetable produce.

Between about 1000 B.C. and A.D. 500 Africa received four important external stimuli leading to the supersession of hunting and collecting by food production (except in the extreme south), and the expansion of the Negroes at the expense of the Bushmen and Negrilloes. It is not known whether the arrival of cattle-owning Hamites in the north-east preceded or followed the spread of iron-working from the Nile valley into central Africa, which can be dated to about the middle of the first millennium B.C. These were the first two external stimuli. By the time Hamites were moving inland from the eastern Horn of Africa, Negroes speaking early forms of Bantu languages had spread eastwards between the forest and the desert, from a region now included in Cameroon. Mingling of Bantu and Hamites resulted in several racial groups of intermediate character, like the Nilotic tribes of the Upper Nile basin, and the Nilo-Hamitic tribes of East Africa. In some of these tribes, a pastoral aristocracy dominates an agricultural lower class. The adoption of iron also gave an impetus to agriculture, by improving the range of axes, knives and hoes needed to clear and cultivate land. From this period must date the general adoption of shifting cultivation or land rotation which is the indigenous African solution to the lack of any reserve of fertility in tropical soils. By cutting down and burning grass and woody plants, the soil becomes temporarily enriched when the ashes are washed into the soil by rainfall. The demand for nutrients by growing cereal crops can be met for a few seasons. Afterwards, yields decline and the natural vegetation must be allowed to regenerate for ten or fifteen years before cultivation is resumed.

The Hamites with their cattle seem next to have moved southwards in eastern Africa where the rain forest is interrupted. Meeting and intermarrying with Bushmen, they evolved into the cattle-keeping Hottentots, who spread ultimately to the southern extremity of the continent, which at the Great Age of Discovery they shared with the Bushmen. They were followed by Bantu, who seem not only to have moved southwards from the region of the lakes from about A.D. 1000 onwards, but to have crossed the Congo forests, possibly along the rivers in large canoes, which they had taught themselves to hollow out of suitable trees by the use of fire and their iron tools. Some Bantu remained within the forest as cultivators, largely absorbing or eliminating the Pygmies. Those who emerged in what is now Zambia and those coming from the lakes were able, on the higher, drier plateaux of eastern Africa, and in tsetse-free temperate southern Africa to conquer and absorb most of the Hottentots and Bushmen, by virtue of superior tribal organisation, expressed not only in the military sphere, but also in the invention of a mixed economy based upon cultivation (mainly by women) and cattle-rearing (mainly by men).

The distribution of languages in tropical Africa arises from its racial history. In the Sudan zone and West Africa generally, indigenous African languages, with distant and uncertain grammatical relationships, have survived from the long period before the coming of the Hamites and of iron, when a small and very dispersed population lived mainly or wholly by hunting and food-collecting. Some languages, especially Hausa and tongues spoken by Nilo-Hamites in East Africa, have been influenced by the Hamitic group.

But the most striking single feature of the linguistic map is the great and continuous extent of Bantu languages, throughout central, East and southern Africa, almost to the Cape. Nearly 200 distinct Bantu languages have been identified. Their common grammar and vocabulary have been preserved because the migration from the original home in the west was (on the historical scale) fairly rapid. At the same time, the absence of writing and the continual movement of population promoted linguistic fission and brought into being many very localised languages spoken by only a few hundreds or thousands of people.

Since the number of non-Bantu languages spoken in the Sudan zone exceeds 200, the total number of languages spoken in Negroid Africa probably exceeds 400. This multiplicity is a great hindrance in education, and governments have had no other alternative than to confine vernacular schools to major languages. Linguistic diversity also is a political weakness, briefly discussed below.

In the Middle Ages, as a result of increasing marine activity on both Indian and Atlantic Oceans, new cultivated plants reached Africa, constituting the third and fourth stimuli to African society before the beginning of European penetration. From India and the Malay Archipelago (borne most probably by the Malay-Polynesian-Melanesian folk who migrated to Madagascar) came the yam, the banana, the oil palm, the coconut palm and the clove, to limit the list to those plants originating in India and the Malay islands which have become important in Africa. The yam spread across the continent and became a basic source of food in the rainforests of the Congo basin and the coastal zone of West Africa. Before the arrival of the yam and the oil palm, these regions were handicapped by a lack of food plants, for the millets, with the possible exception of eleusine, do not flourish in tropical climates with heavy rainfall. For cultivation to become the basis of subsistence, several crops are needed, to give variety in food sources and to permit a cropping system adaptable to climate and soil. Several main crops also reduce the risks arising from dependence upon a single crop. Yams and oil palms, then, accelerated the change from hunting to agriculture in the tropical rain forest, and enabled population to increase. It was after these plants had been introduced to West Africa that tribal organisation became more developed near the coast, and states comparable with those of the Sudan zone farther north appeared. The banana, also, was especially useful in Africa, because it flourished at intermediate altitudes

in East Africa, especially on the rainy highlands, where it became
the chief energy-food of the local tribes.

Not long after the yam, oil palm and banana had been dispersed
across tropical Africa, the Portuguese rounded the Cape of Good
Hope and began also to trade with the New World. From the
latter, they soon introduced maize, manioc, the groundnut,
tobacco and the sweet potato to West Africa, and these plants also
became diffused throughout tropical Africa. (They also introduced
cacao, but this plant remained localised in West Africa.) Manioc
and the sweet potato further strengthened agriculture in the forest
lands. In the savannas of the south-east and south, maize became
the chief cereal crop, rather than the millets, which, grown from an
earlier period in the Sudan zone, still predominate in the belt of
moderate and light rainfall north of the Equator.

It should be noticed that of important plants carried to the
west of the Indian Ocean from the Malay Archipelago, only those
capable of being grown by hoe cultivators were received and
diffused inland. Rice, in particular, did not become a typical
African crop. Where emigrants already skilled in paddy cultivation settled, for instance, in Madagascar, terracing, levelling and
the artificial control of water supply could be practised. Rice,
however, could not be successfully grown by hoe cultivators on
patches cleared from tropical forest. Ignorance of the most rudimentary means of obtaining, controlling and conserving water has
weakened the African's agricultural achievement, and continues
to be so. African society is non-hydraulic, and therefore non-rice-
growing.

The advances in the African economy following the introduction
of plants from the East and from the New World were more than
outweighed by the slave trade. Negroes from the Sudan zone had
been captured and driven northwards across the Sahara and along
the middle Nile valley during the Roman period. When Islamic
states were established in the Sudan during the Middle Ages, the
slave trade was fundamental to their economic life. The main
export from the Arab ports on the East African coast was also
slaves. And from the sixteenth century, Europeans began to ship
Negroes from West Africa to the New World. Both Arab and
European slave traders obtained their captives from African tribes
near their trading centres in exchange for firearms. Chiefs obtaining these weapons could terrorise tribes living farther afield, and
establish strong, despotic states, like Dahomey, Benin and

Ashanti. The mortality in the ensuing intensified tribal wars depopulated whole regions. For instance, in West Africa the intermediate zone between the Sudan and the coastal forests is thinly peopled even today, because it was for so long subjected to slave raiding both from the north and the south. The Ibo hid in the dense forests of the Niger delta. In East Africa, where slave raiding intensified during the nineteenth century, to reach as far inland as the area west of lakes Tanganyika and Nyasa, population retreated to the least accessible places, especially highlands. Here, frequently, the combination of inaccessibility, higher rainfall, and more fertile soils did permit population to concentrate, and gave some immunity from attack; but over much wider areas, a general insecurity prevailed.

The opening of Africa south of the Sahara began with the exploration of the tropical interior promoted by the African Association from 1788. Mungo Park, Barth, Livingstone, Baker, Stanley and many lesser explorers delineated the rivers, lakes and mountains of the last unknown continental interior of the globe. They were soon followed by military forces and colonial officers, pacifying and setting up rudimentary government in the territories falling to different European powers—mainly Britain, France, Belgium, Germany and Portugal as a result of the 'Scramble for Africa' and the Berlin Congress of 1884–5.

Neither the explorers nor the first colonial administrators or missionaries could fulfil their aims without the means to keep tropical diseases at bay, for which Europeans had no natural or acquired immunity or tolerance. Tropical medicine was already advancing early in the nineteenth century; and the discovery, about 1825, that quinine could prevent and cure malaria, and that chlorodyne could overcome many intestinal infections undoubtedly enabled the explorers and their immediate successors to enter the interior and to survive.

The economic motive for colonial expansion in Africa arose from industrialisation in Europe. Colonies, it was argued, could provide raw materials and would offer markets to manufactures. The obstacles to the achievement of these aims were underrated. They were twofold. First, trade demanded modern transport (which in the late nineteenth century meant railways) and ports. Such works are expensive. And in a thinly-peopled continent of peoples living at the subsistence level, how could adequate traffic be generated? Secondly, the conversion of subsistence herdsmen and cultivators to commercial graziers and farmers is not an easy task. Both the technical and social problems are extremely formidable.

Colonial governments were often subsidised, and, even where they contrived to be self-supporting, revenues increased only very slowly. They usually made use of rivers and lakes as far as possible to economise in railway building. The Nile above Khartoum, Lake Victoria, the Senegal, the Upper Niger and above all the Congo and its tributaries were used by river steamers. They also encouraged mineral prospecting, prompted by the growing output from Kimberley and the Rand in South Africa. Not many African dependencies were to become important exporters of minerals, but Belgian Congo and Northern Rhodesia came to share one of the world's great copper orefields. Gold Coast, Nigeria, Tanganyika, Uganda and Kenya in due course became smaller mineral producers.

Agricultural exports were also slow in developing. Some colonies encouraged Europeans to settle and farm. Frenchmen planted coffee in Ivory Coast; Belgians settled on the Rift valley highlands in Congo; the British Government, in consternation after the expensive East African railway had been built, leased land to British emigrants in the Kenya highlands; Germans started plantations of coffee and sisal in East Africa (now Tanzania). Tea was planted by European settlers on the highlands overlooking lake Nyasa, in both British and Portuguese territory. None of these areas of European settlement was large, and most, though not all, were in uplands where the climate is cooler and healthier. In most instances, however, Africans were already in possession of neighbouring land, and when population increased, found the European presence irksome. Since independence, many European farms have been Africanised, on the White Highlands of Kenya and on the southern slopes of Kilimanjaro.

More widespread and on the whole more important as a source of export earnings has been the improvement of native farming. Basically, this has been accomplished by encouraging African cultivators to add cash crops to their range of existing subsistence crops. Cotton and coffee in Uganda, cocoa in Gold Coast (Ghana), groundnuts in Senegal and northern Nigeria, oil palm in (southern) Nigeria and Congo have all contributed substantially to the world's total output. The improvement of roads and tracks with the general adoption of motor transport in the last forty years

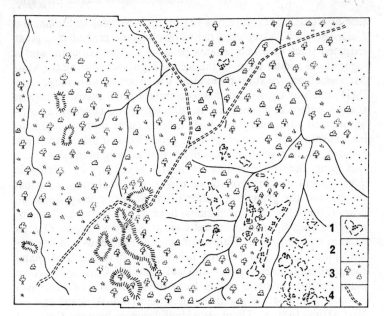

Fig. 12 Shifting cultivation in Africa, near Yei, southern Sudan

1 Homesteads and Current Cultivation.
2 Recently-cultivated land, with partly-regenerated vegetation.
3 Primeval and fully-regenerated high savanna.
4 Roads.

(Reproduced from Monograph No. 4, World Land Use Survey, by permission of Geographical Publications Ltd.)

have enabled produce to be moved from rural markets to rivers, railways and ports. There are, however, limits to this method of expanding crop production. Especially where population has increased (and this has happened in most of the continent), the introduction of cash-cropping has greatly increased the area of land cultivated year by year. The length of the fallow period has been reduced; the land is not sufficiently rested after cropping; erosion and falling yields follow. To transform traditional native cultivation into modern technically-adequate farming is not easy. Customary land tenure and fragmentation of holdings are not the least of the many obstacles to be surmounted. Lack of capital to buy implements, fertilisers, etc., is another; lack of knowledge of scientific farming is a third. But some striking successes have shown that an agrarian revolution is beginning in Africa. In Sudan, the Gezira Scheme has replaced native farming and grazing by a great irrigated tract in which tenants produce cotton, sorghum and a leguminous fodder crop. In the Kenya highlands, during the Mau Mau rebellion, the rural population was grouped into villages and their land was consolidated into compact small mixed farms. In Congo, before independence, Belgian agronomists grouped cultivators into *paysannats*, in which shifting cultivation was systemised, surpluses of some crops were produced and fish ponds were constructed to provide protein previously lacking in the diet.

Among the other results of nearly a century of economic development are the growth of towns, the weakening of tribal society and the growth of nationalism. Major, usually artificial, ports (often also the capital cities) have grown from small beginnings or even upon unoccupied sites at Abidjan, Lagos, Dar Es Salaam and Mombasa. Railway junctions, rail heads and important mines have also become urbanised. There are also many minor administrative posts with small markets. Commonly, town plans exhibit zonation arising from the separation of European colonial administrators and business men from Africans and (in East Africa) Indians. There are wide differences between the street plan, the spacing of houses and the style of building in each zone. Some of the African population is permanent; but often the majority is temporary, and is composed of migrants from tribes, chiefly young men who are earning wages to be able to marry or to support their families. The overcrowded slums in which these men have to live for months or years are among the worst sores of the new Africa.

The relation between town and country therefore remains unstabilised. At present, the basis of living is still mainly in tribal lands. Towns are temporary refuges for tribesmen. Only part of the urban population is composed of citizens. Not until there is more specialisation in labour, so that men can earn their living in either town or country, will migrant temporary labourers disappear, and urban slums at present sheltering them be replaced by homes. Meanwhile, the ebb and flow of migrant labourers is probably increasing.

Political independence in tropical Africa was preceded by the growth of a small middle class of civil servants educated by colonial governments or missionary activity, of small traders (especially in West Africa) and of farmers who had profited by

growing cash crops. The latter often devoted much of their income to their sons' education. Whilst the small parties founded by
this politically-conscious minority had no difficulty in arousing
resentment against colonial governments, they could not create
nations. All the new African states are artificial. None is a nation
state. Tribal ties are still real; and the unchanged boundaries of
former colonies now assumed by African countries, having been
drawn without regard to ethnic distributions, frequently fragment
tribes. The Azande, for example, are divided between the Republics of Sudan, Central Africa and Congo. Often the political party
gaining power when a colony became independent represented
mainly a progressive or numerically dominant tribe or ethnic
group. Its leader became an autocrat. Thus, Jomo Kenyatta in
Kenya is a Kikuyu. This tribe, more closely involved in the
development of the White Highlands than any other, is the most
educated and politically conscious in the country. Tribal rivalry
has erupted into civil war in Sudan, Congo and Nigeria.

Nevertheless, the introduction of modern government and the
money economy has weakened tribalism. The part-Christianising
of tropical Africa has also contributed to this tendency. But the
mother-tongues remain. The federal solution adopted in India was
also applied to Nigeria; but it has broken down. (Though it
should be remembered that the USA underwent a civil war to
preserve its federation.) Federalism, for the larger African countries and based upon major languages, seems to be the avenue of
political development best calculated to bring genuinely self-
governing states into being. It is therefore greatly to be hoped that
Federalism will survive in Nigeria and that the proposed federal
solution for the status of southern Sudan will be included in the
constitution.

In East Africa, Swahili may eventually become the common
medium of communication, and make federation unnecessary;
but this is the only regional second language in tropical Africa.
English and French, essential to the élite, can never become
national or regional languages. They can only be spoken and read
by the small minority graduating from universities.

There remains the problem of states too small to be viable:
veritable ghosts of European colonial competition haunting the
corridors of the United Nations. 'Smallness' in this context means
limitation of population and resources; and this category includes
several African states occupying sizable tracts in the continent,

such as Chad and Niger. Political union, combined with federalism and preceded by closer economic association, seems to be the goal to be striven for. In other words, events in Africa in the twenty-first century should follow the example of Germany in the nineteenth (without its militarism) when the Zollverein, after fifty years, blossomed into the Empire. In the modern world, there is no need in Africa for more than ten or a dozen states. Such political rationalisation could also be associated with land planning based upon the techniques of evaluation already successfully applied in many smaller-scale projects. Capital could then be invested in the most remunerative agricultural and mining areas, and the population could be encouraged to leave lands offering no hope of improved standards of living.

BIBLIOGRAPHY

OLD WORLD CIVILISATIONS

TURNER, R., *The Great Cultural Traditions, The Foundations of Civilization*, vol. 1, *The Ancient Cities*, vol. 2, *The Classical Empires*, 1941.

THE NEAR EAST AND ISLAM

COON, C. S., *Caravan*, 1966

MONTAGNE, R., *La civilisation du désert*, 1947

PLANHOL, X. de, *The World of Islam*, 1959; *Les Fondements Géo graphiques de l'Histoire de l'Islam*, 1968

STAMP, L. D. (Ed.), *A History of Land Use in Arid Regions*, Arid Zone Series, **17**, 1961, UNESCO (especially the chapters by Butzer, K. W., Whyte, R. O., Despois, J., Monod, Th., and Toupet, C.)

WEULERSSE, J., *Paysans de Syrie et du Proche-Orient*, 1946

THE WEST, INCLUDING THE SOVIET BLOC

BROWN, R. H., *Historical Geography of the United States*, 1948

CLARKE, A. H., *The Invasion of New Zealand by People, Plants and Animals*, 1949

COLE, J. P., *Latin America*, 1965 (especially chs 4 and 5)

DEMANGEON, A., *L'Empire Britannique*, 1923 (translated Row, E. F., 1925)

EAST, W. G., *The Soviet Union*, 1963) especially chs 1, 3, 4)

FLEURE, H. J., *Human Geography in Western Europe*, 1918
—*A Natural History of Man in Britain*, 1951
—'The historic city in western and central Europe', *Bulletin John Rylands Library*, **20**, 1936, 312–31

GOTTMAN, J., *Megalopolis*, 1961

GREGORY, J. S., *Russian Land—Soviet People*, 1968, chs I, III, VI, VII

HOUSTON, J. M., *A Social Geography of Europe*, 1953

JONES, E., *Towns and Cities*, 1967

JORRÉ, G. (translated Laborde, E. D.), *The Soviet Union*, 1950, Parts II and III

MARVIN, F. S., *The Living Past, a Sketch of Western Progress*, 1920

MELLOR, R. E. H., *Geography of the USSR*, 1964 (especially chs 3–5)

MUMFORD, L., *The City in History*, 1961

NEWBIGIN, M. I., *The Mediterranean Lands, an Introductory Study in Human and Historical Geography*, 1924

PARKER, W. H., *An Historical Geography of Russia*, 1969

PARKINS, M. F., *City Planning in Soviet Russia*, 1953

PARRY, J. H., *Europe in a Wider World, 1415–1715*, 1966

PLATT, R. S., *Latin America: Countrysides and United Regions*, 1943

PRICE, A. Grenfell, *White Settlers and Native Peoples*, 1950
—*The Western Invasion of the Pacific and its Continents*, 1963

SALAMAN, R. H., *History and Social Influence of the Potato*, 1949

SEELEY, J. R., *The Expansion of England*, 1883

SEMPLE, E. C., *American History and its Geographic Conditions*, 1933

SMAILES, A. E., *The Geography of Towns*, 1966 ed

SMITH, C. T., *An Historical Geography of Western Europe before 1800*, 1967

WATSON, J. W., *North America*, 2nd ed., 1968 (especially chs 5–8 and 18)

HINDU SOCIETY

KOSAMBI, D. D., *The Culture and Civilisation of Ancient India in Historical Outline*, 1965

PANIKKAR, K. M., *The Foundations of New India*, 1963

RAWLINSON, H. G., *India: A Short Cultural History*, 1937 and later eds.

SPATE, O. H. K. and LEARMONTH, A. T. A., *India and Pakistan*, 3rd ed., 1967, Pt. II, chs 4–7

SPEAR, P., *India, Pakistan and the West,* 3rd ed., 1958

WHEELER, Sir M., *Civilisations of the Indus Valley and Beyond,* 1966

CHINA

BOYD, A., *Chinese Architecture and Town Planning, 1500 B.C.–A.D. 1911,* 1962

BUCHANAN, K., *The Chinese People and the Chinese Earth,* 1966

BUCK, J. L., *Land Utilisation in China,* 1937

BUXTON, L. H. D., *China, The Land and the People,* 1929

China Proper, vol. I, *Physical Geography, History and Peoples* (N.I.D. Handbook, B.R. 530), 1944 (especially Part II, chs XI–XIII)

FULLARD, H. (Ed.), *China in Maps,* 1968

GERNET, J., translated Rudoff, R., *Ancient China,* 1968

KING, F. H., *Farmers of Forty Centuries,* 1926

LEONG, Y. K. and YAO, L. K., *Village and Town Life in China,* 1915

MYRDAL, J. (translated Michael, H.), *Report from a Chinese Village,* 1965

SPENCER, J. E., 'The houses of the Chinese', *Geographical Review,* **37** 1947, 254–73

TREGEAR, T. R., *A Geography of China,* 1965

AFRICA

ALLAN, W., *The African Husbandman,* 1965

Ciba Foundation, *Man and Africa,* 1961

HESELTINE, N., *Remaking Africa,* 1961

MURDOCK, G. P., *Africa, its Peoples and their Culture History,* 1959

OLIVER, R. and FAGE, J. D. (Eds.), *A Short History of Africa,* 1959

PHILLIPS, J. F. V., *Agriculture and Ecology in Africa,* 1959

SELIGMAN, C. G., *The Races of Africa,* 1930 and later eds

5

CIVILISATIONS IN CONFRONTATION

Major societies include most, but not the whole, of mankind. They occupy most, but not all, of the earth. Especially where their spheres overlap, we find both relict, autonomous minor societies and also undefined or unaffiliated groups, some quite large.

Ethiopia: a minor civilisation

Unique Ethiopia illustrates the first of these categories. It is now the world's only state which calls itself, and is, an empire,[1] and in it the Amhara are the dominant ethnic group. Their civilisation originated from the fusion of Semitic south Arabian elements and Monophysite (Coptic) Christianity during the Axumite period in the uplands near the present Asmara. The legend that their supreme ruler is descended from King Solomon of Israel and the Queen of Sheba is symbolic. Here, then, is its hearth. Here, also, a peasant society was evolved, in which cultivators were tenants owing services and paying rents in produce to feudal lords, the Emperor or the Church. By southward expansion its core was formed in the lake Tana basin, in which Gondar, its capital from the sixteenth to the nineteenth century, is located. Later stages of this *Drang nach Süden* gave it a domain along the rim of the western highlands overlooking the rift valley where the present capital, Addis Ababa, was founded in 1893. By the conquests of Theodore, John and Menelik in the nineteenth century Ethiopian civilisation expanded its sphere to the present boundaries with

[1]Analogues, however, exist in Morocco, Iran and Thailand.

G

Sudan, Kenya and Somalia. These conquests were concentrated on the eastern highlands occupied mainly by the Galla, on the Red Sea coastal lowlands, inhabited mainly by Muslim nomads, and along the western frontier, peopled, albeit sparsely, by Negroid tribes with kin or affinities in Sudan. The integrity and autonomy of Ethiopian civilisation were preserved by its isolation in its mountainous fastness after Islam had occupied the Lower Nile valley and the Red Sea littoral, and by its successful defence, with Portuguese help, against menacing Muslim invasions during the sixteenth century. Paradoxically, the later expulsion of Portuguese priests was also crucial for the survival of Ethiopian society. If they had remained, the Empire might have been absorbed within the Western sphere.

South-east Asia

What has been called South-east Asia since the Second World War cannot be regarded as culturally autonomous, because of the profound influence exerted upon it by India, Islam, the West and China. Its affinities with these civilisations clearly pose a problem in any attempt to classify major societies. Until recently, Southeast Asia was often called Hither or Further India; and Schmitthenner includes most of the mainland between India and China (except Vietnam) and the Malay Archipelago (as far as the Strait of Macassar and the Sulu Sea) in a zone of 'Indian colonial culture'. Toynbee, however, places Burma, Thailand and Cambodia in the sphere of Indic civilisation; Malaya and Indonesia in the Islamic and the Philippines in the Western. The human geographer must surely agree with Toynbee that South-east Asia is not socially a unity, because it is so diverse ethnically. It is a group of embryonic nations and rather primitive empires, where the more numerous, advanced and advantageously-located linguistic groups are dominant and exercise power over the rest. Some generalisations are applicable to the entire region; but these do not make it a unity.

Among these, three are outstanding. First, its present position in the world balance of power. Just emerging from colonial status in Western (including American) empires, it is now a cockpit of rival adolescent nationalisms and a theatre of competition between Soviet Russia, the USA, Britain, Australia and China. Secondly, its ecological uniformities impart distinctiveness as a home of man. Most of it is insular, for it includes the world's largest tropical archipelago. It also embraces adjoining peninsulas of the mainland, and both are characterised by coastal lowlands backed by ruggedly-mountainous interiors. Most islands, in fact, are composed of half-submerged ranges continuing those of the mainland, apart from Borneo, which is a massif. Insularity has opened South-east Asia not only to prehistoric migrations from the mainland but also trans-oceanic influence from Asia, Europe and the New World. Whilst portions of the mainland, chiefly in the interior, are seasonally dry or receive only moderate rainfall, the greater part is very rainy for much of the year. The entire region is subject to a monsoonal climate, either equatorial or tropical. The original vegetation, almost everywhere, was dense, exuberant, tropical rain forest. Thirdly, the majority of the population is of Mongoloid origin, and is descended from the persistently southward-moving groups which have migrated from eastern Asia by land and sea since the Neolithic Age. Some admixture with the very sparse aboriginal Negrito and Australoid inhabitants took place, but Mongoloid types greatly predominate in the present population. These early immigrants brought the technique of cultivating rice in levelled, flooded fields, and they progressively became more proficient in the arts of navigation and seamanship. Hence, they tended to become concentrated along littorals, in major valleys and upon alluvial, including deltaic plains, where population is often dense; but the extent of land thus occupied is small in relation to the total area of South-east Asia. Interior hills and mountains remain largely forested, and it is here that the numerically—small aboriginal groups live by more primitive forms of cultivation or even by hunting and gathering wild produce. The mean population density is only about a third of that prevailing in China and India. In the prehistoric period (which lasted until the Middle Ages of the West), women were unusually important in society, and descent was reckoned in the maternal line. Early religion combined animism with ancestor-worship and the location of shrines in high places. Musical instruments, modes of concerted playing and puppet shadow theatres are also evidence of common ethnic, though diffused, origins. These social traits, usually termed indigenous, have persisted despite the profound effects of more recent external influence and renewed immigration.

Professor C. A. Fisher and others have argued that these common features of habitat, racial composition and society suffice to make South-east Asia an 'intelligible entity' of geographical study. This may be conceded; but an entity is not necessarily a unity, and this distinction is particularly important in the social sphere. South-east Asia does not have the coherence of Islam proper, India or China. In the South-east Asian mirror, Islamic, Hindu, Chinese and Western images are reflected or distorted in varying degree.

For the linguistic and religious diversity is extreme. Most of the island peoples speak languages of the Austric family, of which some also survive on the mainland. Here, however, the more recently-intruded Burmese, Thai and Annamese (of the Sino-Tibetan family) are in the ascendant. In Indonesia alone

besides the immigrant Chinese, European, Indian and Arab communities, the indigenous population includes speakers of at least 25 different languages and 250 lesser dialects . . . while profound racial, cultural and demographic contrasts exist between coast and interior, between the eastern third and the western two-thirds, and between Java and the outer islands as a whole.   (C. A. Fisher)

A lasting legacy has remained from the Hindu ascendancy exercised over the western two-thirds of South-east Asia from the fifth to the fifteenth centuries. Theravada Buddhism became established on the mainland, where it still persists as the national religion of the Burmese and Thai. Brahmins reduced languages of both the mainland and the western islands to writing, and introduced the rudiments of political organisation into Cambodia, the Malay Peninsula, Sumatra and Java. It has been inferred that the first towns were founded under Indian influence; and the prevalence until today of the Indian type of plough suggests that they fostered agriculture, especially the all-important wet-rice form.

On the islands, the Hindu dominance gave way before the advance of Islam, except in Bali and along the west coast of Lombok. Small groups of Muslim merchants from western India had been settled in various ports since the thirteenth century, but the indigenous peoples were not converted until Malacca began its career as an Islamic thalassic state about A.D. 1400. Its ascendancy over adjoining areas of the mainland, combined with the increasing influence of Muslim traders and *Sufi* (unorthodox Muslim preachers), resulted in Islamisation, though not to the elimination of Hinduism or indigenous beliefs and customs. It is significant that Islamic law (the *Shari'a*) has not displaced local (or *adat*) law; and for this reason the Muslims of Malaya and Indonesia cannot be brought within the domain of Islam, although assuredly they are to be included in its sphere.

Generally in the Malay archipelago, including the Moluccas, Islam was just ahead of the Europeans, represented at first by the Portuguese, whose attempts to Christianise failed. Moreover, under the paternalistic Dutch colonial government that succeeded the Portuguese, and despite the immense expansion of tropical plantation agriculture, especially in Java, what is now Indonesia was effectively insulated from Western education and ideas. But in the Philippine islands, conquered by Spain between 1565 and 1572, the population was small. Both Hindu and Muslim influence had been slight. Animism and nature-worship still prevailed. Andres de Urdaneta, the Augustinian friar who was joint commander of the occupying army, not only converted the inhabitants but shielded them from the excesses that had disfigured the Portuguese domination of the Indies. As an 'empire of the friars' it was a governorship within the vice-royalty of New Spain, and its communications with Europe extended across the Pacific.

> For the most part, the economy was one of great landed estates such as the Spaniards had already set up in the Americas, and huge areas were made over in this way to religious organisations and the individual *conquistadores* . . . the landowning class consisted of *caciques*, descendants of the traditional territorial chieftains whom the Spaniards effectively confirmed in power and with whose families they intermarried freely. (C. A. Fisher)

Although the restrictive Spanish mercantilism retarded economic progress, some 50,000 Chinese were living in the towns, mostly ports, of the Philippine islands by 1850, and internal commerce was largely in their hands. The Church provided fairly widespread elementary education and a University was founded in Manila in 1645. Hence, when Spanish rule was superseded by American in 1899, population had increased to 7 millions; the islands were politically unified and more Westernised than any other country of South-east Asia.

By the Chinese, South-east Asia is called Nan Yang, meaning, the South Sea. Ships from the ports of South China sailed throughout the Malay archipelago for centuries, and Chinese settled wherever there is economic activity. The map showing the distribution of Chinese in South-east Asia mirrors the distribution of the entire population. Though tending to commerce and to living in towns, they have also participated in agricultural colonisation and in new mining enterprises. Proportionately they are not numerous: out of a total population of almost 200 millions in 1956, Chinese numbered about 10 millions, only 1 in 20. Many were descended from mixed marriages; but Chinese social customs are preserved, and also links with clans in China. Hence, they are everywhere a distinct element in the plural societies so characteristic of both town and country. In Thailand 3 million Chinese, or 15 per cent of the population, control much of the trade in rice and are influential in commerce and government in Bangkok, where they are estimated to form half of the population. In Malaya two-fifths of the population are Chinese; in Singapore, three-quarters. The removal of restrictions upon emigration by China itself between 1860 and 1870, and the disinclination of Malays to work in European-directed enterprises, set in motion one of the world's major currents of human migration during the ensuing half century.

Chinese rule in South-east Asia has, however, been much more limited, even in the most expansionist phases of the past. Vietnam was under Chinese suzerainty from 110 B.C. to A.D. 939; and in North Vietnam, especially, agriculture, social institutions and religion received a strong Sinic imprint, without, however, destroying the spirit of ethnic self-determination, which is as strong in the present century after the French occupation as it was in the tenth after the Chinese.

Southern Africa

In southern Africa, which consists of the Republic of South Africa, the Portuguese colonies of Angola and Mozambique and Rhodesia, Western civilisation is dominant; but its position is challenged by emergent Negroid Africa.

South Africa is not unique in the association of two distinct communities of European origin, divergent in economy and tradition. For in Canada, French and British have been associated for nearly two centuries; but a degree of territorial segregation and a wide margin between population and available resources have enabled the two nationalities to maintain a stable *modus vivendi*, reflected in the peaceful course of federal government. But in South Africa, the two White communities—British and Afrikaner —are more intermingled geographically and economically, not only amongst each other, but with the far more numerous Bantu.

Africa is essentially a vast plateau, descending to the sea by bold, rugged escarpments. In South Africa, the edge of the plateau is most clearly defined in the east, where the Drakensberg (Mountains) rise to more than 3,000m (10,000 ft) at a distance of 160km (100 miles) to 250km (150 miles) from the coast of Natal. Sandstones, of which much of the plateau is composed, form tremendous bastions and castellated crests. The seaward slope, eroded by many short and cascading streams, is a land of rolling hills, which continue almost to the shore of the Indian Ocean. Inland, in Lesotho, the hilly relief continues at an altitude of 1,829m (6,000 ft); but otherwise the plateau is unbroken (apart from the valleys of the main affluents to the Orange river system) and declines gradually westwards from 1,500m (4–5,000 ft) to less than 900m (3,000 ft) in the heart of Botswana. In the extreme south, the level plateau continues to the crooked and broken ranges of the Roggeveld Mountains, the Nieuveld Mountains, the Sneeuw Berge and the Storm Berge. These are about 320km (200 miles) from the sea. The intervening zone forms two giant 'steps' (the Great and Little Karroos) each bordered on the seaward edge by a kind of rim (the Zwarte Berge and the Lange Berge).

Only a small part of the country receives a moderate rainfall, and even less can boast of a reliable rainfall. The immediate environs of Cape Town and Cape Agulhas receive cyclonic rains in winter from the west, and, climatically, resemble the Mediterranean Lands in régime (amount 50–75cm (20–30 in), rising to 150cm (60 in) in the hills) and reliability (average deviation fifteen per cent). Northwards, in the Karroos, the amount decreases to but 12–18cm (5–15 in), falling in infrequent showers. Elsewhere, the source of rainfall is the Trade Winds of the Indian Ocean, which are strongest during the summer. Impinging at right angles to the coast, they bring a moderate rainfall (75–150cm or 30–60 in) to the coastal slope and the Drakensberg; but inland the amount decreases, because the winds are descending and distance from the source of water vapour is greater. Over the plateau of the Orange Free State and Transvaal, the annual average fall is 50–70cm (20–35 in); in Botswana, only 25–50cm (10–20 in.) The Trade Winds weaken towards the south. Between the

Orange river and the Little Karroo the annual fall is extremely
light (12–18cm or 5–15 in). These summer rains are accompanied by thunder: indeed, the danger from lightning stroke in the
Orange Free State and the Transvaal is great. Thus heavy rain
falls for a few hours, and is then succeeded by days or weeks of
sunshine. Everywhere, the incidence is uncertain, and the annual
totals fluctuate greatly. Even near Port Elizabeth, where the summer régime of the Trade Winds meets the winter régime of the
Westerlies, the fall is not heavy from either; and both sources can
be deficient in the course of a year, the average variability being
fifteen to twenty per cent. Inland and northwards, the variability
is greater.

The Tropic of Capricorn crosses northern Transvaal, and thus
nearly the whole of South Africa is extra-tropical. It would be
near-tropical, however, apart from the high average elevation.
Exceptionally, the coastal lowlands of Natal prolong the tropical
coastal lowland of Mozambique. Durban, for instance, has a
mean annual temperature of 22° C (71° F); its cool season (July
18° C or 65° F) being short, and its hot season (January 25° C or
77° F) being long. But the southern coast is warm temperate, and
at Cape Town the mean annual temperature is 17° C (62° F.) Inland, the elevation of the plateau offsets the decrease of latitude.
Although Pretoria is seven degrees of latitude nearer the Equator
than Cape Town, its mean annual temperature is only one degree
more (17° C or 63° F). The climate of the plateau is bracing. The
air is dry—often excessively dry—and days are hot; but the air
becomes cool very quickly after sunset. There is a true winter (the
mean July temperature at Pretoria is 11° C (52° F)), and night
frosts are common. South Africa is a 'White Man's Country', in
the sense that people of European stock can maintain their vigour,
and transmit it to their offspring, whilst living fully normal lives;
in particular, engaging in vigorous muscular exercise. The maintenance of vitality is undoubtedly aided by the absence of tropical
parasitic diseases. Malaria, endemic throughout tropical Africa,
persists as far south as the Limpopo valley, which is the northern
boundary of the Transvaal; but ceases where the land rises southwards above 1,000m (3,500 ft). The tsetse fly and sleeping sickness,
likewise, are absent.

The rainfall is only locally sufficient for the growth of forest.
Along the east coast from Port Elizabeth northwards, a low, subtropical forest formerly flourished; but has now largely been

cleared. Patches of similar forest survive on the exposed and inaccessible escarpment of the Drakensberg. In the region of winter rains, near Cape Town, evergreen sclerophyllous forests clothe the mountains, and include yellow-woods, ironwoods, the assegai wood and many smaller bushes, bulbous and tuberous plants; the latter formerly dominant on lower ground. Grasslands are much more extensive, and include both tropical and temperate types. In the former, as usual, trees and bushes mingle with grasses to comprise the Bushveld of northern Transvaal (near the Limpopo). A similar association extends along the east coast, mingling with the subtropical evergreen forest. A true grassland, growing in the temperate climate of the plateau, in the Orange Free State and the Transvaal, dominated by the red grass (*Themeda triandra*), and accompanied by many herbaceous perennials, which beautify vast expanses in summer, is known as the Veld or the High Veld. A somewhat similar grassland, broken by thorn trees and Cape lilac, extends in a zone parallel to the east coast, between the forests of the littoral and the escarpment. The interior of Cape Province, between the Orange river and the littoral, receives insufficient rainfall to maintain a grassy sward, and the plant growth displays the characteristics of semi-deserts. Small, succulent plants, storing water in their tissues and thus able to withstand prolonged drought (such as the mesembryanthemum, euphorbia and aloes, bulbous and tuberous plants, or the Karroo bush) are sparsely scattered, and scattered bunch-grasses are green only after rain.

Like central Africa, which abounds in wild animals, the grasslands of South Africa once swarmed with antelope, of many species, small and large, upon which preyed the greater carnivores. As will be shown later, the earlier indigenous inhabitants, and earlier white settlers, all depended much upon game for their sustenance.

Considered thus apart from its human inhabitants, South Africa may be visualised as a plateau, descending to the sea by escarpments or terraces, and subjected to a warm-temperate or subtropical climate. A light or moderate rainfall, very variable in its incidence, is insufficient, except quite locally, to sustain a forest cover; and the greater part of the country is grassland or semi-desert. The combination of grassland and plateau imparts a spaciousness to the South African landscape which remains among the most enduring impressions of travellers between the Cape and the Limpopo. The veld is an apparently illimitable, gently undulating

plain. South of the Orange river, the broken rim of the African
plateau, and the ranges separating the Karroos, veiled in mysterious blue haze, rise from the plain, and in the clear, dry air may
often be seen from a distance of more than a hundred miles. There
are few obstacles to movement. The rivers, though dangerous in
flood, can be forced when the waters subside. Domestic animals
can be assembled and driven from exhausted pastures to new.
Over the level and normally dry soil, the ox-drawn wagon can
freely go. Thus the past three centuries have witnessed remarkable
human movements: more striking, perhaps, than even the daunt-
less pioneering in the Far West of the USA, before the railways
had spanned the continent. For in South Africa, a people drawn
from the long-sedentary nations of western Europe, turned to a
pastoralism which, at its fullest development, was semi-nomadic.
Its effects upon the land and the social problems of South Africa
have been profound.

It may be postulated, then, that ease of movement in this open
country caused Briton, Boer and Bantu to interlock before the
first railways were built. Modern mining and industry have
accentuated the tendency.

Peoples: (1) *Africans*

Two primitive peoples were being driven southwards and south-
westwards when the first permanent European settlement was established at the Cape of Good Hope in 1652. Ethnologically, the
Bushmen and Hottentot are allied. Both have wandered from the
north, where, in central Africa a thousand years ago, they were
the sole occupants alike of forest and tropical grasslands, with
the Pygmy who now shelter in the Congo forests. The economy
of the Bushmen has already been described on pp. 86–7.

The Hottentot in the sixteenth century lived south of the Orange
river and west of the Kei river. They were pastoralists, fundamentally. They drove herds of long-horned cattle and hairy, fat-tailed
sheep from one pasture to another. Living primarily upon the
milk of cows and the flesh of sheep, they also gathered berries,
bulbs, roots and wild honey. To a certain extent, they were also
hunters. Their encampments were quite large, and contained
(within a thorn fence) pens for domestic animals, and huts (dis-
posed on a plan sanctioned by custom) of grass mats supported
on curved sticks, readily dismantled for transport, and as quickly
capable of re-erection. Like other pastoral peoples in Africa, their

movements were dictated by the need of their animals for water and fresh pasture. Every Hottentot tribe held its own territory, defined not so much by boundary features, but by the location of scarce and valued watering places claimed to be in its possession.

Rock-paintings and place-names of Hottentot origin indicate that these people formerly lived in the region between the Orange and Limpopo rivers, from which they were expelled by the advance of Bantu peoples, whose ancestors began to migrate southwards from the region of lake Victoria about the ninth century A.D. The persisting vanguards drove Hottentot and Bushmen southwards. As more land was needed, the Bantu settled in areas adjacent to those already occupied, dispossessing, and often doubtless killing, Hottentots or Bushmen. To their strong, Negro physique—most writers apply the adjective magnificent to the Zulus and other tribes of the southern Bantu—were allied the advantages of a well-knit tribal organisation and of better weapons, which included well-made spears (for they had knowledge of iron-working) and shields. Unquestionably superior to the other indigenous peoples, they disputed the country with the Europeans, and did not succumb until beaten in a hard struggle. After crossing the Limpopo, they penetrated into South Africa along two well-defined routes.

More important was the coastal zone, through Natal, which, with what is now Cape Province as far as the Fish river, was thickly peopled by the seventeenth century. Although the population of this coastal zone extended to the Drakensberg, the High Veld was largely avoided. The Bantu disliked the cold nights and the lack of shelter. The westward tongue of Bantu peoples accordingly was thrust southwards along the eastern margin of the Kalahari desert and the western Low Veld of Transvaal. For their subsistence they depended upon hunting, pastoralism (for they kept cattle and goats) and simple agriculture. From their domestic animals the men drew milk, which, drunk fresh or sour, was their staple diet. They did not slaughter their animals for food, although they would eat a carcass when death had occurred from natural causes. They normally obtained fresh meat by hunting. Cattle, especially, were the chief wealth of a Bantu family and the standard value in which fines and bride-price (*lobola*) were paid. The men and boys of each family tended the herds on the common pastures of the tribe, in which private rights or ownership were unrecognised. But a tenancy based upon the usufructuary occupation of land for dwelling houses and cultivation was granted by a chief or headman. On land thus allocated, wattle-and-daub huts were erected; enclosures were constructed in which cattle could be penned at night and plots were cleared of natural growth so that cultivation could take place. Care of the gardens was women's work, after the men had cleared bushes and trees from the ground. The women broke up the soil with wooden or iron hoes; sowed sorghum, maize, millet, pumpkins, melons, sweet cane, peas and beans; scared away predators and finally reaped the harvest. Manuring, irrigation and crop rotation were unknown; when the soil was exhausted, it reverted to common pasture, and fresh land, duly allotted, broken elsewhere. For nearly all purposes, each family was self-sufficient, the preparation of skins for clothing, the making of wooden utensils such as pails, bowls, spoons and head-rests by the men, and the weaving of mats or simple pottery by the women being universal. Only metal-working was restricted to a small class of men skilled in smelting and fabricating; but even among these it was a part-time occupation.

For a primitive people, the Bantu were comparatively advanced, and a formidable obstacle in the way of advancing colonists. Unlike the Hottentots, they had some skill in metal work, being armed with assegais. Like Caesar's Germans, whom, in fact, they closely resembled, they did not specially devote themselves to agriculture, living rather on milk—that is, the nutritious curdled milk which they preserve in gourds known as *kalabashes*—on beef, and to some extent on the game they took. Yet even their rough and superficial cultivation of maize and Kaffir corn (millet)—the latter used especially to make their native beer —raised them many stages above the mainly nomadic Hottentots. If their tillage was, and is, wretched, they had in older, roomier days a shrewd eye for the best patches of soil, and habitually settled in one spot for from five to seven years; then, even if the ground was not exhausted, their huts needed to be moved for hygienic reasons, and they moved slowly on 'picking out the eyes of the country' in their progress. This, no doubt, was highly wasteful, but the Bantu were tribally rather than territorially organised, and since land was plentiful, their ideas of boundaries were as vague and rudimentary as their notions of land ownership. Yet they were definitely attached to their own 'country', and the traditional reverence for the graves of their great chiefs suggests that the Bantu were no mere nomads. Thanks to their agriculture, and to the fact that in winter, or in time of drought, their cattle got some sustenance from the stubble of the fields, their food supply was far more regular than that of the Hottentots. This may account for the generally magnificent physique of these Bantu peoples. It also explains how, whatever their actual numbers, they were relatively closely settled, and for that reason more formidable. The Hottentot mode of life under the best circumstances could hardly support as many as three to the square mile, whereas the Bantu system could probably, without undue pressure, maintain a population of at least ten, and possibly more, anywhere in the important Cape-Natal area. Conditions in the north-west or Bechuana area being less favourable, but the country less important, there the rather scanty population has been forced into relatively large villages in the immediate neighbourhood of the stronger springs, whereas in the east, except where they clumped together for defensive reasons, the *kraals* (huts belonging to a family unit) tended to be scattered broadcast. (W. M. Macmillan)

This author goes on to emphasise how this mode of life, which freed many men from continuous and arduous toil not only enabled a part of the man-power to be habituated to hunting, cattle-thieving and fighting, but was sufficiently sedentary (it may perhaps be described as semi-sedentary) to admit of a tribal organisation, the chief being aided by headmen and a council. With other writers, he observes that tribal coherence depended much upon the character of the chief; but that the form of government, in a rudimentary way, was constitutional. He might perhaps have added that the more temperate climate and the absence of parasitic diseases which debilitate so many Negro peoples elsewhere in Africa contributed to the vigour of the South African Bantu.

Their weakness, derived from the long centuries of southward expansion into apparently endless grassland or savanna peopled only by a few Hottentots or Bushmen, was an inexorable demand for land. In the early nineteenth century, when missionaries, traders, administrators and the vanguard of Boer migration were enlarging our knowledge of the Bantu peoples, inter-tribal warfare was commonly attributed to mere savagery. But it was rather due to White aggression against the southernmost tribes, in the basins of the Fish river and Kei river, where the expansive tendency of both races came in conflict, and which (to use a physical metaphor) generated pressure far to the north. Thus the French missionary Casalis, writing from Basutoland in 1848, commented:

Much confusion arises from the limited and erroneous ideas generally entertained. . . . The population is underrated, the actual and future

wants of the tribe are not taken into consideration. . . . The present
lamentable war of the Basutos and the Mantatees, which originated in
nothing else than a land question, shows sufficiently how keen and deep
are the feelings of the natives on the subject.

(2) *Afrikaners*

European settlement in South Africa began in 1652, when the
Dutch East India Company founded Cape Town as a revictualling
station for ships sailing between Holland and the East Indies. The
original intention was strictly limited, and it was conceived that a
population of a few hundreds would suffice to produce the goods
and services required by passing ships. 'Free Burghers' took land
in the Cape Peninsula. This they farmed with such success that
later governors took possession of estates, upon which they cultivated the vine and wheat, or kept large herds of cattle. The free
Burghers were augmented in 1688 by Huguenots from France, and
soon the produce available far exceeded the needs of ships and the
inhabitants of Cape Town. In fact, the estates of the Governor and
other officials were quite able to provide all that was required.
Having a privileged position in the market, they deprived the free
Burghers of the economic function for which, as a class, they were
originally created. The Burghers accordingly began to migrate
eastwards, to be beyond the Company's writ and its powers to tax
or exact rent. Their desire was soon fulfilled; for, reaching the
semi-arid lands where pastoralism alone was practicable, they
helped themselves to land which seemed boundless. They learned
to relish a diet of little else than animal food, hunting game rather
than slaughtering their cattle and sheep. They became accustomed
to live in tent-wagons, and acquired a fondness for a healthy, independent, simple, hardy life. In short, they were bred, in one or
two generations, into a race of frontiersmen and pioneers. Adapting elements in their European knowledge—horsemanship, the use
of the rifle and of the wagon—they made themselves possessors of
the land. It was indeed from the Old Testament that these bold
adventurers gained inspiration. Like the Israelites, they believed
that they were divinely commissioned to subjugate an inferior
race, predestined to a life of servitude. Miscegenation between
Burgher and native was a mortal sin: the two races must for ever
remain distinct.

Hottentot and Bushmen did not succumb without a struggle.
The former stole cattle; the latter stole or hunted cattle and even

stalked men. The earliest strife was with the Hottentot, soon after the foundation of the colony; but it was disease rather than warfare which broke this people. They were almost annihilated by an epidemic of smallpox in 1713, and the survivors submitted to the Burgher yoke. The Bushmen remained, perhaps because their less gregarious life limited the spread of infection, but, continuing to hunt and steal cattle, they were exterminated. Commandos (small bodies of armed horsemen) were formed to pursue cattle-thieves. On interception, the men were shot, and the women taken into captivity. The resistance lasted a century. During the last ten years of the Dutch rule (1785–95), 2,500 Bushmen were killed and nearly 700 were taken prisoner, at a loss of 276 persons—coloured and white—killed by the Bushmen. By then, Bushmen only survived in the most arid northern regions of Cape Colony. Captives, interbreeding with Hottentot and descendants of slaves introduced in the first days of the Company, formed the Cape Coloured community. Till 1833, these remained a class of slaves; since that date, they have been labourers and small tenants.

After the Hottentot had been subjugated, the Boers could occupy land for a considerable distance. They followed the line of least resistance, eastwards from Cape Town, along the longitudinal valleys, and the littoral, more productive because of its higher rainfall. The Great Karroo, baked and arid in summer, was not permanently occupied; but herds were driven there for wintering from the valleys of the Nieuweld Berge and the Roggenveldt Berge. For much of the eighteenth century, the expansion continued. Such was the spirit of independence that no man would settle within sight of the smoke of a neighbour's chimney. It was customary to walk a horse for an hour from one homestead before choosing a site for the next. This, and the preference for pastoral farming, caused the average farm to extend to several thousand acres. Cultivation was restricted to the kitchen garden and a few acres of grain near the house, intended to provide only for home consumption. The country was devoid of effective communications with the ports, and it would have been futile to produce more. Hides and tallow could, however, be carried in ox-waggons to the coast, and it was from the sale of these commodities to traders that the Burghers obtained the means to purchase cloth tools, weapons, ammunition and a few luxuries. But they were not avaricious. They valued their herds more than luxurious living. They preferred independence and a simple life. Yet it would be wrong entirely to attribute their way of life to freedom of choice. Life was too uncertain and dangerous for refinement in the manner of living. Apart from this, they were becoming isolated from the developing European economy.

We may detect, in their mode of living, consequences both of the nature of the land they were making their own, and of their relations with the indigenous peoples. Throughout the eighteenth century, the Bushmen, lurking in the gullies and caves of the mountains, remained an ever-present danger. The lion and the jackal, too, preyed upon herds. The price of survival was ceaseless vigilance. When a Burgher was not serving in a commando, he was patrolling his own lands. He was thus in a quasi-feudal position: ownership of land brought with it the obligation—of natural rather than legal necessity—to be perpetually in arms. The labour of the Cape Coloured servants—living in families in simple huts adjacent to the Burgher steadings—was essential; not to relieve the dominant race from servile toil but to ensure that cattle, White womenfolk and all the Coloured dependents, were protected. It is not surprising, therefore, that the cattle were Afrikaner, of African and not European stock: small, large-boned, large-horned and inured to walking far for food and water. They were reared by Hottentot methods, exclusively by grazing on open range, 'kraaling' at night to give security from wild beasts. To control grazing by means of enclosures would require experimentation and training the coloured labourers in unaccustomed methods. It was far simpler to let the Hottentot go on tending cattle in his traditional way.

The isolation in which this semi-patriarchal economy grew up fostered these peculiarities. Several writers, soon after 1800, commented on the absence of towns or villages. The settlements consisted entirely of scattered, single steadings. Intercourse was confined to neighbours, and even the stimulus of commerce was absent. The traveller Lichtenstein remarked:

In an almost unconscious inactivity of mind, without any attractions towards the great circle of mankind, knowing nothing beyond the little circle which his own family forms around him, the colonist of those parts passes his solitary days, and by his mode of life is made such as we see him.

As if this was not enough, there was no immigration. The Burghers, or Boers, increased rapidly, for they had large families. Were not these open spaces to be possessed by the people of God? Their sons were needed to make good their hold upon the land and aborigines. It is a remarkable fact that the whole Afrikaner community in South Africa today, numbering more than 1,885,000 (1962), is descended from the few hundreds of Dutch, Germans and French who set foot in the continent at the Cape between 1652 and 1707. Between the arrival of the Huguenots (1688–90) and that of the British '1820 settlers' at Algoa Bay, there were few or no immigrants into South Africa. The Huguenots brought viticulture: the British sheep-farming and handicrafts. In the intervening one hundred and thirty years, Afrikaner pastoral society was cast in its tough, refractory metal, and resistant to the roughest usage, it has survived until today.

Towards the end of the eighteenth century, the outposts of Boer settlement had met the van of the southward-moving Bantu along the Great Fish river. The Negroes were checked, and even today, after 150 years of internal population movements, few Bantu are to be found to the south-west, in Cape Province. At the time, the Fish river valley became a no-man's-land. The Bantu stole cattle, and the Boer commandos raided native kraals in reprisal. About this time, sovereignty passed, during the Napoleonic wars, from the Dutch to the British Crown. This brought South Africa into the British commercial system, which was soon to be fully transformed by the Industrial Revolution. British immigrants and British capital began to exploit the country as a source of primary products in exchange for manufactures which were being poured from British factories. The belief in freedom for labour among the middle classes was allied to a humanitarianism evoked chiefly by the brutality of the African slave trade, and considerably influenced the course of events, settlement, migration and thus the present-day geography of South Africa.

(3) *Britons*

To stabilise the Bantu frontier, the new government at the Cape decided to promote immigration to the hinterland of Algoa Bay. The '1820 settlers' numbered about 4,000, and were selected from perhaps 20,000 or more applicants. Of better calibre than the ne'er-do-wells settling elsewhere at this period, they have contributed substantially to the leadership of the British community in South Africa. Farmers rather than semi-nomads, such as were the Boers, they introduced sheep, grew grain and founded some towns, the original nuclei being the forts built to render military control effective in protecting the zone from the Bantu. From the beginning surplus produce, mainly wool, was exported.

About the same time, British missionaries entered the country, soon to penetrate far beyond the previous limits of European settlement. In the interior, after crossing the Orange river, they followed the western axis of Bantu migration in the reverse direction, thus making the 'missionary road' which, passing through Kuruman, provided for Livingstone his approach to the heart of Africa. Missionaries were the heralds, as elsewhere, of the flag; and the annexation of British Bechuanaland was a direct consequence. Later in the century, when German imperialism sought footholds in this continent, the Bechuanaland Protectorate was proclaimed. In the latter territory (which was administered by the Colonial Office and not by South Africa, and is now the independent Commonwealth State of Botswana), the Bantu have to a certain extent been insulated from the full consequences of the European penetration into South Africa.

But the missionaries were also the watch-dogs of the anti-slavery movement in England. Insisting upon the full application of the Emancipation Act of 1833, they helped to provoke the Boers to leave Cape Colony. The latter, depending upon their black servants, whom they generally treated not unkindly, found their economy was undermined by emancipation. They believed that a feudal society was still essential, for they asserted that the government's capacity to police the country and to defend it against the Bantu was ineffective. Moreover, their slaves, if freed, would probably prefer to revert to their original economy, and would become squatters rather than paid labourers. The Boers, having no liking for commerce, had no means to pay wages. In 1836, many thousands of Boers packed their families and household goods into ox-drawn wagons and crossed the Orange river. The Veld lay before them. It was largely unoccupied by the Bantu, and the Boers could live as they desired unhampered by the British colonial government. Their main thrust carried them almost to the Tropic of Capricorn, where, reaching the malarial Bushveld, they stopped. A subsidiary stream of *Voortrekkers* crossed the Drakensberg and entered the hinterland of Durban, which had been previously occupied by the British to deny its useful harbour to the French during the Napoleonic wars. British colonists had been penetrating into the same hinterland, and the desire of the Boers for independence east of the Drakensberg was disappointed when the British government annexed the whole coastal slope shortly after the Great Trek. But on the plateau proper, the *Voortrekkers* and their descendants felt that they had made good their independence when the British Crown recognised the Orange Free State and the Transvaal as sovereign states (1852–4).

But Boer and British rule over South Africa had not quite reached its fullest development. The early British administration at the Cape had sought to stabilise the relations with the Bantu by promoting and recognising small native chieftaincies, across the Kei river in what was then called Kaffraria, in Griqualand East and Griqualand West along the Orange river, and to enable them not only to control their people but to preserve themselves from despoliation by European settlers and traders. The policy did not achieve success; and the colonial government had to assume responsibility. But the chieftaincies have become native reserves within which White settlement has been prohibited. Farther north, in Basutoland and Swaziland, protectorates were established; the former mainly at the initiative and diplomacy of a remarkable native chief who realised that the British Crown alone could protect from ultimate absorption by the Boers and the disintegration of his people.

The present distribution of races in South Africa

Thus the peoples and races of South Africa are today to a great extent distributed in the countryside as they were in 1850 when the tides of Boer migration and British immigration temporarily ceased to flow. And the distribution of communities is reflected both in the ownership and occupation of land, and the political geography. The two tongues of Bantu migration today correspond with the three Commonwealth enclaves, east and west of the Veld, and with the native reserves of Natal and Cape Province. The Boer policy of occupying the whole country, and bringing the natives into servitude, combined with the paucity of Hottentot in Cape Colony and of Bantu north of the Orange river, caused the Orange Free State and the Transvaal to be largely void of native reserves, except in the unwanted Bushveld in the extreme north. The descendants of British settlers are strongest in the districts just inland of Durban and East London. In Natal, where the coastal lowland is tropical, sugar-cane was planted and indentured labourers brought from India to perform the manual tasks in cultivating, cutting and extracting. Their descendants form a sixth distinct racial group in South Africa. They are small-holders and retail traders.

But the distribution of peoples in the countryside gives little indication of the situation in the towns. The Orange Free State and the Transvaal had been recognised for only thirty years when the discovery of gold in the Rand and the foundation of Johannesburg in 1886 disturbed the precarious balance. The diamond mines at Kimberley, discovered in 1870, had previously provided justification for extending the railways into the interior. Now, into the heart of the *Voortrekker's* utopia came British engineers, Jewish financiers, and adventurers from most countries. Within ten years the Boer republics were confronted with a completed railway network and a rapidly growing mining city which might become the economic capital of South Africa. Here, and in older settlements which had become railway junctions, British business men and engineers rapidly increased in numbers and acquired control of commerce and transport. The new towns, from the first, began to suck in the Bantu. They came from the reserves and the protectorates to work as labourers under contract, or to live in native quarters, earning their livelihood by unskilled and semi-skilled work.

A few have become skilled workers, or have entered trades or professions, but the colour bar has undoubtedly hindered economic advancement. Policies of restricting the numbers of Bantu permanently settling in towns have inflated the numbers of migrant workers, and the attendant evils of bad housing, vice and crime.

Nevertheless, the abounding prosperity of South Africa, based both upon gold, diamonds, uranium and a range of other mineral products, and rapid industrial growth is shared by the Bantu, whose average income is much higher than in the purely African countries farther north, and who also have better social services, especially health and elementary education. Extensive African suburbs of permanent brick and concrete houses have been constructed near large towns.

The Bantu Reserves

The Bantu are a vigorous and fecund people. Tribal warfare tended to check their increase before their subjugation by Europeans; but during the past century they have greatly multiplied,

and they now number 11,645,000 (1962). But the European conquest has disrupted their social order and their economy. Tribal
society has largely disappeared in the areas occupied by Europeans. Native families are scattered among the European farmer
and estates, as servants living in quarters close to the proprietor's
house, as labourers permitted to till for their own use small arable
plots near their huts or as tenants of small holdings. They are not
permitted to keep weapons of any kind, and hunting has therefore
ceased to be a means of providing fresh meat. They live nowadays
on millet or maize, with only occasional milk or meat. In the
native reserves or the protectorates, the position is no better.
Hunting, again, has ceased, though small animals or birds may be
snared. The small-scale cultivation of suitable patches close to
kraals continues, with the use of remaining land as common
grazing. But the production of grain is pitifully small and the cattle
half-starved. The cultivation and over-grazing of hillsides are
exposing the soil to severe erosion.

The Chief Magistrate of the Transkei Reserve wrote in
1936:

The native is now primarily an agriculturist and secondarily a pastor-
alist. In other words he exists on mealies grown by himself and regards
his cattle as wealth negotiable only in times of dire need. . . .

He has increased considerably in numbers and the Territories can
now be said to be over-populated and over-stocked, the latter condition
arising out of the former. . . .

Grazing grounds are largely trodden out, seeding rarely takes place
and quality of grazing is seriously impaired.

Every available foot of arable land is used. Lands have been badly
located and frequently occur on very steep slopes.

Indigenous forest and bush have largely disappeared.

The number of stock is far in excess . . . of what it should be . . . but
the number per family is barely sufficient. . . .

Native customs and mode of living render effective reclamation
measures exceedingly difficult . . . drastic steps only . . . will solve the
problem:

1. Reduction in the number of stock.
2. Purchase of additional land to alleviate the over-population.
3. A . . . scheme of stock and grazing control.

At the time the Union was being formed (1903), a survey revealed that such reserves extended to no more than 7 per cent of

the total area. The inadequacy was recognised even then, and an ameliorating act passed in 1913; but little was done until 1936, when the Native Trust was created to acquire land for African occupation. By June 1954, the Trust had increased the proportion of land for African use to 11 per cent.

Since 1900, as already described, over-population has become grave, and with it, soil degradation. On a small scale, remedial measures have been applied; but it has become increasingly evident that the problem is not simply one of agricultural and pastoral techniques; but is of a kind and order that demands re-formulation of the policy regarding the place and future of the reserves in the economic and political life of South Africa. In 1950 therefore, a Socio-Economic Commission for the Development of the Bantu Areas (better known as the Tomlinson Commission) was formed, which reported in 1956, forecasting that South Africa (*including* the three High Commission territories at that date) will have a population of 6 million Europeans and $21\frac{1}{2}$ million Africans in the year 2000. It is proposed to segregate 15 million Africans in seven large areas, which would be transformed into viable units by large investments in communications, industries, new towns and agricultural improvements. The remaining Africans, equal in numbers to the Europeans, will remain in the areas designated for European ownership and occupation.

The outlook for South Africa

It is apparent from the foregoing review of settlement and econo-mic development in the country during the last 250 years that a degree of territorial segregation has always existed. The British and Boer settlers established themselves on the whole in areas un-occupied or but lightly occupied by the Bantu. Native reserves today (and the Commonwealth states) are the successors to areas well-populated by Bantu a century ago, which the British govern-ment at first hoped could be ruled by recognised native chiefs before it was compelled by force of circumstances to assume responsibility itself. *Apartheid,* then, is not new; it is the Afrikaans word for a policy which has been applied for at least a century, and which currently is being redefined, renamed 'Separate Development', and given new impetus.

Race relations in South Africa at the present time are not only unique in complexity. Europeans and Africans have been increas-

ingly associated during the past two centuries, and more especially
as a result of industrialisation; but each racial group has retained
its sense of identity, despite much borrowing by Africans from
Europeans. The cleavage is now widened by the growth of
nationalism among Africans, who want to better themselves to
amend their dependent status and to obtain political equality with
Europeans.

Yet we do not need to look far into the past to discover records
of conflicts which have arisen from interlocked races or nationalities. For this was the situation in Ireland a hundred years ago,
when the Protestant Ascendancy dominated the Catholic Irish in
a way not dissimilar from the current subjection of Bantu to
Afrikaner. Yet by land reform to convert tenants into small owner-
farmers and to compensate landlords, accompanied at the final
stage by the severance of Northern Ireland from the remainder, a
lasting settlement was achieved. In 1920, Greeks and Turks were
at war in western Anatolia, which at that time was inhabited by
both nationalities. By the agency of the League of Nations, Greeks
were exchanged for Turks (to the total number of more than half
a million) and both states became ethnically more homogeneous.
The settlement of Jews in Palestine from 1921 onwards, and the
contemporary rise of nationalism among Arabs, provoked bitter
rivalry which is still white-hot. Measures of partition proposed
first by Britain (as mandatory power) and afterwards, by the
United Nations Organisation, were rejected. A war was then
fought which divided Palestine and more radically separated the
two peoples. Arabs, fleeing from the newly-proclaimed state of
Israel to neighbouring countries, were replaced by expelled Jews.
The state of Israel which then came into existence corresponded
closely with the areas of Palestine where Jewish agricultural
colonisation had been in progress since 1870.

In all these instances, entangled nationalities or communities
were disengaged and largely separated. Moreover, these examples
facilitate judgment upon the Tomlinson proposals, which evidently foreshadow a form of partition for South Africa. Such indeed is
the only solution likely to be attainable, peacefully by a process of
evolution. After all, the Irish land reform took half a century,
from 1870 to 1920. But it may be doubted whether these proposals
provide adequately for population redistribution and for African-
governed territories or states. Even if the three Commonwealth
enclaves are added to the areas designated for Bantu occupation

and rule, there will be insufficient room for some 15 million Africans (if the uselessness of most of Botswana is remembered). And the envisaged equality in numbers of Africans and Europeans in the 'White' area is unlikely to gain the assent of the Bantu. European-descended South Africans should relinquish more territory and aim at a smaller 'White' South Africa in which they would clearly be a majority. They should also become less dependent upon Bantu for manual and menial work.

Equally essential is improvement in Bantu farming, for until land is used conservatively, and the output increased, poverty will continue to impede social progress. It would be unrealistic to ignore the fact that despite much educational effort, agriculture has stagnated in native areas, and until this deficiency is rectified, manufacturing industries cannot flourish and the institutions of the modern state cannot be supported.

Conclusion

We began by inquiring into the nature of human geography. As this quest was pursued, it became apparent that the subject demands insight into the essence of human society; and thus we were confronted by what may be termed the reality of ethnic entities. Mankind is a single species; but the human family consists of societies, differentiated rather than separated or divided from one another; for human societies, unlike those of social insects such as bees or ants, are composite, hierarchical and associative or integrative. The Indian peasant, for instance, is a member of a village community, of a caste represented in most neighbouring villages, a Hindu and a national of India. Among integrating and cohesive influences, language is often supreme, especially when reinforced by the state; but the family and other social institutions sanctioned by religious or philosophical beliefs are not to be underrated; and the universal religions have exercised a magistral rôle in shaping the major societies.

This conception is also dynamic. Small, self-sufficing primitive groups have evolved into larger and more complex societies, economically by the adoption of food production, the use of metals, the application of power, specialisation of labour and living in urban communities; institutionally by the rise of states and the elaboration of legal codes defining social relationships and activities. Among new national societies recently born are the Afrikaner in South Africa and the Israeli in the Near East.

Significantly, both are bonded linguistically: the Afrikaner by the Afrikaans language, derived from Dutch, and the Israeli by Modern Hebrew. In the former, ethnic self-consciousness arose by reversion from settled farming to semi-nomadic pastoralism, aided by migration into the isolation of a continental interior; in the latter, by communal irrigated agricultural colonisation.

Human geography has therefore been interpreted in this book to signify the study of human societies in their habitats or environments. There is a distributional or territorial aspect of societies, and also an ecological aspect often arising from the limits to which resources permit the extension of a customary mode of utilising the soil and from the association of cultivated plants and domesticated animals in the farming system. Hindu society has been confined to the subcontinent of India by the formidable northern mountain rampart, which is reinforced by aridity to the north-west. Chinese civilisation has become rooted in the three great contiguous river basins of the eastern Asiatic mainland. Both civilisations have been profoundly influenced by the juxtaposition of regions suitable for growing temperate cereals in conjunction with rearing such domestic animals as horses, sheep and cattle with warmer, rainier regions where rice and the buffalo flourish. Western society has evolved in response to the proximity of temperate forest lands, steppe and the Mediterranean forest within a peninsula of the Eurasiatic landmass, powerfully stimulated by the use of coal and petroleum as sources of power and by oceanic communications. Its expansion has been directed chiefly to temperate lands which until comparatively recently were but thinly occupied by primitive peoples, now largely eliminated or absorbed to facilitate the transplantation of its own emigrants and the geographical extension of its own form of society.

The phenomena studied by the geographer remain inexplicable apart from analysis of social institutions. In Africa, temporary migration is now an essential feature of life. It arises from the intrusion of western urban settlements and industries into a rural society composed of villages, clans and tribes, in which the individual male's permanent associations and family are rooted in his right to the use of land for cropping and grazing near the place in which he was born, and the sedentariness of his wife and young children. As a consequence, the temporary housing for the migrant workers, often tribally differentiated, form distinctive quarters in almost all African towns.

Human geography, thus conceived, may seem to lack the objectivity to be derived from topographic and other maps or the quantitative approach based upon observation and statistics. But an English autumn scene, half-shrouded in mist and suffused by the pale gleams of early morning sunshine may lack the clarity, definition, and sharpness of detail visible in the Colorado canyon when it is illuminated in the clear dry desert air by the brilliance of a subtropical noonday sun; but both are real. The geography of human societies must be recognised and pursued equally with the analysis of landscape, the localisation of production, the routes and functions of different means of transport and the morphology of human settlements.

BIBLIOGRAPHY

ETHIOPIA

ULLENDORF, E., *The Ethiopians*, 2nd ed., 1965

SOUTH-EAST ASIA

DOBBY, E. H. G., 'Some aspects of the human ecology of south-east Asia', *Geographical Journal*, **108**, 1946, 40–54

FISHER, C. A., *South-east Asia*, 2nd ed., 1966, Part I, chs 1–6, Part II, ch 8, Part IV, ch. 19, Part V, chs 39 and 44

HALL, D. G. E., *A History of south-east Asia*, 2nd ed., 1966, Part I, chs 2–11, Part II, ch 12, Part IV, chs 39, 44

UNGER, L., 'The Chinese in southeast Asia', *Geographical Review*, **34**, 1944, 196–217

SOUTH AFRICA

GREEN, L. P. and FAIR, T. J. D., *Development in Africa, a Study in Analysis with Special Reference to Southern Africa*, 1962

HAUGHTON, D. H., *The South African Economy*, 1964

MACMILLAN, W. M., *Bantu, Boer and Briton*, 1929

POLLOCK, N. C. and AGNEW, S., *An Historical Geography of South Africa*, 1963

SCHAPERA, I., and others, *Western Civilisation and the Natives of South Africa*, 1934

—*Migrant Labour and Tribal Life, a Study of Conditions in Bechuanaland*, 1947

South Africa in the Sixties, ed. H. T. Andrews and others, 2nd edn., 1965

Summary of the Report of the Commission for the Socio-Economic Development of the Bantu Areas, U.G. No. 16, 1955

INDEX

(Exclusive of main topics listed in Contents table)